Il Gigante

Also by Anton Gill

The Great Escape
Peggy Guggenheim
The Devil's Mariner
Ruling Passions
A Dance Between Flames
The Journey Back From Home
An Honourable Defeat

Il Gigante

Michelangelo, Florence, and the *David*, 1492–1504

Anton Gill

Thomas Dunne Books
St. Martin's Griffin ℳ New York

THOMAS DUNNE BOOKS.
An imprint of St. Martin's Press.

www.stmartins.com

Library of Congress Cataloging-in-Publication Data

Gill, Anton.
   Il gigante : Michelangelo, Florence, and the David, 1492–1504 /
Anton Gill.
      p. cm.
   Originally published : London : Review, 2002.
   Includes bibliographical references (p. 325) and index (p. 329).
   ISBN 0-312-31442-6 (hc)
   ISBN 0-312-31443-4(pbk)
   EAN 978-0312-31443-9
   1. Michelangelo, Buonarroti, 1475–1564. 2. Artists—Italy—
Biography. 3. Michelangelo Buonarroti, 1475–1564. David.
4. Florence (Italy)—History—1421–1737. 5. Florence (Italy)—
Civilization. 6. Rome (Italy)—History—1420–1798. 7. Rome
(Italy)—Civilization. I. Title.

N6923.B9G48 2003
730'.92—dc21
[B]   2003043139

First published in Great Britain by Review
An imprint of Headline Book Publishing
A division of Hodder Headline

First St. Martin's Griffin Edition: December 2004

10 9 8 7 6 5 4 3 2 1

to

Marji Campi

and

Anthony Vivis

My guide and I came on that hidden road
to make our way back into the bright world;
and with no care for any rest, we climbed –
he first, I following – until I saw,
through a round opening, some of those things
of beauty heaven bears. It was from there
that we emerged, to see – once more – the stars.

Dante, *The Divine Comedy, Inferno*; Canto XXXIV

CONTENTS

The marble not yet carved can hold the form
Of every thought the greatest artist has,
And no conception ever comes to pass
Unless the hand obeys the intellect.

Michelangelo, Sonnet (opening quatrain)

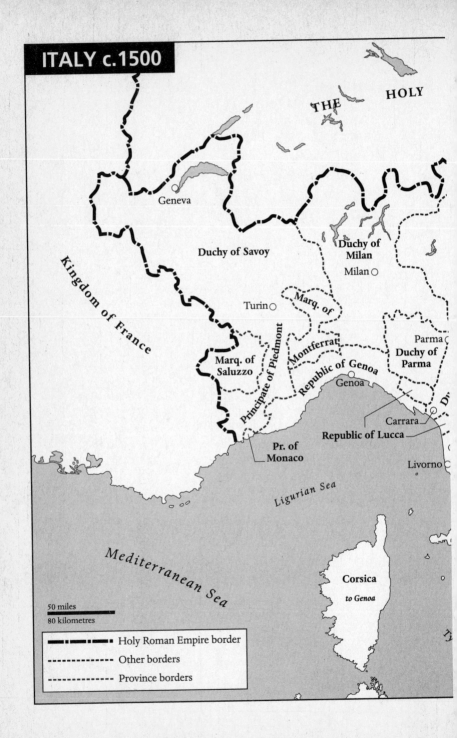

ITALY c.1500

THE   HOLY

Geneva

Duchy of Savoy

Duchy of Milan

Milan ○

Kingdom of France

Turin ○

Marq. of

Duchy of Parma

Parma ○

Marq. of Saluzzo

Montferrat

Principate of Piedmont

Republic of Genoa

Genoa ●

Carrara ○

Republic of Lucca

Pr. of Monaco

Livorno ○

Ligurian Sea

Mediterranean Sea

Corsica

to Genoa

50 miles
80 kilometres

━━━━━ Holy Roman Empire border

---------- Other borders

------------ Province borders

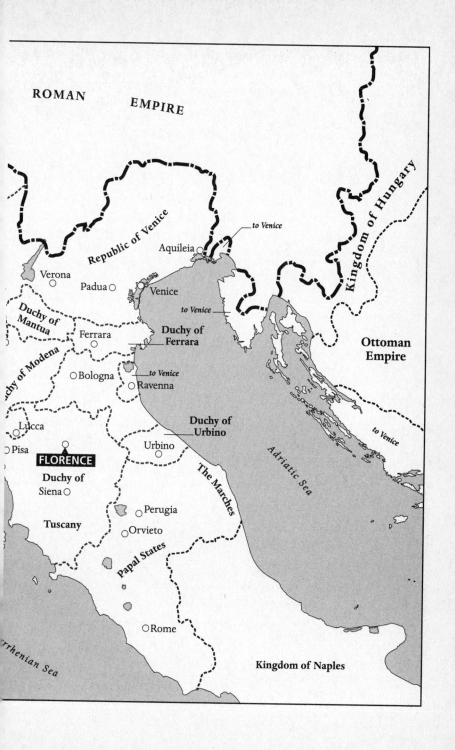

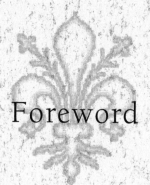

Foreword

M any people and organisations have helped me
with this book. I have to thank the staffs of the
Archive of Florence Cathedral, of the British
Library, the Buonarroti House and the London Library. I
should also like to thank Marji Campi for providing moral
support, and for her patient reading and welcome construc-
tive criticism of the manuscript; Heather Holden-Brown,
editor and friend, for helping me develop the original idea;
Jo Roberts-Miller; Sarah Ahmed; Anthony Vivis for his
unfailing friendship, and Sophia Wickham for helping me
with certain unsolved questions regarding the Medici. I must
also thank all those Michelangelo scholars whose work has
informed this effort.

I have tried to cover every possible established fact in an area where there is still much, sometimes enormous, disagreement about dates, names and events. Even the earliest chroniclers, Michelangelo's contemporaries and first biographers Ascanio Condivi and Giorgio Vasari, are often far from accurate. I have been obliged to make certain choices with which some academics may disagree; but I have done so in good faith. In other words, I have done my best to check my facts. This is not a book, however, for those already in the know. It is designed to give people who do not already know it a taste of a world in which great creativity lived alongside political realism.

All dates conform to the modern Christian calendar.

A select bibliography at the end gives indications of sources, and pointers for further reading. Included in it are the publications from which the translated verses of Dante, Lorenzo de' Medici and Michelangelo's sonnets have been taken.

List of Illustrations

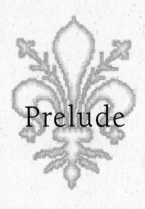

Prelude

T he subtitle of this book indicates that it covers twelve years in Florence, between the death of Lorenzo de' Medici in April 1492 and the placing of Michelangelo's early masterpiece of sculpture, his *David*, in the Piazza della Signoria in summer, 1504. But history doesn't stop and start at arbitrary dates, so this book will go back earlier than 1492 and go forward a little later than 1504 – though the latter date is a good one to end on, since it more or less coincides with Michelangelo's departure from Florence for Rome, where his genius would climb to ever greater heights. Here we are concerned with the flower in bud, not with the flower in bloom: but the former is seldom less exciting than the latter.

The theme here is not only focused on an artist of genius – a man who from his early teens displayed a talent which outstripped his peers and has continued (with honorable exceptions) to outstrip their successors for five hundred years. The intertwined stories in this book are of a man and a city – or rather, of two cities, because there is a space of several years within the chosen period when Michelangelo was absent from his native Florence, working in Rome. Family ties and political and religious preoccupations, however, kept him close to home emotionally, so that for the time between approximately 1494 and 1501 the aim has been to follow the separate, though connected, fortunes of Rome and Florence, and the artist who was to become in later life the honorary son of the former, but would in his heart always remain the true son of the latter – not least because these were not simply separate towns within a country, but in the fifteenth and sixteenth centuries the capitals of distinct and rival states, whose very usage and pronunciation of Italian differed.

One of the main reasons for reaching farther back in time than 1492 is Lorenzo de' Medici. The year of his death may have been 1492 (Michelangelo had just turned seventeen), but this great citizen of Florence, who was Michelangelo's first major patron, deserves a place near the centre of the stage. His short life and the political and social changes it witnessed are a vital ingredient of the scene-setting for the years which succeeded his early and agonising demise. This astute politician, connoisseur, sportsman and ineffective banker was one of the great diamonds in the crown of the early Renaissance. His role, even as a ghost hovering over the action, cannot be ignored in the short, intense story that follows.

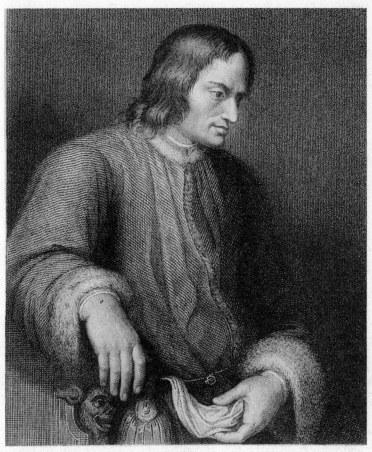

Lorenzo the Magnificent (1449–92) towards the end of his life
(engraving after Vasari)

The reason for choosing these twelve years is simple: they were among the most dramatic in the history of Florence, and they were the most dramatic of Michelangelo's life – the brief years during which he grew from an apprentice of thirteen to a master of twenty-five. After the *David*, he would develop into an artist of awesome maturity, but there would never quite be that rush of blood again, that acceleration of talent which those twelve years witnessed. His contemporaries in Florence at the time included some of the greatest luminaries of the age: Ghirlandaio the master of frescoes; the painters Dom Bartolommeo, Piero di Cosimo and Sandro Botticelli; the philosophers and Neoplatonists Angelo Poliziano, Marsilio Ficino and Pico della Mirandola; and Girolamo Savonarola, the overweening but influential critic of the decadent Borgia Papacy. An influential member of the city's administration was Niccolò Machiavelli; and, a hugely valued and influential presence following his return to Florence in 1500 after an absence in Milan of nearly twenty years, was the great universal genius, Leonardo da Vinci, handsome, tall, dandified and worldly, whose rivalry with the much younger, short, unkempt, ugly and religious Michelangelo would place a strain on the short period that they knew each other during the early 1500s.

Florence, with its long history of republican government and uninterrupted prosperity (principally based on textiles and banking), had never forgotten the classical past of Italy. For a time, during the period of the Great Schism, between

1378 and 1417, when two rival popes each claimed to be sole head of the Church, and Rome was in abeyance, Florence was the principal city of Italy; and it had been a cradle of genius for at least a century before Michelangelo's birth in 1475. Its eminent children could be traced back to the thirteenth century – to the great, arrogant religious painter Cimabue, and after him Giotto and Dante, exact contemporaries, and their younger associate, the storyteller Giovanni Boccaccio, whose *Decameron* provided the principal inspiration for Geoffrey Chaucer's *Canterbury Tales*, one of the first long narrative poems in English.

Lorenzo Ghiberti, who lived between c. 1378 and 1455 was another multiple-talent; a sculptor, goldsmith and architect, as well as a writer on the art of the Florentine School of painting, the *Commentari*. Grounded in the craft of goldsmithry, his crowning glory was winning the competition for the new Baptistery doors in 1402, narrowly beating his nearest rival and close contemporary, Filippo Brunelleschi. Both had submitted a panel showing the Sacrifice of Isaac. The competition had been for the job of completing one new pair of doors, and the twenty-eight panels for these occupied Ghiberti for the next twenty years, after which a second pair was commissioned from him for the Baptistery, the celebrated Gates of Paradise, which took another seventeen years to complete. The name given to the second set of doors is ascribed to Michelangelo, who is supposed to have said that they were worthy to stand as the gateway to heaven. Ghiberti proudly inserted a small portrait bust of his own bald head on the doors that were his masterpiece.

Though his working life was dominated by the creation of the sets of Baptistery doors, Ghiberti was also acclaimed as a sculptor in marble and bronze, and his busy workshop provided a training ground for such mighty artists as Uccello, Michelozzo and Donatello – the last perhaps the profoundest influence on the succeeding generation of Florentine artists.

The Baptistery had been supported and funded by the Calimala Guild – the guild of the wool-refiners – since the twelfth century, and their announcement, in the winter of 1400–01, of a competition for the contract to complete a new set of doors for the Baptistery reinvigorated creativity in Florence and ushered in a long period of creative energy. The doors were to be set facing the cathedral, in other words, on the east side of the Baptistery, the position of greatest symbolic and liturgical importance. The competition was open to 'skilled masters from all the lands of Italy', and its announcement came at a significant moment in Florentine history. The plague had ravaged the city in the summer of 1400, and a war with Milan still simmered, with Milan seeming more than likely to gain the upper hand. Although it might seem that money spent on commissioning new doors for the Baptistery would have been better spent on the war effort, the importance of art both as propaganda and as a morale-booster was well established in Florentine tradition. At the beginning of the fifteenth century, the undertaking of a major, long-term project of this nature symbolised Florence's faith in itself. And it has been argued that the very subject chosen for the competition, the Sacrifice of Isaac, was chosen in reference to Florence's situation at the time: like Isaac, the city might have been on the point of being struck down; but like the biblical hero, there was hope that divine intervention would save it.

Seven Tuscan artists entered the competition, and it may have been optimistic to assume that contestants would enter from a wider field than Florence's immediate locality. Though artists travelled far and wide within the collection of frequently warring states that made up the Italian peninsula, times of trouble and disease frequently curtailed their peregrinations. The committee of judges, which comprised thirty-four leading citizens, narrowed the field down to Ghiberti and Brunelleschi with relative accord, but the competition between the two finalists was fierce. The panels which they submitted still exist, and from them it is clear to see that the artists were obliged to work to narrow strictures, not least in that the form and design of the panels had to accord with those already in place by Pisano on the south side of the building.

The same elements are to be found in both Ghiberti's and Brunelleschi's panels: Abraham and Isaac, the Angel, two servants, a donkey, the ram held in the thicket, and an altar for the sacrifice. Nodding in the direction of Pisano's naturalistic detail, Ghiberti added a small lizard and shows Abraham's cloak lying where it has fallen to the ground at the foot of the altar. Brunelleschi adds only a small tree to the essential elements. Though both artists describe exactly the same moment – the height of the drama, the point at which the angel appears to prevent Abraham, at the very last moment, from plunging his knife into his son's throat – Ghiberti displays much greater psychological sensitivity. Isaac is seen as a beautiful youth, and Abraham steadies him with a hand on the shoulder whose touch is loving, while the hand which holds the knife is drawn well away from Isaac. Abraham's reluctance to perform the sacrifice is completely apparent, as is his emotional and spiritual dichotomy: the agony of having to kill a loved son to prove his love of God is clear, and the angel appearing above needs only to make a formal gesture to dissuade him. There is no such circumspection in Brunelleschi's Abraham, whose unhesitating attack is equally plain. He is full of raw energy as he twists his son's head round with one hand while preparing to strike with the other, and here the angel must intervene physically to prevent the sacrifice. Each interpretation is valid, and perhaps Brunelleschi's has the greater immediate dramatic impact, but Ghiberti's is both more sophisticated and more profound, and no one would contest the jury's decision to award him the contract. Ghiberti's Isaac is of great significance and a clear ancestor of Michelangelo's *David*, for here is a young male nude in the heroic mode.

Like Ghiberti, Brunelleschi, c. 1377–1446, had started his

artistic life by training as a goldsmith. He arrived at architecture via sculpture, and in pursuit of his vocation closely followed the precepts of classical architecture which he learned by observing the buildings of antiquity at Rome in the early 1400s. He was also a major pioneer in the application of perspective to art. His experiments in perspective were born of a desire to represent accurately the buildings of antiquity in drawings. Before the age of photography, since which time accurate reproduction can be effected mechanically (thereby liberating art to be more expressive), it was important to achieve exactly the effect of an object on the eye through drawing or painting, so that you could show a picture of, say, a building to somebody who had never seen it in fact, and convey an accurate image of it to that person. Brunelleschi painted two small pictures, both now lost, one of the Palazzo Vecchio and one of the Baptistery. The Baptistery painting, about thirty centimetres square, was made from a viewpoint just inside the west doors of the cathedral. Taking up a position near the middle door, about thirty-five metres from the Baptistery, he painted on to his small panel in perfect perspective, using a geometrically constructed picture plane, everything he could see that was framed by the cathedral door. In place of the sky on his panel, he set a piece of polished silver to reflect the actual clouds and sky. He drilled a small hole in the centre of the panel where the vanishing point of the perspective occurred. The trick of the device was now ready for demonstration:

an observer, standing two metres inside the cathedral at the exact point where Brunelleschi had painted the picture, held the panel up in front of him, the painted side facing away from him. In his other hand he held a mirror which reflected the painted scene. But as he stared through the aperture in the painting and saw the actual Baptistery, the observer found Brunelleschi's representation so lifelike that he confused the 'real' image seen with his eye, with that of the painted one. Recently, it has been suggested that Brunelleschi may have used an early form of camera obscura (a device which throws an inverted image of an object, conveyed through a small hole in a screen, on to a surface in a darkened room) to complete the work. Either way, the painting must have been a masterpiece of innovation, and the source of much excited discussion among the artistic community of Florence; and Brunelleschi's rationalism of perspective was of fundamental importance to the artists who followed him.

A new way of looking at the classical past to which it was heir began to grow in fifteenth-century Italy.

From the late fourteenth century until well into the fifteenth, Milan's expansionist policies threatened Florence. Under the Visconti dukes, Milan consolidated its hold over Lombardy in the closing decades of the fourteenth century and started to make inroads into the Romagna and northern Tuscany. To counter this, Florence tried to forge an alliance with her neighbouring city-states, but this alliance was never firm enough not to crumble at the slightest test and, by the beginning of the 1400s, Florence stood alone against her powerful northern rival. However, as the city braced itself for an attack which might have broken its power, it was saved by what many regarded as an act of Divine intervention. In 1402, the powerful Duke Gian Galeazzo Visconti, the moving force behind Milanese expansionism in the closing decades of the fourteenth century, was suddenly stricken by the plague and died. For a time Milan lay in disarray, for there was no immediate heir strong enough to take over where Gian Galeazzo had left off, and for nearly two decades the Milanese threat was removed. However, in 1420 Duke Filippo Maria Visconti resumed hostilities and a fierce eight-year-long war ensued. Florence emerged victorious, thanks in part to an alliance forced on a reluctant Venice, but Milan continued to be a problem until the death of Filippo Maria towards the middle of the fifteenth century and the subsequent Peace of Lodi.

In the meantime, the war of the 1420s cost Florence dear. A new and highly sophisticated system of taxation – the best in Europe at the time – was introduced to pay the military costs, and the tax structure remained after the need which had called it into existence had ceased. It, and Florence's ultimate triumph, gave the city a financial stability and a high sense of self-esteem. But Florence was not ruled by a duke; it had developed as a republic. The dukes of the states that had been the city's enemies cast themselves in the role of little Caesars. Florence took a more liberal view. The Roman city had been founded at the time of the Roman Republic – albeit in its closing years – and its citizens had always prided themselves on an allegiance to republicanism and an opposition to imperialism. In the eyes of Florentines, the Roman Republic symbolised all that was good in government, and they saw themselves as heirs to a tradition that embraced not only the best application of democracy, but by extension the *mores* of Athens at the height of its cultural and political development. Florence was the new Rome and the new Athens rolled into one at a time when both the senior cities were in a state of desuetude: Florence was the new home and protector of civil liberty (except for women of the middle and upper classes), equality in law, and equal opportunities in self-advancement. By extension, Florence was also the mother and nurturer of all artistic and cultural activity, and aspired to be the apogee of civilised sophistication in the world.

At the core of these beliefs lay the study and development of humanism, which is the study of mankind's history, social structures and beliefs, and which the scholars of the thirteenth century were already beginning to pick up from their secular classical forebears writing in Latin. In Florence its chief inspiration lay in the recently discovered letters of Cicero, one of the great defenders of the Roman Republic, and it found its greatest early promulgators in the poets Petrarch and Boccaccio, friends and contemporaries whose lives spanned the whole of the fourteenth century, though their trail had been blazed almost instinctively a generation earlier by the great poet and thinker, Dante Alighieri.

But it was through the influence of Cicero that Florentine thinkers found themselves increasingly drawn towards the merits of rationalism. Historical analysis to provide political and diplomatic lessons for the present was one consequence of this, but the recognition that antiquity had much intellectual resourcefulness and that its teaching could be applied to the present also led to new developments of thinking: social systems, such as law and taxation, gained greater sophistication than heretofore; and an interest was born in fields such as archaeology and topography. In the fourteenth century the nascent intellectual instincts of the thirteenth developed. The world was subjected to a scrutiny that sought to establish a rationale for its systems. Greater interest began to be shown in foreign lands, religions and languages; and alongside this came a willingness to be influenced by them. The Church was always the conservative element in all this, but the Church at the time was not the oppressive power it later became, and Florence was remarkably free from oppressive and narrow strictures – it is unlikely that they would have been tolerated had anyone tried to apply them.

Reason meant that there was nothing to be feared: all that existed in nature could be explained if the right approach were taken. Man began to take charge of the world

as he progressively questioned, analysed, and came to understand it.

It was not just a superstitious belief that had led the city
to choose the theme of Abraham and Isaac for the Baptistery
doors competition: the Florentines knew that they had a
fighting chance of surviving the Milanese threat – salvation
didn't merely depend on the whim of a supernatural power.
While by no means as cut-and-dried as abandoning one older,
mystical, gullible belief in forces which control us beyond
our will for a new, crisp, materialistic assessment of any given
situation, the Florentines nevertheless could see, by a newly
acquired ability to analyse through historical precedents, that
Milan's power depended on one man and that its resources
were overstretched. The Duke's death from plague may have
been fortuitous: but the outcome of the war would probably
have been the same even had he lived. Reason, and the ability
through reason to deduce likely outcomes, gave the
Florentines greater confidence and enabled them to estimate
what the future was likely to hold, rather than either guess
at it, or leave matters blindly to chance.

This is not, however, to say that in any way the new
rationalism threatened fundamental Christian belief: that is
a process which is still far from its resolution. However, it
informed the approach to religion, less through ritual than
through artistic expression. Nothing could be more representative of this process than the dome of the cathedral, the
design of which would fall to Filippo Brunelleschi towards

the end of the second decade of the fifteenth century.

That there was to be a dome at all had been determined in the mid-1360s. It should be one that reflected the design of the Baptistery. There could be no question of a hemispherical dome, since such a design would exert too much pressure on the unbuttressed drum. The plan therefore was to build an octagonal structure with ogival ribs. The Florentines aimed, however, to construct something to rival the great domes of the Roman Pantheon, built in the second century AD, and of Aghia Sofia, the huge church of Constantinople, built in the sixth century.

The mechanics of achieving such a structure was another matter, and proposals considered included erecting a massive wooden framework, until it was discovered that there was neither enough money nor enough trees to fulfil such an idea; another involved making a huge mound of earth to support the dome while it was being built. The earth was to be scattered through with coins, like sixpences in a Christmas pudding – the idea being that when the dome was completed, the poor of Florence would be induced to remove the earthen mound in return for the money they found in it.

Brunelleschi did not reveal his own plan in detail, though he did say that the dome could be built without resorting to a central reference point. This was considered mad, but the architect proved his point by applying his method to the construction of the domes of two small chapels, and, with the help of the sculptors Donatello and Nanni di Banco, he built a large brick model of his proposal near the campanile. He undertook commissions in 1419 for the Old Sacristy of the church of San Lorenzo, and for the Foundling Hospital. The dome of the former building looks forward to the great dome of the cathedral, and the conception of the building as a whole, the first centrally planned space of the proto-Renaissance, sets standards of proportion which were taken up subsequently by architects the length and breadth of Europe.

(The Foundling Hospital was a project in which Brunelleschi was involved only during the early years of its building. It was funded by the wealthy Silkmakers' Guild – the Arte della Seta. The Guild was one of the new success stories of Florence. To promote competition with the flourishing wool trade, the city decided in 1419 that the quality of silk-production in the city be improved; until then it had been markedly inferior to oriental imports. In a short time the desired improvements had been met, dependence on oriental culture was reduced, and in order to protect what was a major Florentine asset, silk manufacturers of the city were threatened with the death penalty if they sought to take their skills elsewhere. After 1422, when a technique of weaving silk and gold thread together was developed, Florentine fabrics became the most luxurious and sought-after in Europe. Florence even exported to the Near East, in exchange for oriental luxuries, tableware and spices which were sold to the wealthy of Florence and onwards throughout Europe. At the outset of this successful enterprise, the silk-makers sought to make their mark in the traditional way of the guilds – by endowing a major public work. The Arte della Seta is a good example of commercial and material optimism in Florence as the Middle Ages gave way to the Renaissance.)

Brunelleschi was appointed as the dome's 'head-of-the-work' – *capomaestro* – by the cathedral's board of management in 1420. Ghiberti was also jointly appointed, but this appears to have been a courtesy to him more than anything, for the work on the dome was incontestably Brunelleschi's alone. The two men were always rivals – sometimes bitter ones – and while Ghiberti was never slow to try to take credit where it wasn't due as far as his contribution to the dome project was concerned, Brunelleschi was more than able – at one point famously feigning illness to do so – to expose Ghiberti's shortcomings and downright ignorance of the overall plan, which Brunelleschi was careful to keep to himself. All his co-workers – foremen, masons and workmen – were allowed to know only as much as they needed to know for the project to progress. However, it has also been argued that Brunelleschi was feeling his way as the work went on, relying as much on instinct as calculation.

As early as 1436 the main body of the dome had been triumphantly finished, and Brunelleschi's reputation had eclipsed that of Ghiberti, the man who had beaten him in the competition for the Baptistery doors. On 25 March of that year, Pope Eugenius IV, accompanied by seven cardinals, thirty-seven archbishops and bishops, and nine senior members of the Florentine civic authority, consecrated the dome. The great art theorist, architect and humanist Leoni Battista Alberti, also present, later described the dome in his *Della Pittura* ('On Painting') as 'rising above the skies, large enough to shelter all the people of Tuscany in its shadow, built without the help of any centring or of much woodwork, of a craftsmanship that perhaps not even the ancients knew or understood'. It was Alberti who developed and formalised Brunelleschi's theories of perspective, too, creating a comprehensible and applicable theory for it, using the sciences of optics and geometry.

The dome was not only a solid example of the triumph of reason, it also operated as a powerful piece of propaganda, rising dramatically to dominate the city's skyline as the people of the city continued their struggle against Milan. It immediately became the defining image of Florence which it has remained, and as the city has not changed much in scale over the centuries, we can still appreciate its impact now in much the same way as the men and women of the dawning Renaissance did. Not far away, about twenty kilometres down the River Arno at Pistoia, the site where the dome first comes into view is celebrated in a streetname: the Via dell'Apparenza. The Baptistery still has the greatest height and the broadest span of any masonry dome in the world, and has served, among many others, as a model for Michelangelo's dome of St Peter's in Rome, Sir Christopher Wren's dome of St Paul's in London, and the dome of the early nineteenth-century Capitol building in Washington DC.

Work continued on the dome until its completion in 1467, and a golden orb fashioned by the painter, sculptor and designer Andrea del Verrocchio was placed on top of the lantern in 1472. The story of its construction spans nearly the whole of the fifteenth century, and bridges the long and dramatic period of transition from medievalism to the modernism that found its first full general expression in the art of the Renaissance which such early geniuses as Brunelleschi and Ghiberti so keenly anticipated.

Florence reached an apogee in 1500 – a year charged with significance, for it was the half-millennium, when many believed that the Second Coming might occur. It had already survived some very turbulent years following the death of Lorenzo de' Medici, but it was far from free of troubles, which menaced it from without and within. When Michelangelo returned from Rome the following year and began work on his first and only monumental statue, universally known even before the moment of its unveiling as *il Gigante,* the Giant, Florence was braving threats similar to those posed to David by Goliath. Like David, Florence triumphed, and the nervous, beautiful young man, poised for action and ready for anything, perfectly symbolised the independent and defiantly republican attitude of the city at the time. Harder, disillusioning times were to come, but for the moment Florence and its most cherished son, Michelangelo, could be proud, confident of the past, the present and the future.

CHAPTER ONE

A Prince and a City

D uring Lent, 1492, Florence's most important citizen
lay dying. Lorenzo de' Medici, known, not without
cause, as Lorenzo the Magnificent, head of the
banking family that had grown to prominence in Florence
during his grandfather's time and which now dominated the
city, was succumbing to the gout which he had inherited from
his father. Though he was only in his forty-third year, he had
been unwell for several months, and gravely so since the beginning of January; but ill-health, which he refused to give in to
since it interfered with a full and busy life, had been his
companion for years. Now, despite annual visits to curative
spas and periods of rest at his favourite villa at Poggio a
Caiano, its cumulative effect could no longer be denied.

At Poggio a Caiano, a farm that Lorenzo, always a patron of artists and scholars, had commissioned the architect Giuliano da Sangallo to convert into a luxurious country house, there were activities to distract him. He took an interest in the farmland attached to the villa, he would read his favourite Tuscan authors, Dante and Boccaccio, write fairly conventional poetry on a variety of subjects, from the elevated to the coarse, in the Tuscan dialect, and visit the small menagerie he had established. There, among other exotic animals from Africa and Asia, he kept a gentle, tame giraffe, a gift to him from the Sultan of Babylon. Though Florence had several great families, not many private citizens – for that was what Lorenzo was, officially – could lay claim to such privilege.

From Poggio he would return to Florence refreshed. Seldom in his relatively short life, however, had he had the time to take the advice he gave in his own poem, *The Triumph of Bacchus and Ariadne*:

> *Quant' è bella giovinezza,*
> *Che si fugge tuttavia!*
> *Chi vuol' esser lieto, sia;*
> *Di doman non c'è certezza.*

> [How lovely is youth,
> Always slipping away!
> If you want to be happy, be happy;
> You can't be sure of tomorrow.]

But now approaching death and in increasing pain, which he bore with courage but little patience, were stripping him of both his worldly pleasures and his worldly cares. In February 1492 he could no longer even pretend to work, though for the sake of the city he tried to for as long as he could. Soon afterwards he became unable to walk, or even write. His protégé and friend, the brilliant classicist and humanist Angelo Poliziano, noted graphically that the disease which had gripped Lorenzo was 'eating away the whole man . . . the arteries and veins . . . the limbs, intestines, nerves, bones and marrow'. Gout, which is not brought on by excessive high living but by an often inherited inability of the body to break down deposits of uric acid salts in the various organs of the body, causes severe pain not only in the feet but all over the body. The deposits can manifest themselves as hard lumps in the ear, for example.

Worst of all, Lorenzo's eyesight was failing. He could no longer enjoy the fabulous art collection he had amassed, adding to those of his father and grandfather.

It soon became clear that it would be preferable for him to leave Florence for the better air of the country, but there were duties to fulfil before going. He saw his younger son Giovanni off to Rome, rising seventeen and already a cardinal thanks to some successful political machinations; and appeared at a window of his bedroom in the palazzo on the Via Larga to reassure the people that he was still alive. Then, leaving all his city affairs in the hands of his overweening son, Piero, he quitted Florence for his villa at Careggi in the middle of March.

Careggi had long been the seat of the humanist scholars Lorenzo had gathered around him, and was a little closer to Florence than Poggio. Had Lorenzo chosen it because he wished to spend time in a more serious atmosphere than that at Poggio? Did he guess that his final days were approaching, and that he had seen Florence for the last time? He told his friends that he intended to spend the rest of his days in retirement, writing poetry and reading; but this may have been a ploy to reassure them, and through them, the people of Florence. Lorenzo was a modest man, but he was also a realist: he knew how valued he was in his city, and how little the population thought of his eldest son Piero. He may have pondered on the instability of both the standing of his family and the Florentine state, after his death.

The increasing regard for humanism, as understood in the Renaissance, was no buffer against superstition. And, although the Renaissance was an age of dawning rationalism, it was also an age of contradiction, still to a large extent under the shadow of the medieval world. Towards the end of the fifteenth century belief in portents was greater than it had been a century earlier, when the Church's rule had been paramount and belief in its teachings and tenets unquestioning.

This all goes some way towards explaining the serious-
ness with which certain events in Florence that occurred in
early April were interpreted by Lorenzo and his friends at
Careggi. Just behind the Palazzo della Signoria, the imposing
palace-fortress which was the seat of the Florentine state's
government (now known as the Palazzo Vecchio), runs the
Via dei Leoni. At the end of the fifteenth century caged lions
were kept there – living symbols of the city's guardian, a
heraldic lion known as the *Marzocco*. On 5 April two of
these lions attacked and killed each other, for no apparent
reason. That night, lightning struck the gilded, eight-foot
copper ball which Andrea del Verrocchio had designed to
surmount the lantern at the pinnacle of the dome of the
cathedral. The lantern was damaged, and the ball sent
crashing to the floor of the Piazza del Duomo below. Lorenzo
asked on what side of the piazza the ball had fallen, and
on being told that it was the north side, said, 'I shall die,
for that is the side towards my house.'

There were other signs: a woman ran amok in the church
of Santa Maria Novella during Mass, yelling that a giant
bull with horns of flame was demolishing the building;
wolves entered the city from the countryside and howled in
the night; and Marsilio Ficino, a scholar, theologian and
influential translator from Greek into Latin of recently rediscovered works by Plato and his follower Plotinus, and the
senior member of the group of humanists gathered around
Lorenzo, claimed that he saw spectral giants bawling and

fighting in his garden. These supernatural indications of some catastrophe gaining ground were not the only manifestations of a tumult to come. For the past three years a new religious reformer had been attracting more and more attention in Florence. Girolamo Savonarola, forty years old in 1492 and prior of the Dominican Order at San Marco since the previous year, preached vigorously against the sinfulness and apostasy of the age, and exhorted the people to turn again to a simple faith in God. The art and literature, and the humanist thinking encouraged by Lorenzo was viewed by Savonarola as quite as cynical as the papal rule in Rome.

In spite of his reactionary views regarding the humanities, there was a lot of truth in what Savonarola had to say about the decadent state of Christianity. The prior enjoyed enormous popular support, and he also earned the respect of such sophisticated minds as the humanists Pico della Mirandola and Angelo Poliziano, and the painter Sandro Botticelli. As his success grew, so did the boldness of Savonarola's rhetoric. He believed that God was speaking through him. Mortification of his own flesh through fasting and other measures of deprivation had such an effect on his mind as to induce in him a belief in his own ability to predict the future. A radical denial of free thinking and a total commitment to Christian fundamentals were the only sure means of salvation. He referred to whores as 'meat with eyes' and advocated death by burning for homosexuals. The puny, tallow-faced monk, with his disproportionately large, hooked nose above fleshy lips, had dark green eyes so intense that contemporaries swore that they saw them flash fire. As an old man, Michelangelo, among those affected by the monk's rhetoric, complete conviction and sincerity of belief, told his own biographer Giorgio Vasari that he had never forgotten the sound of Savonarola's voice.

Despite the fact that the Medici family and its control of Florence did not escape Savonarola's swingeing criticism, Lorenzo tolerated him. But Lorenzo was an instinctive diplomat, and on account of this he asked not only Savonarola, but his bitter critic and rival, the Augustinian monk, Fra Mariano, for whose order Lorenzo had earlier built a monastery, to bless him as he lay dying.

In the meantime, Lorenzo's doctor, Piero Leoni, had called in a colleague, sent from Milan by that city's current duke, Lodovico Sforza. Lazaro di Pavia took pestle and mortar and compounded a powder of pearls and gems, which dangerous concoction – one thinks of powdered glass – he prescribed to Lorenzo, who, as all other hope seemed to abandon him, clutched at this straw. Seeing how Lorenzo longed to live, Angelo Poliziano, who was with him then, was unable to restrain his tears and retired to his room. Later in the day, Lorenzo, joined by Pico della Mirandola, resigned himself to the fact that the battle was over. He called for a priest to administer extreme unction, and wanted to have himself dressed for the rite; but he did not have the strength, and was carried back to bed. He tried to remain optimistic in the company of his son and heir, Piero, but no one was fooled any more.

On 8 April he fell into such a deep coma that he was taken for dead until a monk from the Florentine Abbey of Camaldoli held his eyeglasses to Lorenzo's lips and observed them to steam up. But his illness was in its last phase. A Bible and a crucifix were brought, and the story of Christ's Passion was read to him, during which those assembled round the bed noted that Lorenzo's lips moved, showing that he was following the text. The crucifix was presented to him to kiss, which he did, and then fell back upon his pillows. Soon afterwards, he died, probably of heart-failure as a result of the build-up of urate crystals in the kidneys.

Lorenzo's body was taken back to Florence, to the Monastery of San Marco, and was later entombed in the old sacristy of the family church of San Lorenzo, next to that of his younger brother. The city went into deep mourning, and looked uneasily at a future under the sway of il Magnifico's far less charismatic heir. A sad postscript follows Lorenzo's death: his doctor, Piero Leoni, was by all accounts an enlightened man who in all probability looked askance at such suggested remedies as powdered precious stones. Almost to the last he had been convinced that his patient would recover, if only he were kept warm and dry, avoided pears and swallowed no grape pips. After Lorenzo's death, shattered by his failure and broken by recriminatory accusations involving poisoning, black magic, and simple incompetence, he left Careggi and committed suicide by throwing himself down a well.

The early history of Florence is complex, but the development of a proto-democracy in what was by 1300 one of the most important and largest cities in Europe – the population then was around 95,000 – at a time when most governments were autocratic or oligarchic goes some way towards explaining the curious position the Medici held in the city.

The first settlement recorded in the area immediately surrounding modern Florence was an Etruscan trading colony on the nearby hill of Fiesole, founded in about 700 BC. It was situated at a fordable spot where the River Arno narrows just before its confluence with the Mugnone, and it lasted several hundred years before being razed by the dictator, Sulla, in 82 BC in reprisal for its having sided with his enemy Marius. The history of the city of Florence proper begins in 59 BC with a Roman settlement – legend has it that the founder was Julius Caesar – on the north bank of the Arno. Clearly the Romans took their cue from the Etruscans, for the situation was very conducive to trade: the location was perfect for the transfer of goods from small craft coming downriver to larger ones which could take bulkier loads down to the sea at Pisa. The Roman colony was given the name Florentia. Later, Florentines of the

Renaissance would be extremely proud of their classical origins.

The Romans laid out their city as a square with streets on a grid pattern, surrounded by walls each about 450 metres long. The theatre and the amphitheatre stood outside the walls just to the south-east. Many of the later streets followed the lines of those of the Romans, and the vanished Roman walls. Names also recalled their ancestry: the Via Campidoglio derived its name from the Capitol, or principal temple; and the Via delle Terme took its name from the Roman Baths which stood between the south wall and the river.

Early Florence was, however, a modest place – there were few important monuments or great buildings, and what there is of Roman antiquity in the city was imported during the sixteenth and succeeding centuries. During the Renaissance the citizens, aware that they were the heirs more of Roman republican ideals than artefacts, set up Roman monuments and invented myths. An antique equestrian statue was set up near the Ponte Vecchio and called 'Mars'. A legend grew that the Baptistery had been built on the site of a temple to the same god, built to mark the crushing of the Etruscan settlement.

Christianity came to Florence untidily, overlapping the dominion of the pagan city. Greek and Syrian traders who set up businesses and homes outside the walls in the first centuries of the Christian era are thought to have imported the new religion with them. The first churches were built – Santa Felicita to the south and San Lorenzo to the north of the walls. San Lorenzo was dedicated by Bishop Ambrose of Milan in 393 and became the seat of the first bishop of Florence, Zenobius. Over a century earlier the city claimed its first Christian martyr, a Greek businessman called Minias (or Mennas), killed in 1250 during the purges against Christians conducted by the Emperor Decius. Minias was buried on a hillside south-east of the city, on the south bank of the Arno, and a legend quickly grew telling that after his execution by beheading, Minias, carrying his head, climbed the hill that became his last resting-place. A shrine was built there but was lost. Later, when Minias' remains were rediscovered early in the eleventh century, the occasion was taken to build a church on the site. It's unclear when work was begun, but the date 1207 is set in the floor of the church and can be taken as an indication of when work was completed on this exquisite jewel of a building.

Despite the fact that the Arno is not an ideal river, subject to flooding and drying up, the course it runs offered so attractive a trade route that in the early Christian era the nascent city was fought over by Byzantines, Goths, and Ostrogoths. The first church (Santa Reparata) was built on the site of the present cathedral at the beginning of the sixth century. In the centuries that followed Tuscany was ruled successively by Byzantines, Lombards and Franks. As a key trading location, the city continued to grow slowly and steadily, though not without internal ructions inspired by religious disagreement. The city effectively consolidated its position towards the end of the eleventh century under the rule of its leader and principal resident, Countess Matilda of Canossa – from whose family Michelangelo's spuriously claimed descent. During this period such important churches as the Baptistery (San Giovanni) and San Miniato al Monte were begun, and the church of Santa Reparata was rebuilt as the city's cathedral. Meanwhile, extensive trade in cloth, dyes, hides and spices began to develop, and inaugurated a long period of prosperity. A powerful merchant class emerged, disinclined to take orders from any aristocrats who might see themselves as *de facto* rulers.

Following Matilda's death in 1115, a strong militia, financed and run by the city, quickly crushed the local feudal nobility, taking the nearby towns of Prato and Fiesole and more than 130 individual castles. To keep the conquered aristocrats under their eye, the Florentines obliged them to live in the city for at least part of each year, but many took up permanent residence and used their wealth and influence to construct fortified urban residences, from which they conducted feuds, formed alliances and engaged in intrigue.

The merchant class quickly realised that such behaviour would lead to chaos and by 1182 a general merchants' guild had been formed, though long before that, following the death of Matilda, a city administration of twelve consuls controlled by a Council of One Hundred had been set up. This, however, had not met with great success, and despite the merchants' guild and further attempts to construct a cohesive civic legislature, the following century was riven by strife of another kind, caused by the often vicious conflict between the supporters of the Pope (the Guelphs, whom Florence broadly supported) and the Ghibellines, who served the interests of the Holy Roman Emperor. As if that were not enough, harsh antagonism arose within the city between the more extreme Black, and the White Guelphs.

None of this was allowed to affect business, however, which continued to flourish, leading to an economic boom towards the end of the thirteenth century. Specialised guilds had already appeared early in the century, dominated by the prosperous Guild of the Refiners of Imported Woollen Cloth (the Arte della Calimala) and its close rival in wealth, the Wool Merchants' Guild (the Arte della Lana), along with the bankers' guild (the Arte del Cambio). The Calimala imported cloth from France and Flanders, refined and dyed it, using dyes derived from all over the known world, and then exported it throughout Europe.

The population rose rapidly, and building increased. The thirteenth and fourteenth centuries were volatile and busy centuries for the city, which had yet to grow out of medieval turmoil and factionalism and into the rational centre of political, social and cultural sophistication to which its leading Renaissance citizens aspired. However, the guilds imposed a certain order on society, and as economic interests prevailed over more or less misguided ideals, and as the civic pride and ambition born during Matilda's leadership took root, the passage of time brought with it a generally better managed society in the city. Economic success played no small role in this. By 1200 Florence was experiencing a boom through its developing banking interests, and what had been rather a provincial trading centre turned into a city of international importance and power. Its success, however, turned envious eyes on it.

The Holy Roman Emperor, Frederick II Hohenstaufen, resident in Palermo, came to the throne in 1215 and reigned for thirty-five years, during which he pursued enthusiastically the aspirations of his empire to vie with the Papacy for the domination at least of northern Italy. The Vatican countered by threatening city-states with any aspiration to independence with excommunication, and allowed the French to establish themselves in southern Italy – in Naples and Sicily – as a counterweight to the central Europeans. In the 1260s, Charles of Anjou defeated Frederick's illegitimate son and heir, Manfred, and broke the power of the Empire in the north. From being redeemers, however, the French quickly became oppressors. The Papacy found itself under the thumb of a new foreign power, and frictions grew which led to the enforced residency of the Popes at Avignon through the middle years of the fourteenth century.

Florence, however, because of its international importance as a financial centre, remained largely independent of the conflicting powers, and managed to continue to make a profit from trade whatever alarms and excursions might have been happening elsewhere: in a sense it was the Switzerland of its day. Despite the factionalism of the Guelphs and the Ghibellines, building work blossomed in the city, and rich merchants began to vie with each other to commission craftsmen and artists to adorn the churches. The streets were busy with carts carrying all manner of wares. The markets were frequent and noisy, selling cheaper cuts of cloth from bolts, tableware, and a great variety of pungent local cheeses, full red wines (though weaker than they are today), a kind of early grappa, fish from the river and pork and beef and vegetables from the local farms. People who could, spent freely and enjoyed showing off their wealth in the clothes they wore and the parties they threw. The new Orders of mendicant friars, pledged to poverty and sworn to support themselves through begging, rather than live on the wealth of monastic estates, became a feature of the urban scene, and were dominated by the rival Dominicans and Franciscans. The Dominicans' church was Santa Maria Novella, begun in about 1246, not thirty years after the Order in Florence had been established by St Dominic himself. Santa Croce was the church of the

Franciscans, whose Order had been founded in Florence by St Francis in 1211. The church we know now was the third on the site, and it was begun around 1294. It was the result of Franciscan expansionism: each church they had built before on the site had quickly grown too small for their increasing influence. Its design is attributed to Arnolfio di Cambio – the very name, as so often, suggesting a certain anonymity – who is nevertheless one of the first Florentine artist-craftsmen to have established his own individual historical identity. He worked in the shop of the sculptor Nicola Pisano in the 1260s, and followed a career as architect and sculptor in Bologna, Florence, Naples, Orvieto, Rome and Siena before his death in 1302.

The first significant secular building still standing today is what we know as the Bargello, named after the chief of police, but originally the home of the head of the city's administration. It was decided to build it in 1250, work started in 1255, and it was completed by 1261. A utilitarian construction, fortress-like rather than aesthetically pleasing, and always associated with oppression and imprisonment, it is made from the local brown limestone known as *pietra forte*, the favourite building material of the city. Its severe appearance, and it was designed to give that impression, is offset by the incorporation of a pre-existing tower, fifty-seven metres high and co-opted from the private home of a former noble family. The towers of the houses of the nobility of Florence had always been ostentatious status symbols, giving the skyline of the Florence of the twelfth and thirteenth centuries the aspect, as contemporaries described it, of a 'cane patch'. In the middle of the thirteenth century, the new civic government asserted its will over the bickering noble factions, and commanded the reduction of all private towers to a minimum height of twenty-eight metres. The Bargello's tower was deliberately left at twice that height. On the façade of the building the following words were inscribed:

EST QUIA CUNCTORUM FLORENTIA PLENUM BONUM
HOSTES DEVICIT BELLO MAGNOQUE TUMLTO
GAUDET FORTUNA SIGNIS POPULOQUE POTENTI
FIRMAT EMIT FERVENS STERNIT NUNC CASTRA SALUTE
QUE MARE QUE TERRAM QUE TOTUM POSSIDET ORBEM
PER QUAM REGNANTEM FIT FELIX TUSCIA TOTA
TAMQUAM ROMA SEDET SEMPER DUCTURA TRIUMPHOS

[Florence is filled with all wealth imaginable. She defeats her enemies in war and civil strife. She enjoys Fortune's favour and her population is mighty. She fortifies castles and she conquers castles. She holds sway over the sea and the land and the whole world. Under her all Tuscany is happy. Like Rome she is always triumphant.]

As early as 1252 the first gold florins, named after the city, had been struck, bearing the city's name and its emblem, the lily. It contained fifty-four grains of gold and had the purchasing power of at least £100 in today's terms. It soon became the US dollar of its day among the international community. Florentine bankers grew tremendously wealthy and became mini-princes within their bourgeois community. As the city was loyal to the Papacy, the bankers profited from increasingly lucrative Curial accounts. At the same time, the city-state of Florence, in the middle of its expanding territories, was able to take a powerful independent role on the international stage.

The nobles had been the victims of their own arrogance and internecine struggles. What was rapidly emerging in Florence was a merchant/banker middle class – the *popolani*; but alongside them an ecclesiastical element was also growing, dominated by the great mendicant Orders of the Dominicans and their rivals the Franciscans. As mendicant Orders, they depended upon charity for survival, and in Florence they had no difficulty in benefiting from the wealthy Christian population, the more so as merchants and bankers gained status through the size of their endowments to the Orders.

During all this time the city was governed by a more-or-less stable assembly of burghers elected for fixed periods by the *popolani* from among their own class. The first government of limited democracy that really took root – the *Primo Popolo* – concerned itself principally with the city's economic well-being and its defence. A governing body of twelve *anziani* – prominent citizens – each from one of the city's quarters – was elected, to hold office for one year. They were joined by two 'judges' to deal with in the first instance defensive, and in the second administrative and judicial affairs – the *capitano di popolo* and the *podestà* respectively.

The *Primo Popolo* did not last very long, although during its lifetime work on the formidable fortress-cum-jail-cum-police-headquarters now known as the Bargello was begun. By 1258 violent conflict had broken out between Guelphs and Ghibellines in Florence and the region. The result of this was that Manfred, the natural son of the Holy Roman Emperor, took power in Florence and held sway for seven years, but at his death in 1267 in battle against Charles of Anjou power swung back to the Guelphs, and during the fifteen years or so that Charles held sway in Italy, the Guelphs in Florence consolidated their power base. Florentines never forgot the principle of the *Primo Popolo*, however, and when Charles died in 1282 they were ready to set up a new democratic government, though real power was still exclusively in the hands of the most powerful businesses.

This time the ruling council comprised six 'priors' chosen from among the members of the seven major guilds. They served terms of only two months each, but the operation of the city remained firmly in the hands of a Guelph-controlled wealthy elite. Subsequently further democratisation led to the inclusion of smaller guilds' members as priors, and a wider representation of interests. Subsequently the number of priors was increased to twelve; their title was changed to *Signori*, and a palace was built as their office, the Palazzo della Signoria.

The nobility was kept in check by various measures: one of them was the appointment by each *Signore* of a 'standard-bearer', a *Gonfaloniere*, whose responsibility was to enrol twenty companies of armed men to keep the peace. Later the office of *Gonfaloniere* became the most important in the civic hierarchy. In times of crisis or assembly the loyal populace would be summoned to the piazza in front of the palazzo by the tolling of a bell in its tower, known because of its deep, lowing tone as *la vacca* – the cow.

The wealth and the building continued to increase. Three bridges had been constructed over the Arno by the middle of the thirteenth century, and three of Florence's major buildings had been started by the 1290s – the great church of Santa Croce, the new cathedral of Santa Maria del Fiore (the famous campanile by Giotto and Pisano rose during the middle years of the following century), and the new town hall, just mentioned, which was also the state administrative centre, the Palazzo della Signoria. The Ponte Vecchio was built between about 1335 and 1345. A Roman bridge had stood in its position before. The original shops were those of tanners and pursemakers. They were succeeded by butchers. The goldsmiths and jewellers of today first opened up in the 1590s.

The place of the Calimala, the Refiners of Imported Woollen Cloth, as principal guild was taken over by the Arte della Lana, the Wool Merchants' Guild, during the 1300s, when the textile industry as a whole (including the silk-workers' guild) had about 200 workshops employing around 30,000 people, producing up to 80,000 bolts of cloth a year, and with an annual turnover of 1,200,000 florins. The Arte della Lana took responsibility for paying for all works appertaining to the decoration and construction of the cathedral, which is why the guild's emblem of a lamb (usefully tying in with the symbol of Christ) is so evident in the building.

A growing finance industry was now represented by eighty banking houses, and middle-class society was also represented by a large legal profession and a Guild of Physicians and Apothecaries to which the artists, having as yet no formal status of their own, also belonged; they ground their colours much as apothecaries ground their potions. Within the guild they later founded their own Confraternity of St Luke, who'd been the 'first' Christian artist.

There were thirty hospitals whose services were available to all, over one hundred churches and monasteries; and 10,000 children of both sexes were being taught to read and write in the schools. The university was founded in 1321. In a male-dominated society, the smart red outfits worn by

Florentine men were the pin-striped suits of their day. Lorenzo de' Medici's grandfather, Cosimo, bought one for the sculptor Donatello, who wore it for a while, but soon abandoned it in favour of the comfortable, down-at-heel clothes he preferred. Donatello was an exception.

Women were expected to toe the line. If their bent was intellectual and they were not high-born and of independent means, only the Church offered very limited possibilities for self-expression, though some women of the artisan and trading classes also enjoyed a limited freedom of expression, in business as well as in their private life. The ancient world had as yet communicated no information about the position and standing of women in society. Although education was available and access to books possible, women's position in society changed little as the Middle Ages shaded into the Renaissance, and the enlightening effects of the Renaissance were by no means felt everywhere. Women could only fulfil certain rigid roles determined by male concepts: mother, priestess, queen, whore – or the chaste object of a poet's fastidious adoration.

In the opinion of the Florentine priors 'women were created to replenish this free city . . . and not to spend gold and silver on clothing and jewellery'. In 1378 Nicolosa Soderini (an ancestor of a famous *Gonfaloniere*), was prosecuted and fined for wearing a tasselled silk dress bound with black leather. She was ten years old at the time.

Half a century later, in 1433, a law was passed curbing

any showiness in women's dress, and the edict contained a clause reflecting on 'the bestiality of women'. A few decades later, however, if the women in Ghirlandaio's frescoes are anything to go by, this unpleasant law had fallen into disuse. The rich brocades and jewellery the women in his paintings wear begin to vie with the opulent dress only men have hitherto been portrayed in. Botticelli's women are even more free, and perhaps it is worth casting an eye back one and a half centuries to the women in Boccaccio's *Decamerone*: were those liberated attitudes simply imagined?

Florence was also deeply materialistic. Poverty was a disgrace. Everyone gave lip service to the kingdom of heaven, but most were more concerned with mammon.

Mammon paid off. By the end of the 1330s Florence was the most powerful city in Europe; a world-dominating industrial and financial centre. In the middle of the decade building work started, and would continue over the next forty years, on the great church of Orsanmichele. Built on the site of an ancient orchard, the church was a monument both to God and to civic confidence and pride, and every major artist of the day contributed something to it.

But all was not well: two of the main banking houses were badly overstretched in backing the English King Edward III's wars with France. When Edward defaulted on a loan of one million florins, the two banks went bankrupt in England and the ensuing panic among Florentine investors nearly precipitated an economic crash. At the same time, local wars prosecuted by Florence against the smaller rival cities of Pisa and Lucca had drained the treasury. The Arno flooded the city in 1333. The following decade-and-a-half saw civil unrest, a brief dictatorship, the loss of Tuscan possessions and territories to rivals, crop failure and famine, the collapse of virtually every banking house, and, finally, as a devastating *coup-de-grâce*, the arrival of that terrible scourge of Europe and beyond, The Black Death. By 1348 the population of Florence had grown to about 120,000. In six months, the plague killed 90,000 souls. Though it abated, it returned to ravage the city again twice in the following three decades.

Florence was not the only city to suffer. After the plague, its neighbour Siena never recovered its former importance. Florence fought back. By 1380 the population had risen again to 70,000. The citizens clawed their way to prosperity again, the guilds re-formed, the building works resumed, and new banking houses emerged. Among them were those run by the Albizzi, the Strozzi and the Medici families.

The second half of the fourteenth century in Florence saw a major regrowth of artistic, architectural and civic activity, though the city was still far from free of its troubles. The plague revisited the city in the 1370s, and continuing civil unrest culminated at the end of that decade with the *tumulto dei Ciompi*, an uprising of the wool-workers. By 1382, however, an oligarchic government had once more established itself in Florence, in the ranks of which the Albizzi family soon gained a controlling interest. Their hegemony did not, however, go unchallenged: as the miraculously creative fourteenth century had unfurled, during which the Middle Ages gave way to the bright sun of the Renaissance, the Medici opposed them with ever greater tenacity. When, in 1413, the Medici cornered the opulent Papal accounts, the family, though officially remaining mere citizens, became in effect the rulers of Florence. They did this through genuinely patriotic investment in the city and the state, but more simply by dint of becoming the richest family – and it was a family which was almost a clan, with its own internal divisions – in the land.

With plenty of rivals, like the Strozzi and Pazzi families, who had their own supporters within and outside the state, maintenance of power meant survival. With a few interruptions, and culminating in a long decline, the fortunes of the Medici were intertwined with those of Florence for the next 300 years. Descendants would marry into the royal families of Europe, and the family would produce two popes. Not many, however, would disagree that from the point of view of the Medici as patrons of culture, they reached their peak under the rule and in the person of Lorenzo the Magnificent.

The Medici had been quietly involved in Florentine politics since at least the late thirteenth century. Even then their coat of arms, with its seven (the number varied) 'balls' was well known. The balls represented, according to what myth you believed, either the dents the shield of their legendary ancestor, Averardo, received from a demonic tyrant while Averardo fought him to save the Tuscans from his oppression; or cupping glasses, emblematic of the Medicis' origin (as their name suggests) as doctors or apothecaries. The *palle* might even have been coins – the emblems (as we still see in their sign of three 'balls') of pawnbrokers.

It was owing to Lorenzo's grandfather, Cosimo, a skilful politician and an astute banker who was given the honorific *pater patriae*, father of his country, that the family assumed and consolidated their true power. Cosimo the Great started the family tradition, which held firm for the next two generations without interruption, of being lavish and discerning patrons of the arts and humanities, being as much interested in productions of antiquity as in promoting the modern. It was Cosimo, too, who established the power of the Medici in Florence by dint of making the family great patrons of the city's social, cultural and religious life as well, vying in this regard with other powerful families, such as the Rucellai. Under Cosimo work began in 1445 on the massive palace which would bear the family name.

All the great art which flourished in the fifteenth and sixteenth centuries – the centuries which concern us – though inspired by antiquity, was in fact *modern*, and design and art rode hand in hand. Such artists as Verrocchio, Botticelli and Piero di Cosimo thought nothing of designing ephemeral standards and armour and floats for pageants – and

Michelangelo created a snowman for Lorenzo's son Piero in the deep winter of early 1494.

Such contracts went with the territory, and Leonardo and Michelangelo were, in the early sixteenth century, the first creative spirits to establish themselves as artists to be respected and engaged in their own right, no longer to be ranked with artisans and workmen, though the way had long been paved for them by such great forebears in the worlds of architecture, painting and sculpture as Cimabue, Giotto, Alberti, Brunelleschi, Ghiberti, Donatello and Verrocchio.

Most of these men could if necessary turn their hands to any discipline, though Cimabue is remembered for his great religious paintings, Giotto for painting and for his *campanile*. Ghiberti, trained as a goldsmith, is remembered for the famous Baptistery doors, and Brunelleschi, his rival, essentially an architect, for the great dome of the cathedral. Alberti was also an architect, though it is as much for his theories of form and spatial relationships as his buildings that he is remembered. The master sculptors Donatello and, slightly later, Verrocchio, dominated the central years of the fifteenth century. All of them, along with many other masters, like Paolo Uccello, Taddeo Gaddi, Andrea Orcagna, Andrea Pisano, Nanni di Banco, Bernardo Daddi, Andrea dal Castagno, the great Masaccio and many more in this forcing-house of talent, would provide through their works the greatest inspiration for their successors, including, head and shoulders above almost all his contemporaries and surpassed by none, Michelangelo Buonarroti. It is interesting that there was no similar flowering of literature. Dante, Boccaccio and Petrarch stand more or less alone.

Cosimo de' Medici died in 1464, in his seventy-fifth year, and was succeeded in what amounted to an unofficial dukedom (with the consent of the *Signoria*, then fully influenced by or invested with Medici supporters) by his forty-eight-year old son Piero, a valetudinarian with – on account of his chronic sickness – rather less of his father's financial and political integrity. His nickname was *il Gottoso* – the Gouty. Nevertheless Piero held office as a prior, was the last Medici to be elected *Gonfaloniere*; and racked with gout, arthritis and eczema as he was, he remained a good-looking and determined man. He was also a conscientious accountant, and maintained his father's interest in and patronage of the arts and nascent humanism, encompassing the modern secular scholarship which would challenge the tenets of the Church. By his time a generation of Florentines existed who had grown up under Medici 'rule', which in turn had been consolidated by judicious marriages to the daughters of other influential families.

Piero married Lucrezia Tornabuoni, a religious poet of talent and the daughter of another great house. They had three daughters and two sons, of whom Lorenzo was the older. Lorenzo was tall and strong; his ungainly manner and ugly face (his nose was so squashed it looked broken, and he was born without a sense of smell), however, belied a sensitive and acute intellect. He was highly competitive, humorous, and not averse to gorgeous dress on public occasions, though in private he preferred to wear quiet clothes. His taste was exquisite and although he preferred to collect small, easily transportable antiquities, he didn't stint when it came to cost. It was said that a small classical chalice he bought had cost more than a whole series of frescoes. Many of the precious stones, cameos and figurines in the Medici collections cost over 1000 florins each. A painting by Botticelli or one of the Pollaiuolo brothers would change hands for a tenth of that amount.

In his youth Lorenzo enjoyed the games of *calcio*, a kind of no-holds-barred football with twenty-seven players a side, and *palloni* – a precursor of fives. He was a keen hunter, went hawking, wrote poetry, and composed music, for which he also wrote lyrics, which were not always decorous. He played the lute well. He was a good conversationalist and wit, and a kind husband to the bride who'd been chosen for him, Clarice Orsini, a girl from a prominent Roman family, sixteen when she married. He was nineteen, and soon to inherit the mantle of rule.

Lorenzo married Clarice by proxy in Rome, but the official wedding, which took place when she arrived in Florence, occasioned three days of celebrations and feasting in June, preceded by a grand tournament in February. Such lavishness was designed to mollify the Florentines, who looked askance at a bride from Rome, an outsider. At the five banquets which took place over the three days of the wedding festival, 5000 pounds of sweetmeats were consumed, along with 300 barrels of wine. The Medici, always aware of the value of propitiating the populace, gave many grand parties, using the Piazza Santa Croce as their location. Prosperity and a plethora of feast-days and guild-holidays meant that Florentines enjoyed getting on for ninety days' free time a year, so that bread and circuses were the order of the day in the form of balletic (as opposed to earnest and bloody north-European-style) jousts, mock battles, games of football, and, less edifyingly, lions set upon dogs (the lions often got the worst of it, though the dogs were meant to represent Florence's ignoble enemies), and a mare set among stallions, which one male observer thought might be a marvellous entertainment for young girls to see. Festivals of this kind took place with particular brio on such dates as 24 June, the feast day of St John the Baptist, the patron of Florence. Lenten celebrations were more sober, but no less theatrical, with the symbols of Christ's Passion carried through the streets in solemn procession, ritual lamentation and an implicit and pleasurable anticipation of the Resurrection.

A conservative, not a beauty and rather a snob, Clarice was, nevertheless, a strong and attractive person to whom Lorenzo remained devoted and loyal, if not faithful, until her death from tuberculosis in 1478. They had ten children, of whom seven survived infancy, to whom they were devoted.

Piero the Gouty died in the year of Lorenzo's marriage, and his son, twenty years old in 1469, took over the reins of power. It was almost a case of 'the king is dead, long live the king', so vital was it to Florence to have continuity in the liberal but firm influence (to avoid the word 'rule') of the Medici. Twenty seems young, but it wasn't as young then as it is now, and Lorenzo had been groomed for the role of city boss. He accepted a delegation from the city fathers with modesty and dignity, and later noted shrewdly that 'The leading men of the government came to our home to express their sorrow for our loss and to urge me to assume the guardianship of the city as my father and grandfather had done before. Their proposal was against my youthful instincts, and considering that the burden and danger were great, I consented to it unwillingly. But I did so in order to protect our friends and property; since it fares ill in Florence with anyone who is rich but does not have any share in government'. In fact in the interval between Piero's death and the arrival of the delegation, Lorenzo had already written to the powerful Duke of Milan, enlisting a continuation of the traditional support that the Sforzas had lent the Medici. The then duke, Galeazzo Maria Sforza, was a good man to have on one's side, a cultivated and competent ruler who was also, in that curious way that existed between the Middle Ages and the true Renaissance, cruel, debauched and ruthless. Compared with Lorenzo, in many ways he already seemed an anachronism; but Lorenzo was ahead of his time.

Lorenzo managed the affairs of his city in close consultation with his younger brother Giuliano, who was born in 1453. The job was no sinecure, as the Medici were not without rivals who envied and resented their position. Two years after succeeding his father, Lorenzo had visited Rome as part of the Florentine delegation deputed to congratulate the new Pope on his election. This was Sixtus IV, the originator of the Sistine Chapel, a major new building in a reborn Rome still struggling to re-establish itself after the dark age of the antipopes. The chapel would draw on some of the major artistic talents of the day, most of whom came from Florence.

Sixtus was a crude-looking man with a rough manner, who had risen through the ranks of the Franciscans, which Order he had joined early, to the most powerful office on the international scene. His origins were humble, but the Church provided a sure career ladder to any man of capability, regardless of his background, and Sixtus – born Francesco della Rovere – was a popular preacher with a taste for learning, some charm, political acuteness and great luck, which brought him the Papacy at the age of fifty-seven.

As Pope, he quickly indulged in nepotism to a degree which seemed excessive even for that age. He made six of his nephews cardinals, and, more disturbing for Lorenzo, displayed an interest in expanding the sphere of influence of the Papal States. Relations with Sixtus were cordial at first – the Medici were, after all, the Pope's bankers – and Lorenzo was able to buy antiquities from the Vatican collection for his own at friendly prices; but when the Pope asked for a loan to buy the strategically placed town of Imola for one of his secular nephews, one Girolamo Riario, whom Sixtus intended to marry to an illegitimate but acknowledged daughter of the Duke of Milan (the owner of Imola), Lorenzo demurred. Imola controlled the trade route from Bologna to Rimini: Lorenzo had intended to purchase it himself. He was in a difficult position: he didn't want to sacrifice his good relationship with the Pope, but he was all too well aware of the danger to Florentine security of papal expansion in the Romagna and of close ties between the Vatican and Milan, the latter having hitherto been an ally of Florence.

Lorenzo refused to advance the loan, though he must have known what would happen: the Pope promptly withdrew the Curial account from the Medici and transferred it to the rival Florentine banking family of Pazzi, who were delighted to get it, and immediately lent Sixtus the 40,000 ducats he needed to buy Imola.

The political chess game continued, with matters between Florence and the Vatican becoming ever more strained. In 1474 one of the cardinal-nephews, who had earlier been appointed Archbishop of Florence, died (of excess); Lorenzo managed to get his own brother-in-law appointed successor, but the Pope countered by nominating his own man, Francesco Salviati, to the vacant see of nearby Pisa, a town that maintained a bitter rivalry with Florence, with which it was perpetually at war (Pisa was smaller and weaker than Florence, but Florence had no sea-port and coveted the Pisan port of Livorno). The Pope was breaking an agreement that there could be no appointment to the Pisan archbishopric without reference to the Florentine *Signoria*. Thus Lorenzo refused Salviati entry into Tuscany. For the next three years Salviati fumed in Rome, toying with plots against the Medici.

Italy was composed of a number of more or less powerful duchies and republics, the Papal States, and, further south, the Kingdom of Naples. To cover himself and to try to maintain peace in the north, as well as frustrate Papal ambitions in the Romagna, Lorenzo advanced an alliance between Milan, the rich, powerful, but generally aloof Republic of Venice to the east, and Florence. The Pope immediately took this as a slight to himself, and leagued himself with King Ferrante of Naples. Naples and Rome were not traditional allies, but Sixtus had earlier taken the precaution of marrying yet another nephew to one of Ferrante's illegitimate but acknowledged daughters. There was a stand-off which lasted until another crisis hit Lorenzo – his ally Galeazzo of Milan was assassinated just after Christmas, 1476, precipitating a power struggle in the Duchy as his heir was only seven years old. Those plotting against Lorenzo decided that it was time to devise a plan against him in earnest.

Girolamo Riario was unhappy that he hadn't been able to expand beyond Imola; Francesco Salviati not only wanted to take up his post at Pisa but had his eye on the Archbishopric of Florence as well; and the director of the Pazzi bank in Rome, another Francesco, thought that now the Pazzi had the Papal ear and the Papal account, there was no reason why his family should not supplant the Medici at home. This ambition was fuelled by the fact that the Pazzi were a much older family than the Medici, whom they regarded as upstarts. Not all the family were in favour of the *coup* which Francesco de' Pazzi now cautiously proposed, though the advantages which would follow its success were obvious. The Pope, though he could not be seen to be a party to it, gave the project his tacit approval. With Lorenzo out of the way, there would be no obstacle to his own ambitions for expansion. All this took time, diplomacy, and delicacy to achieve.

Riario, Salviati and Pazzi had recruited an at-first reluctant mercenary, Gian Battista da Montesecco, who became more friendly once he knew they had the Pope's backing, which went some way towards persuading him of the justice of the conspirators' cause. His first job was to arrange military backup for the *coup*. The whole plan hung upon the assassination – or murder, depending on how you looked at it – of the key figures of Lorenzo and his younger brother

Giuliano de' Medici in Florence or nearby, under the guise of 'liberating' the city from Medici 'tyranny'. The bait took the form of a seventeen-year-old great-nephew of the Pope, Raffaele Riario, who was entirely innocent of the plot. He had just been made a cardinal and was studying in Pisa. In April 1478, Raffaele was invited by another member of the Pazzi family to stay at a country villa just outside Florence, and once there he was encouraged to write to Lorenzo, expressing the desire to meet him. Lorenzo was then staying with Giuliano at Fiesole. Always generous-natured, he responded warmly to the young man's letter – perhaps even seeing this as a means to patch things up with the Pope – and invited him and his retinue to dine. The plotters hoped to kill both brothers – it was essential that there should be no strong successor to Lorenzo for his supporters to rally round – at the dinner, either by knifing or poisoning them. However, Giuliano was indisposed because of a riding accident and could not attend, so the attempt was aborted.

A further opportunity presented itself soon afterwards. At the dinner, Raffaele had asked Lorenzo if he might see some of the treasures in the Medici art collection. Lorenzo gladly agreed. The young cardinal would be attending Mass in Florence Cathedral the next Sunday and that seemed as good a time as any. A large banquet was arranged and many dignitaries were invited.

It was at the banquet that the killings were to take place;

but once again it looked as if Giuliano wouldn't be there. By now the conspirators were beginning to worry about security and felt sure that if they delayed again their plot would be uncovered – too many people knew about it by now. So they decided to stab the brothers to death in the cathedral during Mass, which they knew Giuliano would be attending. Montesecco's troops were waiting in the vicinity for the order to seal the city.

There were problems. Giuliano's murder was assigned to Francesco de' Pazzi and a down-at-heel gentleman called Baroncelli, heavily in debt to the Pazzi bank. Neither man was by any means a professional assassin. Montesecco, who *was* a professional, had by this time met Lorenzo under a guise of friendship, and found the young man to be very far from the villain he'd been led to expect. Moreover, the idea of committing murder in the cathedral was repugnant to him (though this may have been an excuse to distance himself from the plot), and he refused to take part in the actual killing. Providentially, his place was taken by two priests: one had a grudge against Lorenzo; the other was a tutor in the Pazzi family. These priests were considered a liability as assassins, but there *were* two of them, their loyalty was not in doubt; and if they could take Lorenzo and his friends completely by surprise, it was thought they would have a good chance of killing him. Besides, there was no time to recruit anyone else.

At last everything was ready: as soon as the killings had

taken place, the plan was for Salviati and another conspirator, Jacopo Bracciolini, the ambitious son of one of Cosimo de' Medici's humanist friends, to descend on the nearby Piazza della Signoria with a large armed escort, take control of the Palazzo and kill any members of the *Signoria* who tried to stand up to them.

There was just one more hitch on the morning of Sunday, 26 April 1478: at the last minute Giuliano announced that, after all, he did not feel well enough to go to the cathedral. Francesco de' Pazzi and Baroncelli managed to persuade him that he should. Pazzi even threw a friendly arm around him, in reality to feel if Giuliano was wearing any protective armour under his clothes. He wasn't; nor was he armed.

Everyone took his place near the high altar. Among other friends with Lorenzo was Angelo Poliziano. The conspirators had decided that the sound of the sacristy bell would be their signal for attack, and when it rang, they struck. The two priests botched their effort, giving Lorenzo a flesh wound in the neck but allowing him time to draw his sword, and for his friends to rally round. They bundled him towards the sacristy and managed to get its heavy bronze doors shut against the killers, while the priests lost themselves in the crowd, which by now was in an uproar. Giuliano was not as fortunate as his brother. Pazzi and Baroncelli had hurled themselves on him in a frenzy, stabbing him nineteen times – so ferocious was Pazzi's attack that he managed to stab himself in the thigh. Now Giuliano lay dying, choking on his blood, while his murderers fled. Lorenzo was taken by back streets to the Medici Palace, after one of his friends had sucked the wound clean, in case the daggers of the priests had been poisoned.

At the Palazzo della Signoria, things at first appeared to be going well for the conspirators: the *Gonfaloniere*, Cesare Petrucci, had admitted Salviati, Bracciolini and their cohorts, accepting Salviati's explanation that he had brought a message from the Pope. Petrucci, however, took the precaution of separating the Archbishop from his attendants, largely a bunch of Perugian mercenaries. Alone, Salviati soon lost his nerve, and Petrucci, who'd been suspicious of him all along, called out his own guard. Salviati thereupon shouted to his own men to defend him, but they had been led into an antechamber whose door could only be opened from the outside, and were trapped. Bracciolini attacked Petrucci, but the latter seized him by the hair and hurled him to the floor, shouting orders that the great bell, the *vacca*, be sounded to summon the populace.

After that it was all over for the conspirators. Though some members of the Pazzi family rode through the streets proclaiming liberty and shouting, 'down with the Medici', they were answered by louder and more numerous cries in support of Lorenzo. Medici followers made their way to the Palazzo della Signoria and killed all the mercenaries imprisoned there. As soon as the news of Giuliano's murder reached the Palazzo, Bracciolini was taken upstairs. A rope was put round his neck, its other end attached to a beam, and he was hurled from a window to hang. Salviati quickly shared the same fate, as did Pazzi, who despite his self-inflicted thigh wound had managed to drag himself home to the Pazzi Palace. The mob had hunted him down there, stripped him naked, and brought him bleeding to the Signoria. This was no quick death. Poliziano, an eye-witness to these events, recalled that the dying Salviati, in a paroxysm, sank his teeth into the naked body of Pazzi, hanging near him.

Lorenzo quickly appeared before the crowd that had gathered in front of his palace to reassure them that he was alive. His first action was to take steps to ensure the safety of the innocent Cardinal Raffaele Riario, whose family connection with the Pope would certainly have ensured his death otherwise. In the days and weeks that followed all save one of the principal conspirators were rounded up, tortured, questioned and dispatched. The two priests were castrated before they were hanged. Baroncelli got as far away as Constantinople, but the Ottoman Sultan, Mohammed II, who had taken the crumbling Byzantine city in 1453, sent him back to Florence in chains. He was executed in the courtyard of the Bargello. Mohammed and Lorenzo were on friendly terms, and at the former's request the latter sent him a number of Florentine craftsmen skilled in *intarsia* work.

The ruin of the Pazzi family was complete: their name

was blotted out, their emblem – the dolphin – everywhere torn down, and their property was seized by the state. Sandro Botticelli was commissioned to paint a picture of each of the conspirators in their death throes, for which he was paid forty florins each, and these were displayed on the walls of the Bargello. The twenty-nine-year-old Lorenzo emerged as a hero, and from then on his role as chief citizen, benefactor and *de facto* ruler of Florence was not only assured, but enhanced. He had the sculptor Bertoldo di Giovanni design a medal to commemorate the overthrow of his enemies, and adopted Giulio, the illegitimate baby boy his dead brother had fathered that same year. Giulio would one day ascend the Papal throne as Clement VII.

Rome was furious. Sixtus IV issued orders for the excommunication of Lorenzo and most of the leadership of Florence, demanding that Lorenzo be handed over to Papal justice and that all his property be forfeit. Not content with that, he declared war on Florence, succeeding in getting King Ferrante of Naples to do the same, and threatened the entire city with excommunication if it didn't toe the line. Ferrante's son, Alfonso, marched into Tuscany from the south and occupied the region of Montepulciano, within stabbing distance of Siena, already an enemy of Florence, whence he issued threats and passed on further imprecations from the Pope. Florence responded defiantly, invoking an old alliance with the French king, Louis XI, from whom little material support could in fact be expected, and in rather desperate hope of support from Milan, which did in fact send a small force. Undeterred by their weak position, the Tuscan bishops rounded on the Pope and excommunicated *him,* which must have given Sixtus apoplexy.

For the rest of 1478, however, there was a standoff, but in 1479 power in Milan fell into the hands of the most dominant of Galeazzo's surviving brothers, Lodovico, who was to maintain it for many years as 'regent', and notwithstanding his brutality, become the patron of Leonardo da Vinci. Lodovico calculated that as Florence seemed to be on the brink of collapse, there was no point in continuing an alliance with it. In the meantime, Alfonso stepped up his campaign. Only the heroic resistance of the small Tuscan town of Colle, not fifty kilometres south of Florence, held him up long enough to arrest his advance any further for that winter. It was 14 November when Colle fell.

Lorenzo knew that Florence would fall itself the following spring if he did nothing. He therefore embarked on a diplomatic mission to the court of his enemy, King Ferrante, to negotiate a peace. He set sail in December and arrived in Naples in time for Christmas 1479.

His mission was regarded by the Florentines as one of unexampled bravery and altruism – there was nothing to stop Ferrante from stringing him up if he felt so inclined; but although Lorenzo's move was without doubt as courageous as he'd presented it to be to the *Signoria,* it was also astute, and the risk he was taking was calculated. Although conflict could be brutal and retribution harsh, total warfare was a concept still far in the future. Battles were fought only when necessary, standoffs were common, and antagonists were often that briefly and in name only. The common people only wanted to be left alone; the mercenaries didn't care as long as they were paid, and the leaders were as often as not friends in normal times. There were no standing armies; in all Europe only England had one until the time of Louis XI of France at the end of the fifteenth century.

So it was that when he arrived in Naples, Lorenzo was welcomed affectionately both by Alfonso's younger brother Federigo, a boyhood comrade, and by Alfonso's wife, Ippolita Sforza, an equally old friend. Lorenzo had traded antiquities with Ferrante's senior minister, and, as if all that was not enough, had already carried off half his diplomatic manoeuvre before even setting sail. He'd been in secret correspondence with the Neapolitan court and had established that, while Alfonso would be reluctant to relinquish his conquests in southern Tuscany, Ferrante was worried by the threat from France: the French made no secret of a long-standing claim to the throne of Naples. What was more, Lorenzo was on friendly terms with Mohammed II, and lately a Turkish fleet had been observed along the Adriatic coast.

Ferrante received Lorenzo courteously, but when it came to reaching an agreement he was cagey, and kept Lorenzo in suspense. The expedition had cost Lorenzo a small fortune, paid out of his own purse, which he had raised by heavily mortgaging some of his property. Expected acts of generosity to the poor of Naples had cost more, and the expenses of his retinue as the weeks passed mounted alarmingly. Finally, after nearly three months, Lorenzo had had enough. One day he told Ferrante that he was required urgently back in Florence, and made immediate preparations to return home overland. He hadn't gone far before Ferrante sent a peace treaty after him. It wasn't generous: Alfonso would have to be bought off, the surviving Pazzi released from jail, and, worst of all, some Tuscan holdings in the south would have to be ceded. But Florence would be safe, and in a strong position from which to rebuild its fortunes. With justification his return was to a hero's welcome.

Unfortunately Lorenzo was unable to take up the reins of a cultivated life uninterrupted by cares. Although the family bank had expanded to fourteen international branches at its height, Lorenzo's father had not been the banker his grandfather had been, and Lorenzo too showed little talent for the *métier* that had established the family fortunes. The London branch of the Medici bank had backed the wrong side in England at a crucial point during the Wars of the Roses, and when Edward IV had been kicked out in 1470 to be replaced briefly by Henry VI, their bank had collapsed. The branches in Milan and Bruges also went under, and those in Lyons, Rome and Naples were teetering on the brink. This was not all Lorenzo's fault: shifts in economic power meant that Florence in general was losing its supremacy in international finance.

Lorenzo was unused to going without, and finding himself as good as bankrupt, he dipped into funds held in trust for his two younger second cousins, Lorenzo and Giovanni, the sons of his father's cousin Pierfrancesco, members of the junior but by no means poorer branch of the family. When they came of age he couldn't pay them back the cash he'd taken, and had to part with property in lieu. Interestingly, it was Lorenzo di Pierfrancesco who inherited Lorenzo's artistic sensibility, far more than Lorenzo's own oldest son, Piero. Lorenzo also took money from the state. When this embezzlement was discovered after his death, his direct heirs were ordered to pay back 75,000 florins.

At least peace now seemed assured, though by a coincidence so much to Lorenzo's advantage that people wondered if it hadn't been engineered. In August 1480 a huge Turkish force landed on the heel of Italy and established a base there, with the obvious intention of surging north to Naples and then Rome. Alfonso's garrisons had to abandon their Tuscan holdings in order to head south to protect their own southern frontier, and Ferrante ceded them back to Florence, at the same time persuading the Pope that he should accept Florence's apologies and concentrate on uniting Christendom against the Muslim threat. The scantest apologies were given, and accepted with equally scant grace, but at least peace was agreed on, and for the first time Italy managed to unite. Three major Florentine artists – Sandro Botticelli, Domenico Ghirlandaio and Cosimo Rosselli – went to Rome to work on the frescoes for the newly finished Sistine Chapel. Early in 1481, Mohammed II died, and his army withdrew. With the exception of a few minor spats, however, the peace treaty arrived at in 1480 survived, not least because the various Italian states came to realise, for a time, that their unity provided security against the territorial interests of France, Spain and the Holy Roman Empire.

Lorenzo spent the last twelve years of his life strenuously working to maintain this peace. In the latter half of that period – from 1484 – he was helped by the death of Sixtus, whose small-minded empire-building had been a chief cause of mistrust and dissent. Sixtus was replaced by Innocent VIII, a member of the Cibò family. An unappealing man whose ambitions went little further than a desire to advance his illegitimate children (born before his ordination), his Papacy was distinguished by his declaration of Henry VII as king of England, and Torquemada as first Grand Inquisitor.

He was not difficult to control, though Lorenzo at first experienced difficulties in handling his principal adviser, Cardinal Giuliano della Rovere, another of Sixtus' nephews, a tough and warlike man, who luckily soon fell from favour after prosecuting a disastrous and expensive little war with

Naples. Lorenzo thereafter strengthened his links with the Pope by marrying his sixteen-year-old-daughter Maddalena to one of the Pope's sons, a dull-witted alcoholic of forty, who received as part of Maddalena's dowry the Pazzi Palace in Florence and their country villa at Montughi, as well as a large estate near Arezzo. It was Innocent whom Lorenzo persuaded to create his bright, fourteen-year-old second son Giovanni a cardinal in 1489, though Giovanni would not be publicly inducted until three years later, after a probationary period, in a ceremony conducted at Fiesole on 9 March 1492, almost exactly a month before Lorenzo's death. The ritual completed, Giovanni came down to Florence amid scenes of great rejoicing, to place his new red hat at his father's feet. Lorenzo had crowned his life with a major *coup* for his family, and Giovanni would not disappoint him. In 1513 he ascended the papal throne as Leo X.

After the death of Sixtus IV, Lorenzo could at last spend some time with his friends and his adored children. He had always done so when the possibility presented itself, but he had never been able to fulfil his ambition of withdrawing from the world and devoting himself to scholarship. At least he could play at it at his villas, especially at Poggio and Careggi, where he gathered around him his humanist friends – 'the Academy of Plato' (founded in fact in 1440) – where every year on 7 November a dinner was held in honour of the philosopher's birth. Here he could talk with Angelo Poliziani, five years his junior, a brilliant classicist who had begun translating Homer's *Iliad* into Latin hexameters at the age of seventeen; and who was to write a striking Latin eulogy for Lorenzo following his death; with Marsilio Ficino, the Platonist and senior member of the group, who was to be the longest lived (he died in 1499 aged sixty-six), and whose work sought to reconcile Christian and Platonic principles; and with Pico della Mirandola, the youngest, who was to die in his thirty-first year, but not before he had mastered twenty-two languages, travelling to Greece, Palestine and the Middle East in his efforts to improve them.

Both in the country and in town, according to humanist precepts, Lorenzo established a convention whereby there was no pecking-order in the seating at meals: those first to arrive either took the 'highest' seats, or simply sat where they chose. In addition to the scholars, translators and philosophers whom he subsidised and encouraged, he also gathered round him such cultivated men as the book-dealer and chronicler of his times Vespasiano da Bisticci, the musician Antonio Squarcialupi, the painters Botticelli and Ghirlandaio, the sculptor Bertoldo, now a relatively old man who was the last surviving pupil of Donatello; and, towards the end of Lorenzo's life, the difficult, fiery, teenaged prodigy, Michelangelo.

He provided a forum for all these artists and art lovers, and under his aegis they flourished. The junior branch of the family also commissioned works: Lorenzo di Pierfrancesco probably commissioned Botticelli to paint his *Primavera* on the occasion of di Pierfrancesco's marriage, at the age of nineteen, to Semiramide di Appiano. The painting was certainly in his possession, for it hung in his palace in Florence with other major works by Botticelli from the same period, *The Advent of Venus* and, almost certainly, *Pallas and the Centaur.*

Lorenzo, who was not alone as a collector – many contemporary merchants and aristocrats of wealth followed suit – himself spent money less on modern works of art and architecture than on books and antiquities. Bernardo Cennini set up the first printing press in Florence in 1477, the year after Caxton in London, and much later than such presses had been established elsewhere in Italy and in Germany.

Many Italian scholars regarded printed books as vulgar, and copying provided a livelihood for quite a few people. Lorenzo employed a small army of copyists over his collecting years. The book market was burgeoning, however, and new works began to go straight to print. Since 1204, when the armies of the Fourth Crusade were diverted by the canny Doge of Venice, Enrico Dandolo, to attack his city's chief trade rival, Constantinople, instead of Jerusalem, and sack it, hitherto unknown treasures – those not destroyed wholesale by the crusaders – originating in the Greek world, had filtered through to the west. In 1453, when the twenty-three-year-old Mohammed II took what remained of the once-glorious Byzantium, the last Greek scholars headed west, bringing with them the remains of the

Eastern Roman Empires libraries, as well as antiquities not looted or destroyed by the Crusaders. They made for such havens of scholarship as Florence.

The first printed edition of Homer was published in the city in 1488. Books carried both the Christian message and that of classical thinkers: Bibles and prayer-books became widespread, but by 1500 about 28,000 editions of other works had been produced as well; and by 1600, only thirty-six years after Michelangelo's death, the works of Virgil alone had reached half a million copies each, in the original and in translation. Books also meant that knowledge could be pursued without leaving home, and that distant places, customs, languages and peoples could be learned about and experienced vicariously. And paradoxically the quest for that knowledge, and the ability to communicate it widely and cheaply, led to an increased interest in the outside world, and the possibilities of a world beyond the known one.

Although his small but influential humanist circle dissolved with his death – Pico and Poliziano did not long survive him – and although the cultured and sophisticated world he had engendered would soon be fractured and interrupted, what Lorenzo had created in Florence had a lasting effect. His people mourned him with reason, and despite the rigours to come, they would guard his legacy for ever.

And although he was perhaps not fully aware of what he

had done, Lorenzo had in the last two years of his life made himself the patron of a fourteen-year-old boy who would quickly establish himself as the greatest artist Florence had ever produced.

CHAPTER TWO

A Birth and a Beginning

Michelangelo (or Michelagnolo as he was known in the Tuscan dialect) was born in 1475 in Caprese, a small fortified town about sixty-five kilometres south-east of Florence, now known as Caprese Michelangelo. His father, Lodovico di Leonardo Buonarroti Simoni, was coming to the end of a sixth-month term of office there as *podestà*, or local administrator, of Caprese and nearby Chiusi. He entered the arrival of his son in his notebook in the following way:

> I record that this day, 6 March 1494 [sic: in those days Florence dated the beginning of the calendar year from 25 March] a male child was born to me [sic]. I gave

him the name Michelangelo, and he was born on a Monday morning four or five hours before daybreak, and he was born while I was *podestà* of Caprese, and he was born at Caprese; and his godfathers were those I have named below . . . He was baptised on the eighth of the same month in the church of San Giovanni at Caprese.

Lodovico continues in the same vein, with a pedantic exactitude which characterised not only him but also his brother Francesco, a banker of sorts who might more accurately be described as a moneylender – an occupation fairly recently allowed by the Church to Christians, as businesses boomed and what had been a demeaning way of making a living permitted hitherto only to Jews became attractive, and allowable to Gentiles. It should be mentioned that Lodovico arranged for no fewer than eight godfathers – all local men – to be in attendance. Few princes had as many.

Michelangelo's father had a well-developed sense of his own importance. Though the family was poor, he claimed, without many grounds, descent from a great and ancient house, the Knights of Canossa – a claim which Michelangelo himself, in later life, emphasised to his biographer Ascanio Condivi. Lodovico had never worked, except in honorary positions, and although the Buonarroti had fallen on hard times, he still regarded himself as belonging to one of the foremost families of Florence. Work, in the sense of paid employment, he would have considered beneath him.

The Buonarroti had been established in Florence since the beginning of the twelfth century, and members of the family had held high office in the past. It was during Lodovico's father's time that their fortunes declined to the extent that he had to sell his house on the Piazza dei Peruzzi to raise money for his daughter's dowry. Lodovico now shared a rented house in Florence (though he claimed that he owned it) with his brother and his family, and their mother, Alessandra. The family still owned a farm in the hill village of Settignano, five kilometres east of Florence, which provided them with a modest income, but genteel poverty was the keynote of their life.

Nevertheless, Michelangelo was born under an auspicious star. His biographer Condivi tells us that 'Mercury and Venus were in conjunction with Jupiter for the second time, demonstrating a benign aspect, and plainly showing that the child would be a very extraordinary genius, whose success would be universal, but particularly in those arts which delight the sense, such as painting, sculpture and architecture'. The more reliable Vasari is equally unstinting in his praise, and the introduction to his life of Michelangelo testifies to the accuracy of what the astrological signs prophesied for the artist:

Enlightened by what had been achieved by the renowned Giotto and his school, all artists of energy

and distinction were striving to give the world proof
of the talents with which fortune and their own happy
temperaments had endowed them. They were all
anxious (though their efforts were in vain) to reflect
in their work the glories of nature and to attain, as
far as possible, perfect artistic discernment or understanding. Meanwhile, the benign ruler of heaven
graciously looked down to earth, saw the worthless-
ness of what was being done . . . and resolved to save
us from our errors. So he decided to send into the
world an artist who would be skilled in each and
every craft, whose work alone would teach us how
to attain perfection in design . . . and how to use
right judgment in sculpture . . . Moreover, he determined to give this artist the knowledge of true moral
philosophy and the gift of poetic expression, so that
everyone might admire and follow him as their perfect
exemplar in life, work, and behaviour, and in every
endeavour, and he would be acclaimed as divine. He
also saw that in the practice of these exalted disciplines and arts, namely, painting, sculpture, and architecture, the Tuscan genius has always been
pre-eminent, for the Tuscans have devoted to all the
various branches of art more labour and study than
all the other Italian peoples. And therefore he chose
to have Michelangelo born a Florentine, so that one
of her own citizens might bring to absolute perfection

the achievements for which Florence was already justly renowned.

Lodovico was thirty-one when Michelangelo was born, and his wife Francesca, whom he doesn't mention at all in his note about Michelangelo's birth, twelve years his junior. Francesca's mother was a member of the Rucellai family, one of the most prominent in Florence (they had made their money from the red dye, *oricello*, from which their name derives) and great patrons of the arts and architecture. Michelangelo inherited his artistic sensibility from his mother's side of the family.

Francesca had, however, only brought Lodovico a modest dowry. She had already borne him one son, Leonardo, fifteen months before Michelangelo's arrival, and would bear him three more at regular intervals – Buonarroto in 1477, Giovansimone in 1479, and Gismondo in 1481. None of his brothers shared Michelangelo's artistic bent: Leonardo would become a Dominican monk in 1491, entering the monastery of San Marco; Buonarroto, Michelangelo's favourite brother and the only one to marry and have a family of his own, went into the textile business with his ne'er-do-well brother Giovansimone; and Gismondo, who remained unlettered all his life, became a farmer. Michelangelo, the only member of the family to earn real money, supported all of them all their lives. Sharing his father's longevity, he outlived them.

Lodovico and Francesca returned to Florence from Caprese in April 1575, but Michelangelo was taken to Settignano and put to a wet-nurse there. He wouldn't move to Florence to live with his family until he was about three. It wasn't unusual for children to be put out to paid nurses, and there's no reason to suppose that Michelangelo's other brothers didn't go through the same experience.

Settignano was not only a farming community, but famous for its stone-cutters and trimmers. Michelangelo's wet-nurse was the wife of a stone-cutter and the daughter of a stone-cutter, and in later life Michelangelo would tell Vasari that he took in his feeling for stone with her milk. From his earliest days he was surrounded by the tools of the stone-cutter's trade, the various chisels and punches, drills and mallets, and picked up their uses early. The village was within walking distance of Florence, and after he had left his wet-nurse's family to return home, he kept up with them and visited them often. Not that his father had the slightest intention of allowing him to embark on a career as a stoneworker. Artists were not regarded as any different from artisans – sculptors having less standing than painters – and Lodovico's snobbery wouldn't permit him to countenance Michelangelo's ambitions in that direction. The textile business, or banking, were the careers he desired for his sons. (It is interesting however that the time he spent in rural Settignano didn't imbue in Michelangelo any feeling for the countryside: landscape in his work is cut to a minimum.

From the outset his dominating preoccupation was the male nude.)

Francesca died in 1481, and Lodovico remarried. His second wife also came from a family of standing: she was Lucrezia degli Ubaldini da Gagliano, and she brought with her a slightly larger dowry – 600 florins – than Francesca had.

Though Lucrezia appears to have been a loving stepmother, the loss of their real mother when the brothers were all so young – Gismondo not a year old – must have had a profound effect on the rest of their lives. As far as Michelangelo was concerned, it is fair to say that the harshness of his father and the loss of his mother in early life increased his natural shyness and social awkwardness. It also accentuated his tendency to bottle up private anxieties, dealing with them himself, confiding in no one.

The house the Buonarroti family rented was in Santa Croce, a mixed district of rich and poor, artisans and middle-class businessmen. It was the heart of the wool business, and the large square in front of the church of Santa Croce was used for the frequent jousts and other entertainments chiefly put on for the public by the Medici. Here, in this busy, vital quarter, Michelangelo grew up. Though he had abundant dark hair and intense, amber eyes, he was not a handsome child, and often sick. On the other hand he was sharp-witted and resilient. Intelligent and sensitive, he could also be arrogant and extremely touchy. Quick to anger and slow to forgive, his irascibility never left him. However, he was capable of lasting and deep friendship, and his generosity and loyalty to his demanding family never wavered.

While the sons of Lorenzo the Magnificent had Angelo Poliziano as their tutor, the children of the Florentine middle and upper classes went to one or other of several schools to learn the fundamentals of mathematics, grammar and Latin. Michelangelo was sent to the academy run by Francesco da Urbino. Here he learned some Latin, and to write, in a particularly beautiful hand. Francesco must also have been responsible for imbuing in him a love of literature, which led to a sizable output of letters and poetry, growing as he became older. Above all, it was now, when Michelangelo was about ten years old, that he discovered drawing. It is likely that he had made this discovery even earlier, though we have no evidence for it: but from now on he began to draw in a way which can only be described as compulsive; and as he drew, he found within himself a natural talent in which he became increasingly confident.

His talent was noticed by others. While he was still at the school, Michelangelo was befriended by a boy called Francesco Granacci. Granacci was five or six years older than Michelangelo, the child of a wealthy family, already on his way to a career as a painter, having worked with Filippino Lippi, and now apprenticed to one of the greatest and best established painters in Florence, Domenico

Ghirlandaio, who ran a workshop with his two brothers, Davide and Benedetto. Despite the difference in their ages the two boys quickly recognised kindred spirits in one another, and Granacci admired Michelangelo's talent. His relaxed, even temperament complemented his younger friend's edginess, and far from envying Michelangelo's ability, the rich, gentle and rather self-indulgent Granacci wanted above all to encourage it. Together they went about Florence, looking at and analysing the works of the masters of the immediate past which crammed the great churches' interiors and decorated their exteriors: Giotto's frescoes at Santa Croce, Uccello's paintings in Santa Maria Novella, the work of the Pollaiuolo brothers in San Miniato, of Orcagna at Orsanmichele, and the works of Masaccio, Ghiberti and Brunelleschi, Donatello and Verrocchio.

Michelangelo drew everything – scaffolding, the people in the markets, the goods on sale, buildings, monuments, statues carved in the niches on the exteriors of the churches. Everything was food for his insatiable desire to recreate what existed on paper. The only thing that never seems to have caught his imagination was nature – there are few animals and no landscapes in his work. Ultimately, it was mankind from which he drew his greatest inspiration, and in no greater way than in his celebration of the male nude.

Finally, Granacci took him along to Ghirlandaio's workshop. At the time the master fresco-painter was engaged in a series for the choir of Santa Maria Novella, in which

Granacci, along with the other senior apprentices, was assisting him. Ghirlandaio was at the time at the height of his powers, and it was considered a privilege to become part of his studio. He may have regarded the newcomer to whom the more sophisticated Granacci introduced him with a certain distance. Michelangelo was a nervous, somewhat aggressive boy, unsure of himself except for his talent, and lacking in most of the social graces. The master painter would have known something of the boy's family, which was still famous in Florence even though Lodovico had fallen on hard times, but it is unlikely that this would have swayed him in Michelangelo's favour without the backup of some evidence of artistic talent. This Granacci was able to supply, for he would never have introduced Michelangelo to his own master as a potential fellow-apprentice had he not himself recognised Michelangelo's innate genius in the drawings his younger friend had done during their treks around the city. Ghirlandaio, though apt to be jealous, immediately appreciated Michelangelo's gift and expressed his willingness to engage him as an apprentice.

As soon as he was inside the *bottega*, or workshop, Michelangelo knew that this was where his life lay. From now on he would cut classes at Francesco da Urbino's school in order to spend more time drawing. And among Ghirlandaio's apprentices he found like-minded people with whom he could exchange ideas, and let his own grow. He made friends and some enemies among budding fellow artists, like

Giuliano Bugiardini, Giovanfrancesco Rustici, Baccio da Montelupo and Pietro Torrigiano.

His discovery of a vocation led to trouble with his father and his uncle. Both considered the career Michelangelo wanted to pursue beneath the family's dignity, and the boy's desire to follow it met with recriminations and beatings, but in the long run there could be no denying Michelangelo's will. Backed up by Granacci, and aided by his own stubbornness, he finally won his father over. Lodovico could also reflect that Ghirlandaio was the most highly regarded painter in Florence at the time, and was very well connected. Another bonus was that Michelangelo would be paid by the studio for the projected three years of his apprenticeship – six florins in the first year, eight in the second, and ten in the third. Although he actually started work a year earlier, his official indenture was signed on 1 April 1488.

Later in life, already a legend, and not only wishing to perpetuate the myths that had grown up around him but perhaps also believing in them himself, Michelangelo denied that he had ever had any formal training, but that his genius came directly from God. Because Giorgio Vasari had mentioned Michelangelo's training in his *Life*, first published in 1550, Michelangelo instructed another biographer, Ascanio Condivi, a devoted follower to whom Michelangelo virtually dictated his story, to deny it in a book published in 1553. But when Vasari, who became a friend and admirer of Michelangelo, issued a revised edition of his *Life* in 1568, four years after the master's death, he quoted documentary evidence which proved his original point.

Like many of his contemporaries, Domenico Ghirlandaio's name is a nickname. It comes from *ghirlandi* – garlands – in this case, intricate gold-and-silver garlands designed by his goldsmith father, Tomasso di Currado, for girls to wear in their hair. When Michelangelo enrolled as an apprentice in spring 1487, aged just thirteen – a couple of years older than the age at which apprentices normally started – Domenico was at the height of his powers. He'd returned home in triumph from Rome five years earlier, with Botticelli and Rosselli, where they had been working on the wall frescoes of the newly finished Sistine Chapel. Now aged thirty-eight, an exact contemporary of Lorenzo de' Medici, he had been trained as a goldsmith by his father, but very soon established himself as a fresco painter, work which involved a highly developed technique, and a swift and decisive ability to apply paint. Fresco is the technique of painting on a wall of unset plaster. In true fresco, known as *buon fresco*, layers of lime-plaster are applied. While the final layer, called the *intonaco*, is still wet, the painter applies his colours so that they become integrated with the wall. Fresco was brought to perfection in Renaissance Italy by such masters as Ghirlandaio, and it requires a very exact estimation, for the mixtures of plaster and paint; and the degree of dampness of the plaster must be precisely judged if it is to work. Correctly handled, fresco produces very durable works, given the right climatic conditions. *Fresco secco* is a variant in which the paint is applied to dry plaster. Here, there is a risk of flaking and the range of colours which can be used is narrower, but the light tones which can be achieved made it popular as a technique in the much later Rococo period.

From the time of Giotto di Bondone, the art of fresco in Italy had become increasingly refined and popular. It was a standard mark of status for a great family, by Ghirlandaio's time, to pay for a series of paintings depicting either a Bible story or the life of a saint for a chapel in a church, and the great frescoes which survive are all in public, ecclesiastical buildings. As well as glorifying and perpetuating the names of the families who endowed them, frescoes communicated the essence of religious lore and stories to an illiterate public. They were also great spectacles – the blockbuster movies of their day. People marvelled at the scale and colour of these vast wall-paintings, which seemed to overwhelm them. The art reached its peak in the almost Rococo ebullience and grandeur of Michelangelo's Sistine Chapel ceiling of c. 1509–12, and his 'Last Judgement' on the altar wall of the same building of c. 1536–41.

Ghirlandaio's earliest work in the genre was for the Vespucci Chapel in the Ognissanti Church in Florence, but his reputation was made by what he had done in the Sistine Chapel in Rome. Back home, he decorated a chapel of Santa Trinita commissioned by the banking heir, Francesco Sassetti, with paintings appropriately celebrating the life of

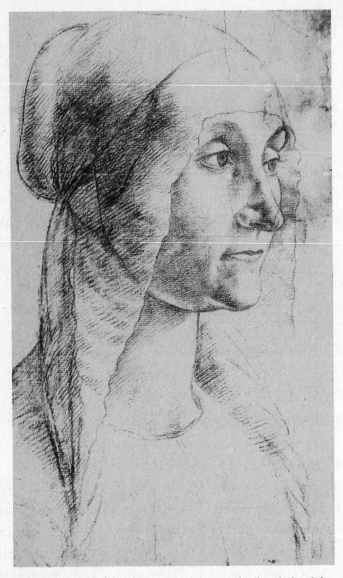

Domenico Ghirlandaio – a study drawing of a female head for
the *Birth of the Virgin* (Church of Santa Maria Novella)

Saint Francis. Never attempting to set religious themes in a historical context, Ghirlandaio's large-scale frescoes depict the life and the people of the Florence that he knew.

He continued an already existing tradition of including in his pictures portraits of the great and the good of Florence: the Medici, for example, are heavily represented in the chapel frescoes commissioned by their friend Sassetti. Ghirlandaio's reputation grew, and he went on to paint the altarpiece for the Ospedale degli Innocenti in autumn 1485, which in turn led to a commission from the Tornabuoni family to work on the choir of Santa Maria Novella. The frescoes were to depict scenes from the lives of the Virgin and John the Baptist. The contract stipulated that work should begin in May 1486 and conclude by May 1490.

Michelangelo joined Ghirlandaio's atelier in time to work on this great project. Early on, he drew attention to himself by making a sketch of the scene in the church, with the scaffolding and the artists on it, working on the ceiling. His precocious talent may have excited envy in Ghirlandaio, though it's unlikely that the master felt more than a disturbing appreciation of his rough young pupil's gift. The story is told by Vasari that when Ghirlandaio saw the drawing, with its mastery of perspective, he said that the boy knew more than he did himself. He probably felt less generous when Michelangelo corrected a drawing he had done for another student to copy, by accentuating the lines of the figure with broad strokes of the pen.

The imprint of work on design remained with Michelangelo: two decades later, he'd paint the shadow of his scaffolding on to the ceiling of the Sistine Chapel.

Apprentices learned as they worked, starting by grinding colours. This involved taking in the solid blocks of pigment delivered by the colourmen and then cutting it into manageable chunks before putting it in mortars and hammering and pressing it to a fine powder until your wrists ached so much that you felt your hands were going to fall off. Even then, the junior apprentices found the powder that resulted could never be *too* fine for Ghirlandaio. The colours were then moistened and blended as required, and this too was a precise science, for the fresh colour was darker when applied than it would be when it was dry; and this change needed to be taken into account. This was unutterably tedious work. Then they mixed the plaster for the frescoes and plastered the walls in preparation for the paint; ultimately they graduated to drawing and painting on the wet plaster some of the scenes in the whole grand picture conceived by the master. Granacci made available as many prints and drawings as possible to his young friend, and Michelangelo was quick to distinguish himself among his fellow apprentices, not without exciting some envy. Famously, he made a copy of an engraving by the contemporary German artist Martin Schongauer of *The Temptation of St Anthony*. Going further than the original, he made his copy in colour, and, fascinated by the demons featured in the Schongauer print, he modelled their scales and their abhuman eyes on his observation of dead fish in the market.

This willingness to copy from nature was shared by Leonardo da Vinci – Giorgio Vasari, the sixteenth-century artist and biographer of artists, tells a similar story about him:

> The story goes that once when Piero da Vinci [Leonardo's father] was at his house in the country one of the peasants on his farm, who had made himself a buckler [a small round shield] out of a fig tree that he had cut down, asked him as a favour to have it painted for him in Florence. Piero was very happy to do this, since the man was very adept at snaring birds and fishing and Piero himself very often made use of him in these pursuits. He took the buckler to Florence, and without saying a word about whom it belonged to he asked Leonardo to paint something on it. Some days later Leonardo examined the buckler, and, finding that it was warped, badly made, and clumsy, he straightened it in the fire and then gave it to a turner who, from the rough and clumsy thing that it was, made it smooth and even. Then having given it a coat of gesso and prepared it in his own way Leonardo started to think what he could paint on it so as to terrify anyone who saw it and produce the same effect as the head of Medusa. To do what he wanted Leonardo carried into

a room of his own, which no one ever entered except himself, a number of green and other kinds of lizards, crickets, serpents, butterflies, locusts, bats, and various strange creatures of this nature; from all these he took and assembled different parts to create a fearsome and horrible monster which emitted a poisonous breath and turned the air to fire. He depicted the creature emerging from the dark cleft of a rock, belching forth venom from its open throat, fire from its eyes and smoke from its nostrils in so macabre a fashion that the effect was altogether monstrous and horrible. Leonardo took so long over the work that the stench of dead animals in his room became unbearable, although he himself failed to notice it because of his great love of painting.

The finished shield was effective: Leonardo tried it out on his father in a darkened room, and it took the man so much unawares that he nearly fainted. Unfortunately it does not survive; nor do many of Michelangelo's early drawings, which he rubbed out or scrapped as being of no value to him once he had learned their lessons. But he kept filling his sketchbooks, and during his short apprenticeship with Ghirlandaio he also gained a thorough grounding in the art of fresco, which would serve him well in later life, though his own natural inclination was always towards sculpture. The key element in his development, however, was a mastery of drawing, and it was from Ghirlandaio that he learned the relatively new technique of cross-hatching, and how to draw confidently with pen or brush, making a few bold lines sufficient to define a figure.

Michelangelo was in the grip of a passion: he worked at night and on holidays – work was always a pleasure, and throughout his life his only real love. Unsure of himself, hating the way he looked, homosexual yet seldom able to express his sexuality, tolerated though it was in later fifteenth-century Florence, he went through life ploughing a lonely furrow. As he grew older he would sleep in his studio to save time, and only slept and ate when he had to. He seldom drank, and his nature, optimistic in youth, became increasingly severe. He was one of the most driven artists ever to have lived.

His own contribution to the frescoes in Santa Maria Novella is uncertain, but one or two figures may be attributed to the young Michelangelo. A kneeling, near-naked young man and two bearded old men in heavy robes beside him in the *Baptism of Christ* could be his work, as may a similar grouping in the *Presentation of the Virgin*. These figures lack the gracile charm normally associated with Ghirlandaio and, if they are by Michelangelo, their bulky, sculptural quality indicates that he developed his particular style early.

Working with Ghirlandaio also brought Michelangelo into contact with the major art patrons of Florence, and it wasn't long after beginning his apprenticeship that either

Granacci or Ghirlandaio himself introduced him to Lorenzo de' Medici.

At the time Lorenzo, aware that since the deaths of Donatello in 1466 and Verrocchio in 1488 (though Verrocchio had left for Venice ten years earlier) the art of sculpture in Florence had fallen into a decline, had developed a sculpture garden near San Marco, already established by his grandfather on the advice of Donatello, and appointed the aging sculptor, Bertoldo di Giovanni, to run it. Lorenzo was now on the lookout for art students of talent to train as sculptors: in the Florence of the day, the field was wide open.

The garden contained a small casino housing Cosimo de' Medici's superb collection of antique gems, as well as the Medici collection of classical sculpture. Only recently had anyone bothered to look into the heritage of ancient Rome, which had been neglected for hundreds of years. Now, as Rome began its long process of regeneration, antiquities which were beginning to be appreciated as such began to influence modern thinking and modern aesthetics. However, medieval thinking still made its incursions. An antique statue was discovered in Siena and, after hesitant discussion by the city fathers, placed in the market square. But Siena was in the middle of a petty war with Florence at the time, and soon after the statue had been set up, things began to go badly for the city. Attributing this to the malevolent influence of a pagan idol, the Sienese authorities decided that the statue should be pulled down and smashed into tiny pieces. These were subsequently smuggled into Florentine territory and sown in the fields, thereby transferring the curse.

The early Renaissance was a confusing mixture of Catholic fundamentalism, which was represented on the one hand by a decayed Papacy and on the other by the medieval throwback of the Inquisition; of pre-Christian superstition; of a dawning humanism, and (ahead of its time), of rationalism.

Bertoldo, now approaching seventy, had been a pupil of Donatello and later his occasional collaborator, and though neither a major nor an original talent himself, was dedicated to his art and steeped in its technique. He was an ideal tutor to the young aspiring sculptors who now came to him for instruction. Among them were Granacci, Michelangelo and Pietro Torrigiano, who was three years' Michelangelo's senior.

Granacci and Michelangelo left Ghirlandaio's studio before completing their apprenticeship to make this move. Possibly Lorenzo himself requested that the painter release them – a request which Ghirlandaio could scarcely refuse. Michelangelo's father, however, was further outraged. Despite Granacci's efforts to persuade him otherwise, a sculptor, in his mind, was no different from a stone-cutter, and on a far more humble level than a painter. It seems extraordinary that he should not have been gratified by the attention his son was receiving from the leading man of the city.

In the event, Lorenzo won him round, and also offered to find him a post. Lodovico said candidly that he had no experience of working for a living (he believed that work was no pastime for a gentleman), but that he'd heard of a vacancy in the Customs House which he'd like to fill. The post he asked for was so modest that Lorenzo was taken aback, but granted it to him, observing that Lodovico would probably never become a rich man.

Drawing remained the basic discipline the students worked at, and they frequently went to copy the frescoes painted nearly a century earlier in the Brancacci Chapel of the Church of the Carmine by Masolino and Masaccio, and latterly by Filippino Lippi. The little side-chapel, one of the greatest jewels of the early Renaissance – indeed a wonder of the world, and miraculously preserved – was funded by Antonio Brancacci late in the fourteenth century in accordance with his father's wishes for 'the foundation of a family chapel as a certain and acknowledged testimony to the standing of the family and a symbol of its solid prosperity'. Work on its building had begun by 1390 and its wonderful decoration was undertaken by Masolino and Masaccio in the 1420s. It was the work of Masaccio (Tomasso di Giovanni) which interested Michelangelo and his fellow students (and many others) most.

Masaccio was one of the most important painters of the

fifteenth century. He was the heir of Giotto and the fore-runner of Michelangelo. He played a key role in the early development of Renaissance style and his work typifies the interest shown by his contemporaries in the architecture and sculpture of the ancient world. Although a painter, Masaccio was always very receptive to sculpture, as the monumentality of his work attests. It is possible that as a very young man he studied in the *bottega* of Donatello, for his work betrays the influence of the seminal sculptor to a high degree.

The son of a notary, he was born on the Feast of St Thomas, 21 December 1401, at San Giovanni Valdarno, south of Florence. His brother Vittorio, five years his junior, also became a painter. Vittorio's was a lesser talent; however, he lived to his eightieth year. It is regrettable that Masaccio didn't even reach the age of thirty.

Masaccio is first mentioned in a document as a painter in Florence when he was sixteen years old, and a few years later, at the age of twenty, he joined the Guild of Physicians and Apothecaries – the Arte dei Medici e Speziale. Artists, in those days still held to be craftsmen, were hard to categorise. Since apothecaries frequently manufactured the blocks of pigment used by artists, they were lumped in with them. Soon, Masaccio had joined forces with Masolino, a painter some seventeen years his senior, whom he probably met through the Guild, and it was in partnership with Masolino that Masaccio created the frescoes which are his masterpiece – his contributions to the decoration of the

Brancacci Chapel in Florence, which were made around 1425. The extraordinarily solid, sculptural quality of Masaccio's work was greatly admired by Michelangelo, who imparts the same quality to his own paintings; but Donatello, who may well have been one of Masaccio's teachers, also influenced Michelangelo profoundly.

'Masaccio' was yet another nickname, translating roughly as 'Mr-Head-in-the-Clouds', on account of his unworldliness, as Vasari tells us, though the nickname literally means something like 'Big Tom'. He was a genius and a true innovator. Dying, probably of the plague, in 1428, in his twenty-seventh year, Masaccio was the first painter to give his figures true, three-dimensional substance. His influence was immense, not least on Michelangelo, to whose own taste and artistic striving Masaccio directly appealed. It was during a drawing session in the chapel, however, that Michelangelo got into a row with his fellow apprentice Pietro Torrigiano. Tact was never a strong suit of Michelangelo, and, aware as he already was of his own superior gift, he was becoming quick, impatient and ruthless in his criticism of shortcomings in the work of others.

Years later, Torrigiano told Benvenuto Cellini what happened. Cellini recorded it in his *Autobiography*:

This Buonarroti and I used to go along together when we were boys to study in Masaccio's chapel in the Church of the Carmine. Buonarroti had the habit of

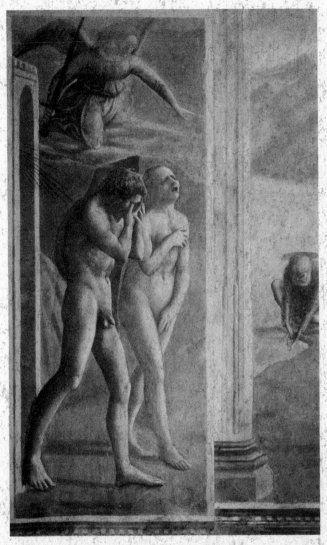

Masaccio – *Adam and Eve driven from Paradise* in the Brancacci Chapel of Santa Maria dei Carmine. Masaccio's contributions to the chapel, made late in his short life, show the artist at the height of his powers

making fun of anyone else who was drawing there, and one day he provoked me so much that I lost my temper more than usual, and, clenching my fist, gave him such a punch on the nose that I felt the bone and cartilage crush like a biscuit. So that fellow will carry my signature till he dies.

Cellini adds: 'This story sowed in me, who used to see Michelangelo's divine masterpieces every day, such a hatred for Torrigiano that . . . I could not bear to look at him.'

As a result of the fight, Torrigiano was banished Florence. His subsequent wanderings took him all over Europe, and he worked among other things as a mercenary soldier. He died in Spain, a prisoner of the Inquisition, in 1528. Few of his works remain, but he was the most important Italian Renaissance artist to work in England, and his surviving masterpiece is the double tomb of Henry VII and Elizabeth of York in Westminster Abbey, London, on which he worked from 1512 to 1518. As for Michelangelo, Torrigiano's boast proved all too true: he did carry the signature of a badly broken nose for the rest of his life, and it added to his ugliness.

His disfigurement does not seem to have been a serious source of distress to him. There are few references to it in his considerable writings; but there can be little doubt that he disliked his appearance, not least because a broken nose tends to rob a face of its individuality. He was, however, a member of a curiously long line of ill-attired, ill-favoured artists. Ghiberti was thickset and bald; Brunelleschi was short, bald, and aggressive-looking, with thin lips, a beaky nose and a receding chin. Like Donatello and Michelangelo, he dressed badly. One might be tempted to suspect that a disregard for clothes may have been a conscious affectation, were it not for the fact that Leonardo and Raphael, for example, did not subscribe to it, and for the fact that such men as Donatello and Michelangelo would have had no time for affectation of any sort. Nevertheless, they may be the source for the cliché-view of the unworldly, unkempt and absent-minded artist. Vasari, himself an ugly, pock-marked man who suffered from flaking skin, was at some pains to point how unusual a thing it was that Raphael was a handsome man. So enthusiastic is he that he doesn't hesitate to do a little oblique character assassination on Michelangelo, who is otherwise his hero:

Nature sent Raphael into the world after it had been vanquished by the art of Michelangelo and was ready, through Raphael, to be vanquished by character as well. Indeed, until Raphael, most artists had in their temperament a touch of uncouthness and even madness that made them outlandish and eccentric; the dark shadows of vice were often more evident in their lives than the shining light of the virtues that can make men immortal. So nature had every reason to display in

Raphael, in contrast, the finest qualities of mind accompanied by such grace, industry, looks, modesty, and excellence of character as would offset every defect, no matter how serious, and any vice, no matter how ugly.

Earlier painters had also been notably unattractive physically: the name Cimabue means, literally, 'ox-head'. Giotto was so ugly that Boccaccio wrote a tale in the *Decameron* (Sixth Day, Fifth Story, told by Panfilo) about it: 'Messer Forese da Rabatta and Master Giotto, the painter, returning from Mugello, poke fun at one another's disreputable appearance.' Panfilo points out that, 'Nature has frequently planted astonishing genius in men of monstrously ugly appearance', and reminds us that, just as Giotto was 'a man of such outstanding genius that there was nothing in the whole of creation he could not depict with his stylus, pen or brush', so Rabatta 'was a jurist of such great distinction that many scholars regarded him as a walking encyclopaedia of civil law', though he was 'deformed and dwarf-like in appearance'. The little moral tale tells how the two men, in a hurry to get back to Florence, get caught in a storm and, bedraggled, borrow dry but wretched clothes from a friendly peasant. They look worse than ever, and, as they ride on, Rabatta, 'shifting his gaze from Giotto's flank to his head and then to the rest of his person, and on perceiving how thoroughly unkempt and disreputable he looked, giving no thought to his own appearance he burst out laughing, and said:

'"Giotto, supposing we were to meet some stranger who had never seen you before, do you think he would believe you were the greatest painter in the world?"

'To which Giotto swiftly replied:

'"Sir, I think he would believe it if, after taking a look at you, he gave you credit for knowing your ABC."'

If physical ugliness or deformity had been popularly associated in the medieval mind with spiritual degeneracy, this was no longer the case in cultivated Italian circles by the time Boccaccio was writing in the mid-fourteenth century. Ugliness and a lack of dress sense were never hindrances to Michelangelo.

In the meantime, however, Michelangelo had been given the great honour of being invited by Lorenzo to live as a member of his family within the Medici Palace. This represented a significant step forward for Michelangelo. He was able to escape the lack of privacy and the suffocating atmosphere of his father's house, with his snobbish conservatism and genteel poverty, and exchange it for a palace in which the tone was of the highest liberal cultivation and sophistication. Lorenzo's patronage permitted the young man's social sensibility and independence of spirit to expand and develop. Michelangelo had been strongly affected by his father's claims of noble descent – he would claim it stubbornly himself throughout his life – and his disdain for humdrum work. Lorenzo gave Michelangelo the means to begin what turned out to be an obsession (which lasted all their lives) for the welfare and standing of his none-too-talented family. He was able to begin to see himself as an independent artist, with no need of a workshop and its associations with the trade. Association with the Medici family enabled him to broaden his horizons in the fields of politics, literature, philosophy and fine arts, and to take a more cosmopolitan view of the world, though he never became a great traveller. He also attained the freedom to establish himself in a position where he could do the work which pleased him without compromise – a very fortunate position for any young artist and most unusual in those days, when an artist was broadly regarded as a craftsman expected to turn his hand to anything within an 'artistic' field. In the palace he would have come into contact not only with Lorenzo's sons and daughters, who were close contemporaries of his (the canny young Cardinal Giovanni was only nine months younger than the artist), but also with the sophisticated humanists of the Platonic Academy. There is every reason to suppose that, although he would have received no formal instruction from any of them, their thinking influenced him. The informal seating arrangements at table (there was no priority; the first to arrive took the best seats) would often place Michelangelo, who'd inherited at least some of his father's punctuality, close to them; and though still in his teens, his talent earned him their respect.

Michelangelo was always a Christian, but his belief was tempered by humanist considerations. He read widely, both contemporary secular works and the Bible; his favourite poet was Dante. He had his own room, was given an allowance of five ducats a day, and presented with a violet cloak. He used the money to help his family out – once his older brother Leonardo became a monk, Michelangelo more or less assumed the role of head of the family. It is ironic that his success in a career his father so opposed and looked down on should have provided the impecunious family with an income for the rest of their lives. Caring little for his own needs, and far from materialistic, Michelangelo constantly stinted himself to look after his family, though this tendency was not without its masochistic side, and he frequently moaned about the burden he carried. In this he mirrors his father Lodovico's nature.

Within the palace, he had access to Lorenzo's library, and to all the Medici collections, and was able to open himself to their influence. Donatello's bronze *David* of the mid-1420s, the first nude figure designed to be viewed from all sides since antiquity, stood at the centre of the courtyard, which also contained many reliefs by the same sculptor. The palace contained many tapestries, as well as paintings by Fra Angelico, Botticelli and the Pollaiuolo brothers (with their extraordinary feeling for painting textiles). The chapel had frescoes by Benozzo Gozzoli. Though nominally the home of a private citizen, the palace of the Medici was known throughout Europe as 'The Hotel of Princes and All the World'.

Michelangelo had escaped the anxious and claustrophobic atmosphere of his father's house and found in Lorenzo, who was only five years younger than Lodovico, a new father. Within the two families there were discrepancies: Michelangelo's older brother Leonardo was by now sixteen, a shy and devout Christian. Piero de' Medici, the seventeen-year-old oldest son of Lorenzo, was already married, and a tough, spoiled and arrogant young man who rashly regarded himself as heir apparent to what was to all intents and purposes – though crucially not in fact – the 'dukedom' of Florence.

Michelangelo's adoption in 1489, aged fourteen – in those days fourteen implied far greater maturity than it does today – into this august family was formal, and he could never hope to be on equal terms with the Medici, but his affection for Lorenzo and his loyalty to him ran deep, and never wavered. At the same time, Lorenzo's condescension was well placed. There were no rivals to Michelangelo's ambition to become a great sculptor in the Florence of the late 1480s. Leonardo da Vinci, about twenty-five years Michelangelo's senior, was in Milan and would remain there until 1500; and though he was working on the model for a giant equestrian statue of Francesco, the father of the present duke, it was not as a sculptor that he was known.

In the sculpture garden Bertoldo di Giovanni had

introduced Michelangelo to the art of making models of wax, clay or gesso before he first cut stone; but from the moment he held a hammer and chisel in his hands, his ability to carve smoothly and without hesitation was apparent. He might have been cutting butter. The antique statues of the sculpture garden provided him with plenty of inspiration, but he brought to his work, almost from the first, a vitality and fluidity that had not been seen before, and could certainly not be matched by Bertoldo. There is an apocryphal story that Michelangelo's first attempt at sculpture was of a faun's [or satyr's] head, copied from an antique original. His faun was meant to be old, and when Lorenzo saw it, though impressed, he said jokingly to the teenager, 'But he still has all his teeth. Don't you think that by his age he would have lost one or two?' Michelangelo took the criticism on board, and as soon as he had the opportunity he chipped a tooth out; not content with that, he worked away at the marble gum to wither it, so that the loss of the tooth looked realistic. Popular myth relates that this so impressed Lorenzo that it was then that he decided to take Michelangelo into his household. Unfortunately the faun, and any record of it, are lost.

His desire to sculpt the human body, above all the naked male body (as the ultimate expression of God in Man), grew early, but not before a desire to outdo his conventional masters in the use of intricately draped folds of clothes. Nudity in religious art was still permissible – this was half a century before the Council of Trento, which, in its retort to the Reformation, tended, among other things, to clothe figures in churches that hitherto had been innocently naked. The great painting of Michelangelo's old age, the *Last Judgment* in the Sistine Chapel, was disfigured in his lifetime, when Pope Paul IV ordered Daniele da Volterra (the 'Breeches-Maker') to paint loincloths on all the nude figures in it.

Michelangelo was tireless. As well as the faun, he produced two other pieces of sculpture that have survived, before the death of Lorenzo threw his life and the future of Florence into confusion. These two are the first pieces in marble indisputably by him. The first is a shallow relief of the Virgin, sitting in profile at the foot of a flight of steps and nursing a very muscular Christ Child on her knee. The *Madonna of the Steps* is clearly an early piece, and some of the execution is clumsy, but there is no denying the vitality of it, nor the debt the sculptor owes to Donatello, a master of low-relief who was also, as we've seen, Bertoldo's teacher.

Bertoldo, Donatello and Antonio del Pollaiuolo all share credit as influences for the next piece, the *Battle of the Centaurs*. The idea for the subject was probably suggested to Michelangelo by Poliziano. The centaurs, invited to the wedding of King Pirithous and the Lapith princess Hippodame, became drunk and tried to make off with the princess and other women present. A fierce fight ensued during which Theseus, who was one of the guests, killed

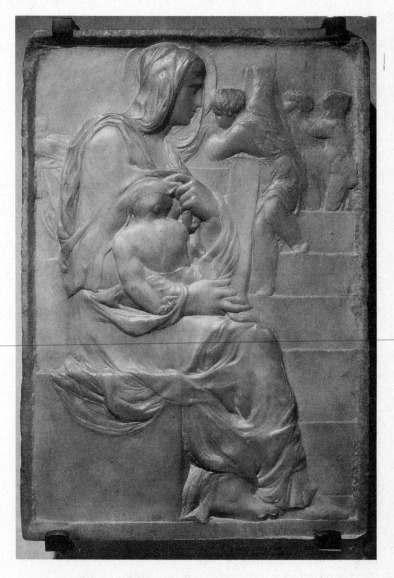

Michelangelo – *Madonna of the Stairs*. An early relief sculpture
which shows the influence of Donatello

the centaur Eurytus. Michelangelo uses this story as an excuse to create an energetic tangle of male nudes – a theme to which he was to return again and again throughout his long life – in a piece reminiscent of a Roman sarcophagus, though it owes something to Bertoldo's more academic *Battle of the Horsemen*, executed in 1475, as well as to Antonio del Pollaiuolo's didactic drawing entitled *Battle of Naked Men*, which was done ten years earlier, and perhaps also to Donatello's vigorous, leaping angel on the *cantoria* he did for the cathedral in Florence during the 1430s.

As recently as 1963 a naked Christ Crucified was discovered in a corridor in the monastery of Santo Spirito. This large, slender wooden polychrome figure, though very different from all his other work, has now been attributed to Michelangelo, and it may be that he carved it as an expression of gratitude to the prior, Niccolò Bichiellini. Santo Spirito ran a large hospital which cared for the poor. Its mortuary often contained unclaimed corpses, and the liberal Bichiellini permitted Michelangelo, in his quest for a greater understanding of human anatomy, to dissect them, which he did at night, alone and secretly, by candlelight, when his work in the sculpture garden was finished. It's been assumed that Bichiellini and Michelangelo were taking a great risk by indulging in this activity, though dissection was not forbidden by the Church: what was prohibited was obtaining corpses for dissection by exhuming them.

But the period of dissecting corpses followed the death

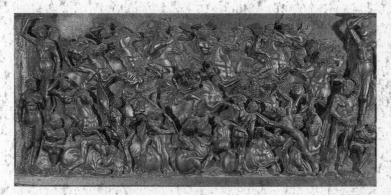

Bertoldo di Giovanni – *Battle of the Horsemen*

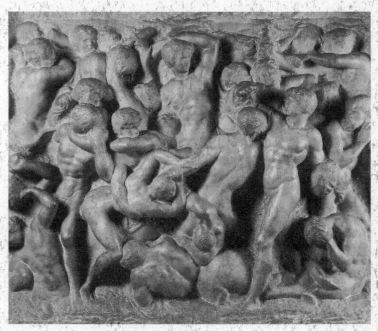

Michelangelo – *Battle of the Centaurs*

of Lorenzo, when Michelangelo found himself briefly back at his father's house; and although Lorenzo's son Piero recalled him to the Medici Palace, it had become a different place, just as the atmosphere in Florence had also radically changed; and for all his interest in simply pursuing his career as an artist, Michelangelo could not ignore what was happening around him.

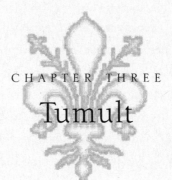

CHAPTER THREE

Tumult

P iero di Lorenzo de' Medici was only slightly older than his father had been when he took over power in Florence, but he had little of his father's diplomatic ability and none of his charm. Worst of all, he made the mistake of taking up the reins of power tactlessly. Lorenzo had always been sensitive to the strong democratic principles which governed the people of Florence, and was careful to play his role as a private citizen who happened to be first among equals, judiciously deploying his wealth to the benefit of the city as much as for his own well-being. Piero, a strong, handsome, well-built man of twenty-one, behaved from the first like a prince: but he didn't have the gravity to carry it off. It wasn't all his fault – he'd been brought up, as he saw it, to a privileged position which he owed to no one. The fourth Medici to assume the leadership of his city, he did so as of right.

He may have been aware what a hard act to follow his father was; but he was unaware how inept he would be in the part he'd been brought up to play. He'd had the best tuition and grounding possible, but, as is often the case with the children of prominent parents, he was only a shadow of Lorenzo. It was his younger brother Giovanni who'd inherited il Magnifico's quick-wittedness and political skill; and though it may be wrong to blame Clarice for his shortcomings, Piero did have more than his fair share of Orsini arrogance. He was also imperious and short-tempered. If Lorenzo had been aware of the shortcomings of his heir, any attempt to rectify them had failed.

All in all, Piero's reign proved disastrous from the start. Aged seventeen, he had himself married an Orsini, Alfonsina, a Roman girl who regarded Florence as a provincial backwater and didn't care who knew it. She exerted a strong influence over her husband, and contributed to an unpopularity which only the affectionate memory of Lorenzo held in check for a while. But it was only a matter of time before Florence realised that the man in charge of the city's fate was incompetent and talentless. He had no inclination at all towards either business or administration, preferring to indulge in hunting and the writing of poetry – the latter, in its poverty, symbolising how far short of his father he fell.

He left all matters of civic management to his secretary, Piero Dovizi da Bibbiena, and turned over the running of the family's crumbling banking house to Giovanni Tornabuoni, a great-uncle by marriage, who could do little to stop the rot.

Even if he had been a man of integrity, he'd inherited a tricky situation. Apart from the damaging loss of wealth during Lorenzo's time, the family was at war with itself: the junior branch was represented by Lorenzo di Pierfrancesco de' Medici and his younger brother, Giovanni. Despite il Magnifico's plundering of their inheritance, they were richer than Piero. They were also older, more influential, and cleverer than he was. Lorenzo di Pierfrancesco had much of il Magnifico's artistic acumen, and would soon play a key role in Michelangelo's life. These two cousins of Piero made no secret of their dislike for him, and he knew that he could not rely on their support in any power struggle with either the Signoria, the Pope, or any of the other powerful families within the city.

Added to this was a problem which even Lorenzo the Magnificent had had trouble dealing with: the gathering power and influence of Girolamo Savonarola. Born in Ferrara in 1452 and brought up largely by his grandfather, a doctor who believed among other things in the restorative properties of alcohol, which he thought would guarantee long life if taken in large quantities, as a boy Savonarola already inclined towards a rigorous asceticism.

He became a Dominican monk when he was twenty-three, and dedicated himself to fighting the devil wherever he might be found – not least within his own body, which he zealously mortified.

His principal weapon in the fight was the sermon, though his early efforts in this medium were disastrous; apart from his unprepossessing appearance, his voice was harsh and his manners ungainly. A first appearance in Florence, in 1481, met with failure. However, he returned to the city in 1490 to take up residence at the monastery of San Marco, ironically an endowment of the Medici, where he became Prior the following year, and where he remained from then on. Florence was the city he intended to conquer for Christ, and he set about his task with dogged determination, despite the disapproval and enmity of the Franciscans and the Augustinians.

His greatest adversary was the Augustinian Fra Mariano, whose own elegant sermons met with wide approval; but Savonarola's dedication, sincerity and unquestioning belief, quite apart from his formidable energy, gradually began to win people over. Some of his themes struck strong chords. Cynicism and an interest in pagan classicism were wrong. God would punish those who did not believe in Him simply and unquestioningly. And in a superstitious age, Savonarola's claim that he could foretell the future – like many fanatics, he saw himself as a channel for God's word – attracted the people's nervous attention. After all, the Church was in disarray, the Papacy had little credibility; popes fathered children and placed them in positions of secular power, and were more concerned with secular and temporal matters than with Holy Writ. What Savonarola failed to appreciate was that this tendency was also due at least in part to the exigencies of the times.

Florence itself had become too liberal, too lax, too fond of entertainments and show. Wealth was a curse, and the rule of the city by one family a disgrace. Savonarola held up to the people the example of the Republic of Venice as a true republic. The city-state should regain its democratic administration, and acknowledge no king but Christ. The members of the *Signoria* who were allied to the Medici should be rooted out, and there was no lack of enemies of the Medici who would be only too glad to see this happen.

So convincing was the monk that although Lorenzo had tried to contain him as best he could during the last three years of his life, Savonarola's teachings had even affected men in Lorenzo's inner circle – men like Pico della Mirandola and Poliziano, whose own humanist principles were being preached against. The sublime painter of pagan themes, Botticelli, now turned to religious subjects, though it would be wrong to overestimate the influence of the preacher on the painter.

Lorenzo knew better than to try to suppress Savonarola, but the power the monk was beginning to accumulate alarmed him. Piero, whose arrogance and lordly behaviour made him a far more precise target for Savonarola's criticisms than Lorenzo had been, fuelled the flames which would engulf him. Lorenzo's popularity and selfless activity on the part of his city could keep Savonarola's influence in check to a certain degree. With his death, virtually no opposition was left, and, eerily, it was known that Savonarola had told Lorenzo that he would be the first of the two of them to leave the city. Unthinkable as such a prospect had seemed at one time, it had in fact come to pass. Lorenzo had died.

No doubt rigorous fasting and isolated meditation had made the monk a little crazed, but he knew when to seize the advantage. After Lorenzo's death, Savonarola's credibility grew as further predictions came to pass. He had said that Pope Innocent VIII would die, and that Ferrante of Naples would die. Both men duly did so – Innocent in 1492, Ferrante two years later. (Innocent was succeeded by a Spanish cardinal, the vigorous, sixty-year-old Rodrigo Borgia, elected on 11 August, who took the name Alexander VI. Pope Alexander – 'Alexander the Libertine' – would prove a match for Savonarola; but that still lay well in the future.)

Starting with the Easter sermons of 1492, Savonarola stepped up a campaign already begun during the Lent sermons. In vivid terms he depicted the destructive storms, plagues and wars which would break over Florence if God's word were not heeded; and Florence was very familiar with all three disasters. He urged the citizens to clothe themselves in 'the white garments of purification', and to repent while there was still time; if, indeed, it were not too late already. He spoke of a black cross, the cross of God's wrath, rising up from Rome; and of a golden cross rising to the heavens from Jerusalem. He urged the people to turn to the golden cross, unless they wanted to be attacked by enemies from north of the Alps, barbarians armed with 'giant razors', who would bring the pampered age to a horrible close. The ferocity of his imagery – he was a true hell-fire preacher – stirred up great anxiety in his listeners, though it would be an exaggeration to say that he instilled widespread panic for long, and much of what he said, especially his attacks on the Papacy, which became more and more explicit, were heard by the Vatican less with fear than in anger.

Savonarola was a man who bridged the worlds of the Middle Ages and the Renaissance. There was enough super-stition and enough genuine concern at the decadence of the Church to sweep him along for a time, even though his predictions became ever wilder. He said, for example, that within the lifetime of his congregations the Turks would be converted wholesale to Christianity.

But his was a flame destined to burn fiercely, and not for long.

Lorenzo had worked hard to maintain a tenuous alliance between the Italian states and kingdoms, and had enter-tained a delicate friendship with the French king, Louis XI. But the cultivated Louis had died in 1483. His son Charles was thirteen at the time. Now, rising twenty-two, King Charles VIII showed signs of wanting to flex his military muscle, using the standing army Louis had raised to keep the peace and subdue rival elements in France.

Charles was an unlikely general. He was minute in stature, had sparse reddish hair and beard, a beaky nose and wet, fleshy lips which were constantly open since he was obliged to breathe through his mouth. Some nervous dysfunction caused his head and hands to twitch constantly, and on the rare occasions that he spoke it was to do no more than mutter monosyllabically. He was deformed, having both a humpback and a limp, and it was thought that each of his splayed feet had six toes. He was a glutton and a sexual profligate. Oddly, given his father's interest in learning, Charles was poorly lettered; however, he'd managed to woo and win the Duchess of Brittany, a charming and intelligent woman, if ambitious, when she was already engaged to someone else; and although people professed to be uneasy in his presence, his nickname was 'the Affable'.

Above all, Charles wanted to be a worthy successor to his father. Louis had been preoccupied with consolidating his position in France. Charles, imperilling what his father had achieved, had foreign ambitions. The Kingdom of Naples was viewed as one of the hereditary rights of the House of Anjou. Charles decided that he would claim those rights when King Ferrante died early in 1494. In this he had already been encouraged by the Regent of Milan, Lodovico, who had no desire to hand over power to the rightful heir to the Milan dukedom, his nephew Gian Galeazzo, who had now reached his majority. Gian Galeazzo was weak and unambitious, but his wife's grandfather had been King Ferrante, and he'd promised her help in toppling Lodovico. Lodovico was prepared to sacrifice any Italian alliances to hang on to his power in Milan. Lodovico's spies had, however, also made him aware of a secret treaty made in 1492 between Piero de' Medici and Ferrante to take and divide Milan between them.

Charles' campaign was ready to go into action by the late summer of 1494. It looked as if Savonarola's prediction of an invading army laying waste to Italy from the north was about to come true. Florence was directly in Charles' path. Charles had a huge professional army, at least 30,000 strong.

The French crossed their frontier, entered Lombardy, and were soon made welcome by Lodovico in the Duchy of Milan. As soon as they headed south, the army divided into two flanks. The rightful Duke of Milan, Gian Galeazzo, who had fallen ill in mysterious circumstances a short time earlier, sickened and died. His wife and four children were arrested, and Lodovico had himself proclaimed Duke. Meanwhile the vast French force penetrated further into Italian territory. Venice wisely declared its neutrality; within the Papal States and Tuscany there was no force to oppose it – armies of mercenaries were usually levied under *condottieri* whenever the occasion arose, and there had been no opportunity or money to do so this time. Matters were made more difficult for Piero in Florence when Alexander VI issued a Papal Bull authorising Charles' safe passage through Rome on his way south.

Charles halted at the Tuscan frontier and sent envoys to Piero to ask him to back the Angevin claim to the throne of Naples, as well as to allow the French army to pass through his state unopposed. Piero dithered frantically, keeping the envoys waiting for five days, while he secretly pledged support to Ferrante's successor, Alfonso. Finally he told the envoys that Florence would remain neutral; but this was not what Charles wanted to hear. He needed Florence on his side, so that he could use the state's fortresses to secure his line of retreat back to France. To show Piero he meant business, he sacked the fort at Fivizzano, about 100 kilometres north-west of Florence, and killed everyone in the garrison without pity.

This brutal act stirred Piero into belated activity. He wanted to keep Charles out of Tuscany at all costs. He sent mercenaries to his other fortresses. The Florentines, however, under the influence of Savonarola, regarded Charles' advance with gloomy fatalism. By now Savonarola had persuaded many citizens to fast 'three days in the week on bread and water, and two more on wine and bread', according to the Mantuan representative in the city.

The threat posed by Charles caused most of the women to hide in the convents. When Piero asked the city fathers for money to finance a campaign against the French king, it was refused. The city would be financially ruined, and it would fall anyway. Better to give it up. In the meantime, Piero's cousins Lorenzo and Giovanni di Pierfrancesco sent a private emissary to Charles, dissociating themselves from Piero and his actions, and expressing solidarity with the French. The emissary was intercepted by Piero's men, however, and the two cousins duly arrested; but they managed to escape and made their way to Charles' camp, where they assured him that if Piero could be assassinated, Florence would rally behind the French king.

By now Florence was isolated, it was clear that Naples hadn't the strength to be a useful ally, and the French were close to Pisa. Piero decided that he would try to emulate his father in bringing off a diplomatic *coup*. Without talking to the *Signoria*, early in November he set off to meet Charles and offer him terms. Charles held all the cards and contemptuously demanded, and got, four key fortresses, the towns of Pisa and Livorno (the port), and Piero's agreement to a huge loan. The humbled Piero returned to Florence to report to the *Signoria*, who were aghast at the deal he had agreed to, and had the door of the Palazzo della Signoria shut in his face. There was a nervously charged stand-off between Piero and his men and the city fathers, who had the town bell, the *vacca*, rung to summon the citizenry. Unable to drum up sufficient support for himself, Piero retreated to his palace. That night he fled Florence with his family, and made his way to Venice, via Bologna, taking with him as much of value as he could carry.

When they learned that he had gone, the city fathers hastily and angrily passed a decree that no Medici should ever be allowed to live in the city again, and placed a sum of 4,000 florins on Piero's head, and 2,000 on his brother Cardinal Giovanni's. The Medici Palace was ransacked by the people, and by the French when they arrived, while the *Signoria* appropriated a vast amount as well, including cash, jewels, paintings and statues. The collections built up over three generations were laid waste. Meanwhile, Charles had arrived in Pisa, which he declared 'liberated' from Florence. This was another blow, and an ambassadorial delegation was put together to meet Charles at least to try to mitigate the terms brokered by Piero. Among the ambassadors was Savonarola, who had viewed all the events of the last few months with grim satisfaction – all that he had said would happen, had happened, and now the city would hang on his every word.

But it was Savonarola more than anyone who saved Florence from any worse fate that might have befallen. He greeted Charles as 'the Minister of God, the Minister of Justice. We receive thee with joyful hearts and a glad countenance . . . We hope that by thee Jehovah will abase the pride of the proud, will exalt the humility of the humble, will crush vice, exalt virtue, make straight all that is crooked, renew the old and reform all that is deformed. Come then, glad, secure, triumphant, since He who sent you forth triumphed upon the Cross for our salvation.' The Dominican cannily asked for Charles' forgiveness towards those who had opposed him, since they had not realised that he was the agent of God. Charles might have been a little nonplussed by some of this, but the ugly and vainglorious young man felt hugely complimented, and agreed to spare the city. However, he was determined to enter it as a conqueror, and he would bring his army with him. Lorenzo and Giovanni di Pierfrancesco de' Medici would return too, quietly, and tolerated, quickly changing their name to one which reflected their own new-found democratic adherence: Popolano, and taking down the Medici coats-of-arms from their palace.

On 17 November 1494 Charles, brilliantly attired in golden armour and a golden cloak, rode into the city at the head of his army. His tall, red-haired Scottish archers attracted especial attention, but so did the king's diminutive, misshapen form. The next eleven days were surprisingly quiet – there were a few brawls and a handful of killings; but in view of the size of the foreign contingent billeted on the town, it could have been much worse.

The only serious contretemps arose over the terms agreed between the king and the city. The *Signoria* was happy with every particular, including the retention of Pisa by the French until the campaign was over, but when it came to money, Charles found himself offered 120,000 ducats instead of the 150,000 he'd expected. He exploded with anger and said that the missing 30,000 must be restored or he'd order his trumpeters to call his men to arms, and he would sack the city. One of the city fathers, an elder statesman called Piero di Gino Capponi who had once been ambassador to France and remembered the young king as a peevish infant, famously retorted, 'If you sound your trumpets, we will ring our bells.' There was a moody face-off, but then the French king climbed down. This was just as well for Florence – if Charles had called Capponi's bluff, the Florentines might have found themselves victims of the same treatment that had been handed out at Fivizzano.

Agreement having been reached, Charles left the city and went on his way south. It was only after he had gone that the city realised how much money his stay had cost, and how many debts the French had left unpaid. Charles' brief popularity – based as it was on relief that he hadn't sacked the city – soon waned.

The Medici had been good to Florence, but their benign dictatorship had blocked any real democratic development, and the city was effectively leaderless. The times were uncertain, suddenly. In the political confusion that followed the way was clear for Savonarola to consolidate his grip on power in the city, and he would hold on to it for the next four years. His one disadvantage was that he was not a native of the city. But for the moment he had a half-hopeful, half-fearful population in the palm of his hand.

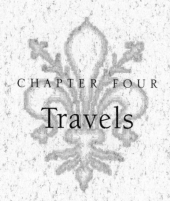

CHAPTER FOUR

Travels

Lorenzo's death had marked the end of an era. Under Savonarola, gone were the costly displays, the public games and the jousts so luxurious that at one, in 1468, Lorenzo could appear in an outfit covered with pearls, bearing a banner of purple and white taffeta designed by Andrea del Verrocchio. Artists thought nothing of designing ephemeral pageants, and Verrocchio was joined in this business by Botticelli, Antonio Pollaiuolo and Piero di Cosimo among many others. Even so, the silver suit of armour designed by Verrocchio for Giuliano de' Medici in 1475, for a joust at which he followed a standard made by Botticelli, must have been a particularly splendid sight.

But it wasn't just passing display that had flourished. The

years of the first three great Medici, and especially those
which passed under Lorenzo's rule, had been times of
burgeoning economic success together with a long period
of peace and stability. Soon after Lorenzo had taken over
as head of the family and the city, a Medici commercial
agent, Benedetto Dei, noted that in a population of 40,000
there were 270 wool shops, ninety-six artisans' workshops
working in woodcarving and inlay work, eighty-three manufacturers of silk, sixty-six apothecaries' shops, fifty-four
dealers in decorative stone and marblework, forty-four
goldmiths' and jewellers' businesses, and thirty-three banks.
Fifty town squares had been laid out, and there were 108
churches.

Added to these were the palaces that were being built by
the principal families. The years of peace meant that taxes
had remained low, so that money had accumulated in fabulous quantities. Lorenzo had introduced tax relief on private
building programmes to encourage investment in the city.
The mighty, fortress-like palazzi, which are such a feature
of Florence, grew up during this period, and architecture,
already an established art in Florence, flowered in the
persons of such men as Benedetto da Maiano, 'il Cronaca'
(the nickname of Simone Pollaiuolo) and Giuliano da
Sangallo. Savonarola may have been able to chip away at
the ephemeral manifestations of Florentine wealth, but the
solid foundations of which they were an expression could
not be removed, even if he had wished it.

On the death of Lorenzo, Giovanni de' Medici had written a letter to his brother Piero which contained words both of condolence and advice:

What a father we have lost. Allow me . . . to express my hope that in your behaviour towards people, especially those around you, I may find you as I would wish – kindly, liberal, friendly and humane.

It is clear from this that Giovanni knew his brother and – reading between the lines – feared the worst.

The city and the Medici family had lost a benevolent father, and things would never be the same again. But Michelangelo had lost more than a father, he had lost a patron, and at a time – he was just seventeen years old – when his career was beginning to take shape. Now, he was obliged to return to his father's house. Bertoldo had died in 1491, aged 70. The sculpture garden had fallen into disuse, and Michelangelo, not having the means to work on his own, and not yet being fully established enough to solicit clients – apart from the fact that such unsettled times were hardly ripe for the commissioning of works of art, from which in any case Savonarola was encouraging people to turn away – busied himself with his anatomical studies at Santo Spirito. It was at about this time that he carved the large wooden Crucifixion for Niccolò Bichiellini.

The anatomy studies were of great value to him, because

he believed that to reproduce the human body, whether in paint or stone, you should understand your subject from the inside out, and know what was going on under the skin, just as clothed figures needed to show the limbs and torso they covered. Michelangelo was far from the only artist to practise dissection. The classical sculptors whose work had once again begun to attract attention were admired for the vitality of their work. Renaissance artists sought to emulate this, and free themselves from the stiffness of medieval representation. It is evident from the work of Antonio Pollaiuolo and Leonardo da Vinci that they, too, dissected bodies in order to attain a greater realism in their work, though Leonardo would have been equally inspired by his interest in anatomy per se, and his scientific spirit.

In 1493, Michelangelo was able to buy a marble block from which he intended to carve a *Hercules*. He could only afford a weatherbeaten block, but the family finances, for which he had effectively become responsible since joining Lorenzo's entourage, demanded that he work. He planned an over-life-size figure, about 2.5 metres high, an ambitious project for one still relatively inexperienced, despite the talent he knew he had within him. Hercules, a pagan figure who nevertheless represented courage and fortitude, was a subject who often figured in Florentine sculpture, along with John the Baptist, and the biblical David, the slayer of Goliath, with whom Florence had identified in the past as it stood up to its more powerful enemies. Charles VIII could hardly be called Goliath, but he had represented a towering strength which might have obliterated the Republic if the Republic had not stood its ground. (For all Piero's cack-handed diplomacy, he should at least be given credit for making the right decision in the nick of time and going to Charles to intercede for a peace which, however dishonourable, at least saved the city from being looted, if nothing worse.)

It is possible that the *Hercules* was a commission, but it is certain that Michelangelo sold it, because after it was finished it stood for many years in the courtyard of the Palazzo Strozzi, which was being built at the time. The Strozzi were another of the powerful families in the city. With the disgrace and fall of the Medici, whose monopoly on power they had opposed, they became, for a time, ascendant, though they took care to play this down in the face of Savonarola's vigilance for hubris. A further connection between the Buonarroti and the Strozzi was that at the time Michelangelo's younger brother, Buonarroto, worked for the Strozzis' wool business.

The statue was a major undertaking. Michelangelo made at least one model for it, and when it was finished – the work took six months to complete – it stood two metres high, and portrayed the hero with his club. It was inspired by Donatello's bronze *David*.

The *Hercules* is now lost. It was taken to France during the reign of François I, for whom it was acquired by the dealer Giovanni Pattista della Palla, and was eventually placed in the Jardin de l'Etang at Fontainebleau – an engraving of it there still exists – but it disappeared when the garden was redesigned in the early eighteenth century.

Piero de' Medici may not have had a fraction of his father's cultivation or taste, but he still wished to emulate him, and soon invited Michelangelo to return to the Palazzo Medici, on the same terms as before. He gave the young sculptor no commissions, however, except one that Vasari tells us about. Vasari also tells us – to Piero's credit – that Piero 'often used to send for Michelangelo, with whom he had been intimate for many years, when he wanted to buy antiques such as cameos and other engraved stones'. It would be nice to believe him.

Piero was four years older than Michelangelo, and even during the latter's two-year residence at the palace when Lorenzo was alive, it's unlikely that they had become friends; but they would have been well aware of one another's existence. Living once more in the palace, Michelangelo must have missed the sophisticated people who had sat at Lorenzo's table. Now, people took their places according to an aristocratic pecking-order, and the talk was merely of hunting and pageants. There was less money, too; and Piero's appreciation of talent is indicated by his boast that the two retainers of the greatest value in his household were Michelangelo and a Spanish groom, who was not only astonishingly handsome, but able to outrun on foot Piero riding at a gallop.

The commission Vasari recounts seems a strange one, until one remembers that at the time artists were considered artisans capable of and expected to do any work required of them. Goldsmiths became painters or turned their hand to sculpture or bronze-casting and even architecture. The winter of 1493–4 was a hard one, and in January there was a heavy snowfall in Florence. What Piero wanted was a giant snowman. Vasari, who cannot have seen it since he was not yet born, describes it as 'very beautiful'; but apart from that nebulous account there is no clue about its appearance. However, it is likely that Michelangelo didn't simply dash something off for this ephemeral creation, and it may be that he profited from the experience, as he had from the *Hercules*, in experimenting in the difficult task of scaling up human proportions for a colossal work. Interest in colossi had been growing since huge fragments of classical Roman and Greek statues had been excavated, and accounts of the Colossus at Rhodes had been translated; but no one had attempted to carve one in modern times.

Whatever stimulation this work gave Michelangelo, the political and military events that began to preoccupy Florence and the twenty-three-year-old Piero as 1494 progressed left little time for him to think about the fortunes of a budding Tuscan sculptor. As Michelangelo was personally concerned increasingly with the problems of portraying the male nude, and since it looked as if, as long as Savonarola's views and taste were in the ascendancy, there would be little room for such expressions in art, the artist decided that the time had come to leave. By mid-October of that year, well before Charles VIII made his grand entrance into the city, Michelangelo, in the company of two companions, had left the city for neutral Venice.

Ascanio Condivi, to whom Michelangelo related his memoirs, tells an odd story which is quite in keeping, however, with the portents reported surrounding the death of Lorenzo. According to one version of this story, Lorenzo's ghost appeared to one of his former entourage, a musician called Cardiere, in a dream. Lorenzo, dressed in nothing but a ragged black cloak, told him of the impending expulsion of the Medici from Florence and ordered him to pass this information on to Piero. Cardiere, naturally, hesitated to do this, though he confided his experience to Michelangelo, who was a close friend, and who told him that he should do as Lorenzo's ghost had said. A few nights later Lorenzo appeared to Cardiere again and, awakening him with a slap on the face, asked him why he hadn't done as he'd been bidden. This time Cardiere plucked up the courage to approach Piero, and set off on foot along the dusty road to see him at his villa at Careggi, four kilometres outside Florence. He met Piero and his party on the road, as they were returning to Florence, and told them about Lorenzo. Piero, not surprisingly, laughed him to scorn, and his chancellor, the future Cardinal di Bibbiena, asked the logical question, that if Lorenzo's ghost chose to appear to anyone with such an important warning, why not to Piero himself? Cardiere withdrew, but according to the story Michelangelo was sufficiently impressed by the whole affair to decide to leave Florence.

It's more likely that Michelangelo was sensitive to the mood of the city and, having sold nothing but the *Hercules* in the previous two years, and unable to practise his craft, he simply decided to go to seek his fortune elsewhere. It was not unusual for young artists and artisans to wander from place to place, going where the work was, though in Michelangelo's case the unsettled atmosphere in Florence was a contributory factor. It's been suggested that his companions were Cardiere and Granacci, but as Michelangelo was paying everyone's expenses and Granacci was rich, he, at least, seems an unlikely candidate.

The three young men reached Venice without difficulty. It is tempting to imagine Michelangelo passing the young Albrecht Dürer on one of the *calle*, since the young German artist was also there at the time, but there's no record of their ever having met, and at that stage in their lives there would be no reason why they should know of each other's existence. What Michelangelo certainly would have seen was Verrocchio's great equestrian statue, the *Colleoni*, which had only two years earlier been placed in the square outside the church of SS Giovanni e Paolo. (In 1493 Leonardo da Vinci, who had by that time been working in Milan for over ten years, had erected an eight-metre-high model for a bronze equestrian statue of the first Duke of Milan for Lodovico Sforza. At the same time he was working on his *Last Supper*, using new techniques of applying paint. It was the model for the bronze that excited the greatest discussion in Florence when word of it reached the city, but Leonardo's great statue was never cast.)

Venice provided no commissions for Michelangelo, and after only a short stay in a city whose atmosphere he found unsympathetic, he made his way westwards again, stopping at Bologna, where by coincidence Piero de' Medici had taken temporary refuge at the start of a lengthy period of exile in various cities.

Money was running out, so the need to find work was pressing. The companions had almost certainly passed through Bologna en route for Venice, and perhaps on the way back they only intended to break their journey there before returning to Florence; but they unwittingly infringed a local visa regulation, and, unable to pay the fifty Bolognese *lire* fine demanded as a result, they were detained. The visa – a dab of red sealing wax on the thumbnail – was a device for registering visitors to the city: if they had visited Bologna on the outward journey, it seems odd that they weren't aware of this.

They were rescued by a prominent local citizen who served on the city's governing Committee of Sixteen, and who may have made Michelangelo's acquaintance earlier, in Florence, while a guest of Lorenzo. Gian Francesco Aldovrandi was himself a patron of the arts, and pulled strings to get the three travellers released. He then invited the artist to stay at his house. Michelangelo declined, because he couldn't abandon his companions, but neither could he expect Aldovrandi to invite them too. Aldovrandi was impressed by this loyalty, and said jokingly, 'Then I'll join you in your travels, since you take such good care of your friends.' But Michelangelo's companions in any case wished to continue their journey, rather than stay in Bologna, so Michelangelo gave them what money he had left to enable them to do so. While he stayed with Aldovrandi, he read, at the latter's request, the poetry of Dante to him aloud, since Aldovrandi delighted in hearing the great poet's words spoken in his native Tuscan accent. Michelangelo also read to him from Boccaccio and Petrarch.

Bologna was a city-state in its own right, ruled by a *condottiere*, Giovanni II, whose main aesthetic preoccupations were his beautiful Spanish and Arab horses, and the gardens of his palace. He maintained his city's independence because its strategic position meant that it could bar the way for any invader from the north. Giovanni thus had Florence and Rome, Naples, Milan and France courting his alliance. In the same way as Pope Alexander, Giovanni managed to play each off against the other in order to preserve his peace until the danger, in this instance represented by Charles VIII, was past.

At the time Bologna had its own major native artist in

Francesco Francia, a goldsmith turned painter who was in charge of the Mint. There would have been no rivalry between the older man and the young visitor since their disciplines were different, and Aldovrandi, knowing Michelangelo was a sculptor, wanted to show him the principal churches of San Petronio and San Domenico. The west porch and lunette of San Petronio were decorated with statues and reliefs by the Sienese contemporary of Donatello, Jacopo della Quercia, a man whose solidly vigorous forms Michelangelo greatly admired. (En route for Venice, Michelangelo, making the first of his rare journeys, would have passed through Padua, and seen the works Donatello, the great master, had left there.)

The church of San Domenico contained the great sarcophagus of St Dominic, which had been carved by Nicola Pisano and his school in the second half of the thirteenth century. This was now surmounted by a late fifteenth-century ornament, the work of Niccolò dell'Arca, who had died leaving the work unfinished. Three statues, small in stature in keeping with the other decorations of the pinnacle, had yet to be carved, and now Aldovrandi asked Michelangelo if he felt ready to take on the job.

He certainly did. St Dominic was the founder of the Order to which his elder brother belonged, and whose prior in Florence was Girolamo Savonarola, whom Michelangelo admired. Although he was steeped in the humanist tradition that he had learned at the court of Lorenzo the

Magnificent, Michelangelo was too firmly grounded in the Catholic tradition to relinquish it; nor did he ever show any sign of wanting to. Savonarola's ideology appealed to many intellectuals – humanists among them – who felt that a new rationale was needed to reform the Church; and there was an austerity in the monk's world-view which appealed to the strong moralism of Michelangelo's own nature. But alongside the important religious aspect of the work, Michelangelo was also aware that not only was this commission a great honour and a great responsibility, but that it might lead to further commissions, though the recent *Hercules* was a truer indication of the scale in which he preferred to work. The work involved carving two saints, a Petronius and a Proculus, and an angel holding a candlestick to complement one already in place by dell'Arca. The saints were to be about sixty centimetres tall, the kneeling angel somewhat smaller.

The statues show a marked development already from the *Madonna of the Stairs* and the *Battle of the Centaurs*. The angel, grave and dignified, with a distinct personality, is deliberately less finely carved than dell'Arca's corresponding one, and the carving gives the marble a buttery quality. The figure itself shows the bulkiness Michelangelo favoured from his earliest days, and the cutting of the draperies seems almost like an advertisement for the sculptor's skill, though Michelangelo was to show greater flamboyance in carving folds of cloth within the next three years. Interestingly, the inside wings of the figure are not carved at all. As both the earlier *Madonna* and the *Battle of the Centaurs* have similar unfinished areas, a feature which much of Michelangelo's later sculpture shares, it has been suggested that the unfinished quality, the so-called *non-finito*, has an aesthetic origin. In this case it seems likely that it was more a question of the sculptor not having the time to put the finishing touches to the work. One must also take into account contemporary notions of what *was* finished. Michelangelo typically took on more work than he could handle. He could also lose patience with the task of polishing something which, by the time he has brought it to a point which satisfies his creativity, he has moved on from.

The saints – Petronius and Proculus – are realised in great detail, and there is an indication that Michelangelo may have seen and been influenced by the work of Cosmè Tura, which he would have seen if he'd passed through Ferrara, which lies directly between Bologna and Venice. The *Petronius* is a dignified elderly bishop, fully robed, holding a model of the city of Bologna in his hands, his bearded face grave. By contrast the *Proculus*, a young disciple of the third-century martyr St Valentine, is bursting with energy, his face vividly expressive. Both saints are formally attired, and the fact that they are reminiscent of the work of painters who were popular in Bologna may indicate that Michelangelo was not given entirely free rein; *St Petronius* shows the influence of della Quercia, whom Michelangelo

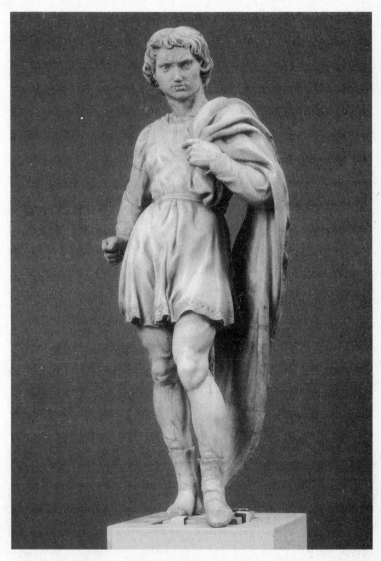

Michelangelo – *St Proculus* from the *Arca di San Domenico*,
Church of San Domenico, Bologna. Sculpted in 1495, the pose is
close to the one Michelangelo would adopt for the *David*

greatly admired. *St Proculus'* physical attitude, though he is clothed, looks forward directly to the *David* which Michelangelo would begin to release from its marble only six years later.

Unfortunately the commission led to a row with an unnamed local artist who claimed that it should rightfully have been his; and as no further work was forthcoming in Bologna, and the atmosphere in Florence was calm once again, Michelangelo, after a year away, decided to return home late in 1495.

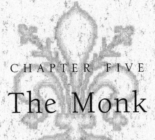

CHAPTER FIVE

The Monk

Charles VIII of France entered Rome on the evening of Wednesday, 31 December 1494 – a wet, miserable day on which the streets had turned into muddy quagmires. It stuck in Pope Alexander's craw to have him there, knowing as he did that Charles had among his advisers Cardinal Giuliano della Rovere, a nephew of Sixtus IV and also Alexander's most bitter enemy and rival.

Charles rested his troops in Rome before setting out once more for an early campaign, attacking Naples in February 1495 and taking the city after a battle which lasted just a few hours. Alfonso having abdicated and fled, Charles had himself crowned king, taking the two other titles that went with Naples: Emperor of the East and King of Jerusalem.

In Naples he was at first hailed as a liberator, but his triumph did not last long. His success had depended on the disunity that existed between the various Italian states; but they now realised that they would have to pull together if they wanted to rid the country of what they all saw as an unwelcome presence. Venice, Milan and Rome formed a league against Charles. They were abetted by King Ferdinand of Spain, who ruled Sicily and didn't want a French presence in Italy, and by the Holy Roman Emperor, Maximilian I, who had married a daughter of the Duke of Milan, and looked equally askance at French expansionism.

Worried by this turn of events, and suddenly aware not only of how far away from home he was, but how tenuous was his line of retreat, Charles left Naples under the control of a garrison, and in the summer of 1495 started to lead the remainder of his weary army home. Many of the men were also suffering from syphilis, which they would now spread along the whole route of their journey. The introduction of 'the French disease' did nothing to endear the invaders to the rest of Italy. Charles was intercepted near Fornovo, not far from Parma, by Giovanni Francesco Gonzaga of Mantua, who surrounded the French army with a much larger force. The hugely outnumbered French managed to fight their way out, and after a bloody struggle continued their march, though the Italians managed to capture their baggage-train and claimed a victory.

Gonzaga had Andrea Mantegna paint a picture to celebrate

the event, but Charles had got away effectively unscathed, and when he reached Milan, Lodovico promptly abandoned his new allies and came to terms with him. Charles returned safely to France, but he had achieved nothing. The Spanish soon saw to it that the French hold on Naples was broken; and Charles himself had only three more years to live: in April 1498, at his château at Amboise, he inadvertently struck his head on a wooden beam and died of concussion soon afterwards. Lacking a direct heir, he was succeeded by his cousin Louis, a descendant of the Dukes of Orléans, who consolidated his position by marrying Charles' widow. An abler ruler than Charles, Louis XII himself invaded Italy in 1499, and soon put an end to Milan's independence. As a result of that, the painter-turned-architect Donato Bramante went to Rome to work for Alexander; and Leonardo da Vinci (who had long since lost the metal for his huge equestrian statue when it was sent to Ferrara in 1494 to be turned into cannon for use against the French) returned briefly to Florence.

In Florence, meanwhile, unrest and uncertainty continued, while revenue was drained by a costly and long-drawn-out war with Pisa, which clung to the independence proffered it by Charles, and would not bow to the Florentine yoke.

Within the city itself, factionalism was rife, but the supporters of Savonarola, the *Frateschi*, had the upper hand over both their aristocratic and their republican opponents, who in turn were at odds with one another, though there were shifting alliances. Savonarola's opponents sneeringly called his supporters *Masticapaternostri* and *Piagnoni* – prayer-mutterers and whiners. By comparison with some of the other blood-and-thunder preachers operating in Florence at the time, Savonarola was both rational and intellectual. It was these qualities which enabled him to control the city for as long as he did, while his lurid sermons gained him popularity. The sermon as a piece of theatre is something we have long forgotten.

Although priests were specifically excluded from partici-pation in state politics, Savonarola was effectively in charge of the city, and, implementing his own republican ideals, the Prior set about the restructuring of the government of the state with a new constitution which drew its inspiration both from Venice and from the pre-Medicean form of Florentine popular rule. He cleverly appealed to the Florentines' pride in their city as a cradle of republican liberty.

A Great Council was established and plans were set afoot for the construction of a new Great Hall, annexed to the Palazzo della Signoria, to house it. This was to be the most significant building of the entire Savonarola period, and so keen was the Prior to have it completed that he diverted to it resources from the ongoing work on the cathedral. The Great Hall would have to accommodate 1,000 delegates. Work on this huge space – the room measured fifty-three by twenty-three metres, and is now known as the *Sala dei*

Cinquecento – began in July 1495. Though not completed, the room would be functioning by April 1496. Asymmetrical in plan to maximise the space available, it had a low ceiling, and a loggia at one end with carved and gilded seats for the *Gonfaloniere* and the *Priori*. At the west end, opposite the loggia, were a pulpit and an altar. The other walls were lined with stalls, and benches filled the central area. The whole austere space was lit by twelve windows. As the city's principal architect, Giuliano da Sangallo, had left in the wake of his Medicean patrons, it was Simone del Pollaiuolo, '*il Cronaca*', a pupil of his and a supporter of Savonarola, who undertook the job. Some years later Michelangelo and Leonardo would undertake two vast frescoes for its walls.

The Great Council would be modelled on the similar Council in Venice, to which a large number of ordinary citizens could be elected, but there would be no equivalent of the Doge. In practice it wasn't a straightforward system. Though Savonarola claimed to be its instigator, it may have been the brain-child of the Florentine upper-class, the *Ottimati*, which had far more governmental experience than the Prior. Allowing more of the people a say in running the city was, according to your point of view, a liberal and progressive thing to do, or a sop to the masses to keep them from rebelling: actual power would be wielded, as usual, by a small oligarchy. The Florentine upper class would have wanted a smaller senate, answerable to the Great Council but actually the ruling executive; Savonarola envisaged a democracy whose true leader was Christ. Piero Capponi, who'd stood up to Charles VIII over the sum to be paid him, wrote privately to a friend that the state needed a body of twenty-five to thirty men of wealth and absolute integrity (given that such people actually existed) to rule the city. Most politicians think they know what's best for everybody, and most therefore lose patience with the democratic process once they are in power.

In one sense democracy exerted itself in the form of the various parties that evolved. There were the *Bianchi* (the Whites), who supported the new constitution, and the *Bigi* (the Greys), who opposed it and remained supporters of the Medici. Those most opposed to Savonarola were known as the *Arrabiati* (the Rabid Ones). Outside the city, Piero de' Medici was still a threat. He would assemble small armies (on one occasion no more than a band of mercenaries) and besiege the city in an attempt to take it back by force three times in the 1490s – in 1496, 1497 and 1498.

However democratic things seemed outwardly, policy was still determined by Savonarola, because he had the ear of the people. His was a severe rule, conducted from the pulpit; and now he was convinced that God reigned in the city through him. A proto-Calvinist of sorts, he demanded that all supporters of the Medici be executed (five in fact were); that churches be stripped of their gold and silver ornaments, and that fasting should be the order of the day for everyone. Savonarola's views on religious art were naturally austere, and he disapproved of the beautiful and elegantly dressed Madonnas of Botticelli and Filippino Lippi, though the imagery he used in his own sermons was extravagant and melodramatic. His principal interest, in which he prefigured Luther, was in reforming the Church. In that he was without compromise.

New laws were introduced to restrict extravagances in everything from dress to conduct. Public festivals, games and races were forbidden. In the end such extreme measures proved unpopular, and Savonarola made matters worse for himself by seeking to shame errant citizens and priests by training youths and boys, clad in white, in the way of pious discipline. These last roamed the streets in bands, their hair cut short, singing hymns and collecting alms for the poor. They also collected such wicked objects as mirrors, scent, earrings, necklaces, bangles, make-up, fans, wigs, chessboards, lutes, dice and cards. Brothels and alehouses either closed or went underground.

Savonarola introduced his own 'festivals', of which two took place, at the traditional time for those things, Shrove Tuesday, in 1497 and 1498, on the Piazza della Signoria. Great bonfires were erected, on to which the populace were encouraged to throw their 'vanities' – paintings, jewels, dresses, books of poetry and so forth. Luca Landucci, an apothecary of the time who kept a diary, recalls on 27 February 1498 that 'On the Piazza de' Signori was made a pile of vain objects, such as nude statues, boards for games, heretical books . . . looking-glasses and many other vain things, all very valuable, and reckoned to be worth many thousands of florins. The procession of boys was made as the year before: they collected in the four quarters, holding crosses and olive-branches, each quarter drawn up behind its tabernacle, and each quarter went in the afternoon to burn its pile. Some disapproving people caused trouble, throwing dead cats and other rubbish on it; however, the boys set it alight and burned it all.' The flames rose as choirs sang hymns and bells pealed.

These 'bonfires of the vanities' seemed ridiculous to many of the more sophisticated of Florence's population, and as the sacrifice of treasures was voluntary, not too many items of aesthetic importance were destroyed in this way. By 1498, Savonarola was beginning to overreach himself.

He had long since begun to irritate the Pope. The worldly, political and nepotistic Alexander VI had, at first, tried to silence Savonarola by offering him a cardinal's hat, but the Dominican had replied loftily that he preferred the red of martyrdom. It is easy to see during the progress of the four volatile years when he held sway in Florence that the monk was absolutely set on such an end: a painful death being the logical conclusion of the mortification that had always been at the centre of his life. Like all fanatics, he was only able to take his followers with him part of the way – people might have been enthusiastic for his policies and beliefs at first, or they may have simply used them for political reasons:

getting rid of the Medici, or reforming the Church, for example; but in the end they would tire of them and of their champion. Also, working in Rome against Savonarola was the Augustinian, Fra Mariano da Gennazzano, now General of his Order, and enjoying the ear of the Pope.

Alexander, having failed to seduce the monk into silence, now resorted to force. As early as 1496 he summoned him to Rome, but Savonarola refused to go. Edicts followed from the Vatican forbidding him to preach, but although he obeyed for a time, substituting a devoted follower in the pulpit for himself, he could not deny himself for long, and returned to preach all the harder, as the populace, half-fearful, half-zealous, packed the cathedral to hear him.

In summer 1497, the Pope excommunicated him; but, after several months of fasting and soul-searching, he refused to recognise the Pope's authority to do so. At last, after a threat from the Vatican to put the whole city under an interdict, the Council, among whom there were many who wanted Savonarola removed, moved against him. A short time earlier, Savonarola had written to Alexander:

You have not listened to my expositions . . . I can no longer place any faith in Your Holiness, but must trust myself wholly to Him Who chooses the weak things of this world to confound the strong. Your Holiness is well advised to make immediate provisions for your own salvation.

There was clearly no way that Alexander would tolerate this 'son of iniquity' any further. He timed his final intervention well. Support for Savonarola was fading; except for a few disciples who shared his ardour, the population was becoming sick of his joyless régime, which brought no material benefits at all, however godly it was. Towards the end of his rule the Prior became the butt of unpleasant practical jokes: a group of rich young men, the *Compagnacci*, ('Ruffians') smeared the pulpit of the cathedral with grease and draped it with a rotting donkey hide; and managed to send a great wooden chest crashing down from the clerestory into the congregation, scattering the people in panic.

The Council moved against the Prior early in March 1498, requiring him to preach no more. He acquiesced, but only on condition that he be allowed to give one more sermon in self-justification. On 18 March he let fly: he said that he had every right to resist unlawful authority, that his prophecies had been fulfilled, and that the Church had become a Satanic cradle of every kind of prostitution and vice. By now he was in the grip of an ecstatic madness, an exultation which was the result of years of self-denial, the light-headedness that came with semi-starvation, and a compulsive desire to embrace a martyr's death, though what he hoped to achieve by it, and who he thought would view it as genuine martyrdom, is hard to say. His imagery is wild: he preached because of a raging fire within his bones: 'I feel myself all burning, all inflamed with the Spirit of the Lord!

O, Spirit within! You rouse the waves of the sea, as the wind does. You stir the tempest as you pass.'

This last sermon incensed the already impatient Franciscans, who disliked and despised the Dominicans, calling them *domini cani* – the dogs of the Lord. A Franciscan monk, Francesco da Puglia, spoke out and said that all Savonarola's claims to a special relationship with God were false and that he, Fra Francesco, would walk through fire or take on any other ordeal in the Prior's company to prove that the latter was under no special divine protection. Savonarola refused to take part, but undertook that his devoted disciple, Fra Domenico da Pescia, would perform the ordeal for him. Fra Francesco retorted that he would only undergo the trial with the Prior. In a situation which was becoming farcical, another Franciscan monk was found to replace Fra Francesco.

The whole idea of such a barbaric practice as trial by ordeal was repugnant to the modern minds of the *Signoria*. One of them suggested that rather than trial by fire, couldn't the monks attempt to walk on the water of the Arno? At least all anyone would then risk was a wetting. However, the trial, the idea of which unfortunately had excited the people, had to go ahead. It was agreed that if Fra Domenico perished, Savonarola should be banished; if the Franciscan died, Fra Francisco should go. No one seems to have thought about what to do if both monks perished. A date was set, 7 April, and a corridor a metre wide and thirty metres long was laid out in the Piazza della Signoria, made of wooden staves soaked in oil, which would be lit. Through this flaming corridor the two monks would pass. The two monks duly arrived, supported by their Orders, on the appointed day at the appointed time, in front of an eager mob. There was some bickering, and it was clear that neither monk was eager to go ahead; but at last everything was made ready. Then, out of an already louring sky, a thunderstorm broke.

This might have been seen as divine intervention on the part of both the Dominicans and the Franciscans, but as it caused the ordeal to be called off, the mob was furious. The next day was Palm Sunday, and the congregation that had gathered in the cathedral to hear a sermon by a Dominican monk was set upon by an angry crowd. Pursued by the mob, the adherents of Savonarola fled to San Marco, where the monks, unknown to Savonarola, were already prepared for a fight. There was a pitched battle, with monks hurling masonry down from the monastery walls, while the mob tried to set the place alight. Several people were killed on both sides before a troop of guards arrived from the *Signoria* with orders to arrest the Prior, who had retreated to the library. With his two most loyal and close followers, Fra Domenico and Fra Silvestro, he was led through the streets, mocked and pelted with refuse and stones, and imprisoned in the tower of the Palazzo della Signoria. Not content with that, the mob then sought out Savonarola's two principal lay supporters, Francesco de Valori and Paolo Antonio

Soderini. The *Signoria* was able to protect Soderini, but Valori was not so fortunate: encountering him in the Piazza della Signoria, the mob beat him to death. They then made their way to his house, broke in, murdered his wife and all the members of the household, and pillaged the place.

In prison, Savonarola was severely tortured: the *Signoria* had, it appeared, no qualms about barbaric practice when it came to the *strappado,* that horribly simple torment so beloved of the Inquisition by which a person is raised by his arms tied behind his back and then jolted downwards so as to dislocate the shoulders. His arms nearly torn out of their sockets after seven sessions, the Prior confessed to his 'crimes', but later repudiated his confession, which he had committed lengthily to paper. This made no difference to his fate. After six weeks of interrogation and torture, together with Fra Domenico and Fra Silvestro, he was given a summary trial, found guilty of heresy and schism, and condemned to death. A new bonfire was erected in the Piazza della Signoria, and a scaffold placed over it. Here, the Prior and his two faithful monks were hung in chains as the fire was lit under them. The apothecary Luca Landucci wrote:

In a few hours the victims were burned, their legs and arms gradually dropping off . . . Part of their bodies remaining hanging in the chains, a quantity of stones was thrown to make them fall, as there was a fear of the people getting hold of them; and then the hangman and those whose business it was, hacked down the post and burned it on the ground, bringing a lot of brushwood, and stirring the fire up over the dead bodies so that the very last piece was consumed. Then they fetched carts, and accompanied by the mace-bearers, carried the last bit of dust to the Arno near the Ponte Vecchio in order that no remains should be found.

The period of Savonarola's ascendancy had been a poor one for the arts in general, not only because of the austere proscriptions emanating from San Marco, but because the same handful of years, much to the monk's initial advantage, saw a spate of crop failures leading to famine, the continuing war with Pisa which drained money and morale, outbreaks of bubonic plague, and, the legacy of Charles' troops of syphilis which Landucci graphically describes as 'French boils'. The French had helped themselves to whatever they fancied of Florentine works of art, and the effects of Piero de' Medici had been auctioned off. Florence in the mid-to-late 1490s was in a state of relative impoverishment.

It was not the most propitious time for Michelangelo to return, but when he did so in the winter of 1495, coming back to his gloomy family house in Santa Croce, he was not entirely without hope of a patron. The cadet branch of the Medici, now called Popolano, was still in Florence. Lorenzo and Giovanni di Pierfrancesco de' Medici knew Michelangelo from when he had lived at the Medici Palace, and Lorenzo had for some time been an active patron of the arts. His patronage of Botticelli has been mentioned, and he was involved in the commissioning of a long series of drawings to illustrate Dante's *Divine Comedy* from the same artist. In 1495, Lorenzo was a wealthy, cultivated thirty-two-year-old little affected by the political volatility of the city, but rather keeping his head down after the dramatic events surrounding Charles VIII in which he'd been involved so recently. It would have been the most natural thing in the world for Michelangelo to make his way to Lorenzo's palace.

Lorenzo was a connoisseur and had no difficulty in recognising the twenty-year-old sculptor's talent. He immediately commissioned a small figure of the young St John-the-Baptist (a *Giovannino*) in marble, which is probably lost, though a *Giovannino* in the Bargello once attributed to Donatello may be this one. Lorenzo was also involved in the creation and sale of another statue, and this involvement would radically affect the next months of Michelangelo's life.

Whether as the result of a commission or, more likely, as a piece created speculatively for sale, Michelangelo had by the spring of 1496 carved a life-size *Sleeping Cupid*. When Lorenzo saw it he suggested to Michelangelo that it would fetch more money if it could be passed off as a classical statue on the Roman art market. The story goes, though it runs counter to Michelangelo's honest and strait-laced personality, that the artist 'antiqued' the *Cupid* by burying it for a while. Vasari suggests that he may not himself have perpetrated the deception, but that it was done by an art dealer who became involved, Baldassare del Milanese, who 'took [the *Cupid*] to Rome and buried it in a vineyard he owned and then sold it as an antique'.

Baldassare certainly does seem to have shipped the statue to Rome, where he sold it to Cardinal Raffaelle Riario for 200 ducats. Riario was the same nephew of Sixtus IV who'd been present in Florence cathedral when the Pazzi had tried to murder the Medici brothers, and he'd now grown into a noted epicure. Michelangelo, who didn't learn of the purchase price until later, was paid a mere thirty ducats. Vasari comments that 'Milanese sold the Cardinal the statue that Michelangelo had made for him, and then wrote to [Lorenzo di] Pierfrancesco saying that he should pay Michelangelo thirty crowns since that was all he had got for the *Sleeping Cupid*; and in this way he deceived the Cardinal, Lorenzo di Pierfrancesco, and Michelangelo himself'.

Not long afterwards the Cardinal discovered that the 'antique' was in fact no such thing, but he still admired the work, and having established that it came from Florence, sent one of his own men there to find the artist. Very few sculptors were working at the time and Michelangelo's reputation was in any case beginning to grow, so it wasn't long before the Cardinal's man ran him to ground. Asked to give an example of his work, Michelangelo did a perfect drawing of a hand. This was enough to convince Riario's servant that here was the author of the *Sleeping Cupid*, which Michelangelo admitted; upon which the servant suggested on behalf of his master that Michelangelo might wish to come to Rome and work under the Cardinal's patronage. Eager to broaden his horizons, and aware that there was a greater chance of commissions in Rome under Alexander than in Florence under Savonarola, no matter how much respect he had for the latter priest, Michelangelo accepted. Lorenzo wrote a general letter of introduction for him to his own friends and contacts in the city. As for the *Sleeping Cupid*, it may have found its way into the collection of Isabella d'Este, wife of Giovanni Francesco Gonzaga, and, if so, it was later purchased by Charles I of England, who acquired the Mantua collection. It was lost when the Cromwellians sold off the royal collections.

Michelangelo arrived in Rome on 25 June 1496. Though it has been suggested that he was an *avid* supporter of Savonarola, it is unlikely, if that were true, that he would have left Florence at a point when the Prior was reaching the height of his powers. In fact, Michelangelo was never deeply concerned either with church or secular politics, though within him there would always be both a broad humanism and a deep belief in Christianity. For the moment, though, he was a twenty-year-old artist out to do nothing more complicated than further his career. When he found out that Baldassare had got 200 ducats for the *Sleeping*

Cupid but only paid him thirty, he was livid, and determined to recover either the piece, or its proper value.

As for Florence, Savonarola left it, ironically, with the model of a new secular republic, whose operation harked back to its pre-Medicean days. Men like Niccolò Machiavelli, the first modern, fully documented, pragmatic civil servant and politician, who entered the service of the *Signoria* in 1498, would successfully continue to manage the city and the state's affairs, even though the pre-eminence of Florence would dwindle, until the Medici returned as *ipso facto* rulers in 1512.

CHAPTER SIX

Rome

Michelangelo arrived in Rome in search of work; but he also wanted to clear up the business surrounding his *Sleeping Cupid*. Vasari tells us that once Cardinal Riario had discovered the deception, he compelled Baldassare del Milanese to refund his money and take the *Cupid* back.

Although the Cardinal has been accused of lacking perception, if not taste, this is based on the fact that he was taken in by the *Sleeping Cupid* and that he gave Michelangelo only one commission. But this is flimsy evidence on which to condemn a man who was an acknowledged connoisseur, and whose sumptuous new palace (which is now the *Cancelleria*), designed by Bramante Lazzari, was nearing completion in Rome, under the watchful eye of the Pope, who didn't like to see too much grandiosity in his cardinals, especially if it affected his own. But Riario came from a powerful enough family to stand his ground, even against the Borgia. Most of the rich in Rome vied with each other in patronage of the arts, though the murder rate among the ruling class at its peak reached five or six a day. Riario was among the richest in the College of Cardinals, and managed to survive this bloodbath.

Michelangelo was not slow in trying to sort the matter of the *Sleeping Cupid* out. On 2 July 1496 he wrote to Lorenzo di Pierfrancesco, who was quietly becoming one of the most influential men in the new Florentine Republic, about it. (There was no formal postal service then; people entrusted their mail to friends, itinerant merchants, and bankers' couriers to deliver inter-city and international post. The system worked very well.)

This is the earliest letter we have in Michelangelo's own hand. He is impatient, and scarcely bothers about his first impressions of Rome. He cuts straight to the business in hand, mentioning some of those friends with whom Lorenzo had put him in contact, which means that he made the rounds with his letters of introduction and recommendation soon after he arrived, though he apologises for not having delivered other business letters Lorenzo had entrusted to him. Mentioned in the letter are Paolo Rucellai, a member of the wool-dyers family related by marriage to Michelangelo, and

Cavalcanti and Balducci, Florentine bankers in Rome. The letter also contains one obvious and simmering reference to the *Sleeping Cupid* and the fact that it had been palmed off on the Cardinal as an antiquity:

I beg to inform your Magnificence that I arrived here safely last Saturday, and went at once to the Cardinal . . . to whom I delivered your letter. He seemed well inclined to me, and desired at once that I should look at different statues [antiquities in the Cardinal's collection], which I spent the whole day in doing, and have therefore not yet delivered your other letters. On Sunday the Cardinal came to the new building [the *Cancelleria*] and sent for me. When I came, he asked me what I had thought of all I had seen. There are indeed, it seems to me, very beautiful things here. The Cardinal now wished to know whether I would venture to undertake any beautiful thing. I answered that I would make no great promises, but he would see himself what I was able to do. We have purchased a fine piece of marble for a figure as large as life, and next Monday I begin work on it. Last Monday I gave the rest of your letters to Paolo Rucellai, who paid me the money [for the repurchase balance on the *Sleeping Cupid*?] I required, and that for Cavalcanti. I then took Baldassare del Milanese your letter, and demanded the *Cupid* back, promising to give him his money [presumably only the thirty ducats Michelangelo had been paid] in return. He answered furiously that he would rather break the *Cupid* into a thousand pieces; he had purchased it, it was his property, and he could prove in writing that he had satisfied him from whom he had received it. No man should compel him to deliver it up. He complained of you, that you had slandered him. One of our Florentines here interposed to smooth things over, but proved ineffectual. I am now hoping to arrange the matter through the medium of the Cardinal's good offices, for so I have been advised by Baldassare Balducci. I will write you whatever takes place further. So much for this time. Farewell. God keep you.

Michelagniolo in Rome

No one will ever know for certain what resulted from this very Italian-sounding row; but it is unlikely that Michelangelo had the time to pursue the matter of the lost *Cupid*. Despite some fascinating theories that have been advanced, it's most likely that Milanese did have a receipt from the Cardinal attesting to its resale; that he kept it, and subsequently sold it on.

Rome in 1496 was a strange place, part seething town, part slum, and part farmland. It's unlikely that Michelangelo, or any Florentine, would have felt like a provincial there. Many of the great palaces and churches now on the seven hills were not yet built. Most of the ruins of antiquity still awaited excavation. There were great tracts of wasteland within the old Aurelian Walls, inhabited by gangs of bandits.

Pope Alexander VI followed Pope Sixtus' IV lead in pursuing a programme of regeneration, which would reach new heights under Alexander's close successor, Julius II.

The huge, crumbling buildings of the old empire, the Colosseum, the Forum and the Pantheon rose like giant ghosts in a town which had, since their day, fallen into ruin and was now, slowly, rising again. There was already evidence of this: rubbing shoulders with the remains of Roman baths and theatres were the symbols of the Christian age: the great churches of St Peter (the old basilica), St Paul-without-the-Walls, Santa Maria Maggiore and San Giovanni Laterano, as well as dozens of lesser churches, monasteries and convents. Although the buildings of antiquity were beginning to be appreciated (Nero's Golden House had recently been excavated, and its wall-paintings influenced many contemporary artists), they were still pillaged for materials to be used in the reconstruction of the city and particularly the palaces of the rich. And stone was not all they appropriated. At the palace of Cardinal Giuliano della Rovere, currently in exile on account of his enmity for Alexander, Michelangelo would have been able to see, and naturally would have been influenced by, the magnificent Greek *Apollo Belvedere*, a work of the second century BC. However aesthetically devalued the *Apollo* may be today, his effect on early Renaissance thinking was profound; not least on that of Michelangelo. The very stance of the *Apollo* foreshadows the physical attitude, the *contrapposto*, of the *David*.

But any jewels such as this still found themselves surrounded by mud. Despite its growing importance as an international urban centre, Rome still had three uninhabited hills; and teeming slums stood cheek-by-jowl with vineyards, farmland and wasteland. There were two centres. The port, on the banks of the Tiber, was the centre of the business district. The Vatican was about a quarter of the size that it is today, surmounted by the old basilica of St Peter with its attendant chapels. The Vatican itself was like a fortress, and was connected by a covered walkway with the Castel Sant' Angelo. This complex was the military and political centre of the town, and had only a nominal concern with religion. Cardinals, like Giovanni de' Medici and Giuliano della Rovere, were temporal appointees, not ecclesiastical ones; and the Vatican was far more concerned with the pragmatic Kingdom on Earth than the theoretical Kingdom in Heaven. The palaces of cardinals were also strongholds.

Rome was a dangerous place. The crime rate was high, and it was matched by a degree of corruption rarely met with since the city's foundation. In the seventeen days between the death of Innocent VIII on 25 July 1492 and the election of Alexander VI on 11 August, 'while the city was under the rigid rule of the white-faced Cardinal Riario'

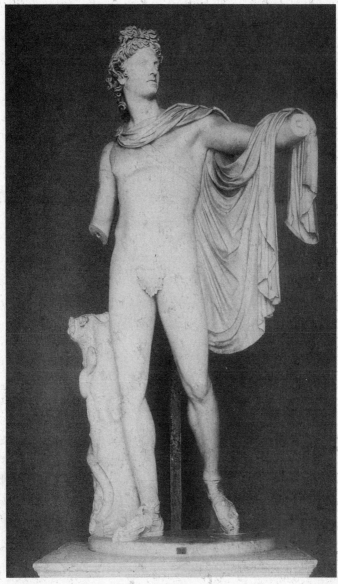

The *Apollo Belvedere*

(as Frederick Corvo, the historian of the Borgias, tells us), 'a matter of some 220 assassinations took place: in such order had the deceased Pope left His capital that more than nine murders were committed every day among a population of a mere 58,000 . . .'

Alexander VI, whose ambition was to impose some kind of order on the city and the lands which were vassal to it, was faced with a huge task. He had murderers, when caught, hanged, and left their bodies to hang among the ruins, adding to the general stench of the city. Those caught in any kind of political skulduggery (except anything to the benefit of the House of Borgia) were forced to see their houses razed to the ground – the worst possible disgrace for a Roman citizen. They themselves were then hanged and displayed until their rotting corpses fell from the scaffold and had to be cleared away by the dung cart.

Alexander appointed a Commission to settle disputes which had formerly been decided by murder. Inspectors of the privately run prisons were appointed, all official salaries, fallen into arrears during the weak reign of Innocent VIII, were paid up to date; and a judicial Bench was established. Nevertheless, Rome remained a hotbed of vice and intrigue, to which the Pope himself contributed. Florence by contrast was sophisticated, ethical and civilised. Michelangelo's own moral outlook was always rigid and of a high standard. He cannot have found the atmosphere of Rome sympathetic, but he knew that in the interest of his career he would have to stomach it.

Alexander was naturally no stranger to sharp political practice, but a more idealistic leader might have been unequal to tackling the job in hand. The Pope understood the principles of compromise, and of divide and rule. Within the city, as in external affairs, he sought to sow disunity among factions which, united, would have stood against his own family and interests. His was a coarser version of the rule of the Medici at their height; conducted with less finesse and a more cynical grasp of *Realpolitik*, a response to the necessity posed by the place and the times.

He was a worldly Pope; rich, powerful and ruthless. He had fathered several children already, and, after ascending to St Peter's throne, he remained a profligate. He was astute, adaptable, charming and tough. In an early move to break the monopoly on power held by the Italian cardinals, he created others from abroad in 1493, the year following his election. There were two Frenchmen, a Pole, a Spaniard; and the English John Morton, Archbishop of Canterbury and remorseless controller of the finances of King Henry VII. Alexander also raised to the purple his own eighteen-year-old son, Cesare, whose ruthlessness matched his father's, and who would prove a useful weapon in the maintenance of the rule of the Borgia.

During the years of Charles VIII's incursion, Alexander made and broke alliances as the political situation dictated. He was quick to curb the threatening power of Savonarola, and achieved it without letting any mud stick to him. At the same time he commissioned the Umbrian painter Pinturicchio to decorate the Castel Sant' Angelo, where Alexander had taken refuge while Charles VIII was in Rome, with frescoes celebrating his own life; and he had the same painter embellish the Borgia apartments in the Vatican. Pinturicchio also painted the Pope's portrait – a jowly politician in jewel-encrusted vestments, seen in profile in an attitude of prayer, fat hands clasped together, his intelligent expression and eyes the apogee of insincerity.

Despite everything, Rome under Alexander was a healthier place for the arts than Florence under Savonarola.

Alexander was also concerned with strengthening and renovating Rome's defences, and had Giuliano da Sangallo's brother and fellow-architect, Antonio, overhaul the Castel Sant' Angelo; but in this period of refurbishment and renewal, continued after 1503 by Giuliano della Rovere (Julius II), he was not alone. Several moneyed cardinals were building palaces to their own aggrandisement, not without the risk of attracting the jealous eye of the Pope. Prominent among them was Raffaelle Riario.

The cardinal who had bought the *Sleeping Cupid* now expected something more of Michelangelo to match the statues which adorned his new palace, and the sculptor responded with a slightly over-life-sized nude of the young *Bacchus*. The marble bought for this piece is referred to in the letter of 2 July from Michelangelo to Lorenzo di Pierfrancesco.

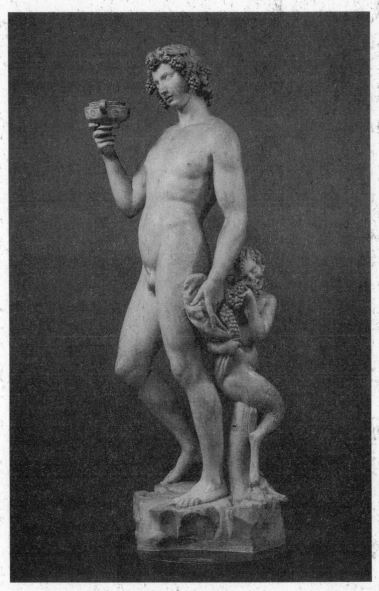

Michelangelo – *Bacchus*

At first glance the statue seems to draw heavily on the classical pieces Michelangelo would have often seen in Rome, but a closer look reveals how modern and original the twenty-one-year-old sculptor's concept is. The psychological and physical impact is huge: this god is a real drunk; though he's a young man, his body is sloppy, and his belly and arm muscles are already slack from drink. Vasari says, 'In this figure it is clear that Michelangelo wanted to obtain a marvellous harmony of various elements, notably in giving it the slenderness of a youth combined with the fullness and roundness of the female form'. It may also be that the *Bacchus* gave for its creator an early expression of what he thought of the state of Rome.

Standing upright, Bacchus seems only just able to keep his balance, holding up a wine-cup on which he tries to focus. As a comment on and corrective to drunkenness the statue would be hard to equal. Bacchus' emblem, the leopard skin, falls slack and unheeded behind him, loosely held in his left hand, and next to his left leg a panisc, or little satyr, nibbles at a bunch of grapes by a tree-stump. The whole piece is designed to be viewed from all angles, a revived concept of statuary resulting from the study of classical sculpture, lending itself to the habit of placing a piece in the middle of a courtyard (and it may have been intended for such a position in Riario's new palace), rather than against a wall. It is giddying to walk around it, an effect Michelangelo may have intended, though there is one optimum view, threequarters right front, which shows the god and his panisc to their best advantage.

Unfortunately the statue did not please Riario – perhaps it was too realistic, perhaps it too obviously represented the defeat of the spirit by the body – and it ended up in the collection of Jacopo Galli, a Florentine banker in Rome who became Michelangelo's friend and occasional agent. However, the choice of subject was always that of the commissioner, not of the artist. In this context one is bound to wonder why Riario asked for a *Bacchus*; but the answer may be simply that he lacked one in his collection, and needed a reproduction. What he got, and rejected, was an early work of genius. The *Bacchus* shows Michelangelo for the first time in full and confident command of his powers: it represents a profound turning point, demonstrating an ability on the part of its creator to scale-up effortlessly, as well as to communicate a state of mind accurately, and sets Michelangelo on the path to greatness.

Galli was a neighbour of Riario, and there is a suggestion in both of Michelangelo's early biographies that it was in fact Galli who commissioned the *Bacchus*, as well as a now lost *Eros*. The facts of the commissioning remain uncertain, but we know that the *Bacchus* ended up in Galli's garden at Rome among his collection of antiquities, because it was drawn there by Maerten van Heemskerck in the early 1530s. Heemskerck drew it minus the hand holding the cup, perhaps to make it look more like an antique, damaged statue.

There is an interesting footnote to the *Bacchus* story. In about 1511 the sculptor Jacopo Sansovino, who adopted the surname of his master, the more famous Andrea Sansovino, was commissioned to carve a *Bacchus* himself, in Florence. This has little of the mastery of Michelangelo's sculpture, though its elements are identical: a paunchy Bacchus raises his left hand holding the cup, not his right; and the panisc crouches behind his right leg. The most impressive element of the statue is that Jacopo has extended the raised arm almost in defiance of gravity – it is hard to believe that he could have judged so finely the limit after which the marble would have broken off under its own weight. But the ensemble is less sinister: here is simply a boozy, amiable young man, not an alcoholic. Sadly the model for Jacopo's statue, Pippo del Fabbro, later went mad, and in his madness identified himself with the statue so closely that he wandered around Florence naked, adopting the pose of the *Bacchus* for hours on end, when he was not draping himself in wet sheets and taking up the poses of other neo-classical statues for which he had modelled.

It isn't known for sure what, if any, pieces – the *Bacchus* may have been the only one – were actually commissioned by Riario from Michelangelo. It wasn't unusual for a great prince (ecclesiastical or temporal) to summon an artist to join his staff and then ignore him. During the period that Michelangelo was with the Cardinal, it may have been that Riario had his mind on other things. But although it seems clear that the Cardinal commissioned the *Bacchus*, there is no record of a payment for it. By the summer of 1497 Michelangelo was running short of funds. He was also being badgered by his family: his father in Florence was, as usual, in financial difficulties. His second wife had just died, and he wrote urgently asking his son to come home, even if it meant leaving unfinished work to others. Michelangelo tried to reassure him, but it was clear that he would not be able to return to Florence quite so easily. It is interesting that Michelangelo, in his correspondence with his father, always refers back to 1497 as the year when his troubles began, but it is hard to square this view with the fact that at about the same time his career really began to take off.

In the meantime, he was visited by two of his brothers in turn: first his younger brother, Buonarroto, arrived from Florence. Michelangelo had no space to put him up in his own modest digs, but found a room for him in a nearby *pensione*. That the brothers were broadly sympathetic to Savonarola is attested to in a letter written in a disguised hand with a false signature by Michelangelo to Buonarroto in March 1497, a year before Savonarola's fall. Michelangelo would have been aware of the machinations in Rome of Fra Mariano against Savonarola, and knew that he would get into trouble if a letter over his signature, expressing sympathy for the Dominican, should fall into the hands of his enemies. The artist writes:

. . . From thy brother Michelagniolo I have received your letter, from which I derived the greatest comfort, chiefly because it contains news of your seraphic Fra Girolamo [Savonarola], who has set the whole of Rome talking. They say here that he is a vile heretic: so much so that at all costs he ought to come to Rome and prophesy a little for these people here; then they would canonise him. Wherefore let all his friends be of good courage.

. . . Fra Mariano has nothing but evil to say of your prophet . . . In my next letter I will give you more information, for now I am in a hurry. There is no other news to give you, save that seven paper bishops [ie, legal offenders who were to be pilloried wearing paper mitres] were made yesterday, and five of them were hanged by the neck . . . When you write hither, commend me to Michelagniolo. No more. Written in the dark

Your Piero, in Rome

But when he arrived in Rome, Buonarroto's main news was of a bad debt that was rebounding on their father, and, with understandable irritation, but never flinching from his keen sense of duty to family, Michelangelo agreed to help – though it would mean that he himself would have to borrow money to clear his father's financial obligation.

Leonardo, Michelangelo's older brother, the Dominican monk, had run into difficulties through his uncompromisingly puritanical line, had possibly been unfrocked, and had fled to Rome from Viterbo, where he had been preaching, to seek help from his younger brother, who gave him a gold ducat to enable him to return home to Florence. Michelangelo wrote to his father on 1 July 1497 about this encounter, and mentions other business difficulties by the way, from which it becomes easier to see why he felt that 1497 was such a bad year for him:

. . . I have failed in all my attempts to settle my business with the Cardinal, and I have no wish to leave Rome until I have received satisfaction and have been paid for my work. [A reference to a down payment – for materials? – on the *Bacchus*?] With these exalted personages one has to go slowly, for they cannot be forced into action. I believe, however, that the end of the coming week will certainly see all my affairs arranged. [It didn't.]

I must tell you that Fra Leonardo [Michelangelo's brother] has returned here to Rome, and says that he was obliged to flee from Viterbo and that his frock has been taken away from him. He wished to return to you, wherefore I gave him a gold ducat for his journey, which he asked of me. I think you must already know of this, for by now he ought to be with you . . . Commend me to my friends.

Michelagniolo, Sculptor, in Rome

If there is one positive note struck, it is in the proud signature that identifies Michelangelo as a sculptor. Whatever else may have happened, whatever financial and ethical difficulties he faced, there is no problem with his sense of self as an artist.

As far as the debt his father had incurred was concerned, Michelangelo was again in correspondence with Lodovico towards the end of the summer (August then was harvest-time, and the beginning of autumn).

On 19 August 1497 he wrote to his increasingly self-pitying father regarding the debt of 'ninety broad florins of gold' owed to a draper called Consiglio d'Antonio Cisti, that 'you must satisfy him and pay him something on account; and whatever you agree to pay him for the balance, let me know, and I will send it to you, if you do not have it; although I myself have very little, as I told you. I will manage to borrow it, so that you will have no need to take money out of the Monte [bank account] . . . It is no wonder that I have sometimes written irritably, because I often get very wrought up, owing to the many annoyances one encounters when away from home.' His father's anxiety needed to be assuaged, however, since Lodovico seems to have been in serious danger of going to the debtors' prison, a disgrace he would scarcely have been able to face. Lodovico wrote pathetically in the margin of the letter, 'He says he will help me to pay Consiglio.'

Michelangelo was also getting involved in work again, or

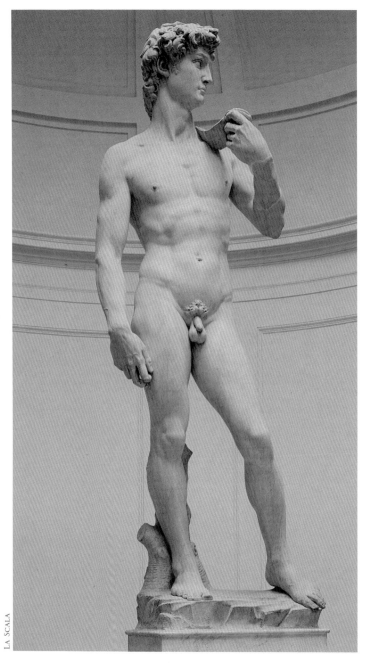

'DAVID'

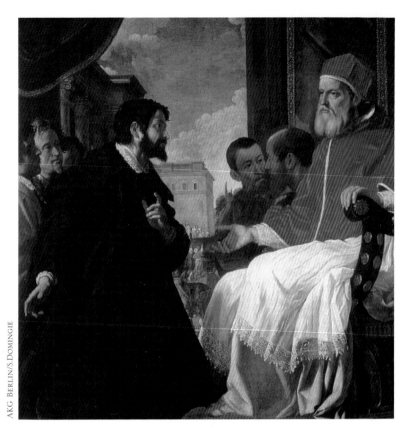

'MICHELANGELO WITH POPE JULIUS II IN BOLOGNA (1506)'
BY ANASTASIO FONTEBUONI — A PAINTING EXECUTED IN
ABOUT 1620

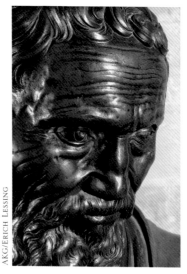

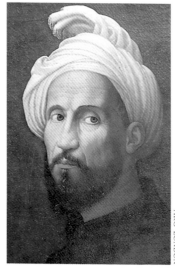

BUST OF MICHELANGELO BY
DANIELE DA VOLTERRA, MADE
AT THE END OF
MICHELANGELO'S LIFE

'PORTRAIT OF MICHELANGELO
IN A TURBAN' BY GIULIANO
BUGIARDINI,
ABOUT 1522

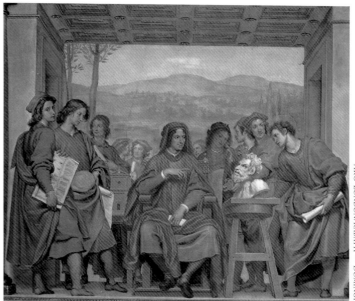

'LORENZO DE' MEDICI AMONG THE ARTISTS' BY OTTAVIO VANNINI
— THIS FRESCO OF 1635 DEPICTS MICHELANGELO
PRESENTING HIS FAUN'S HEAD TO LORENZO DE' MEDICI

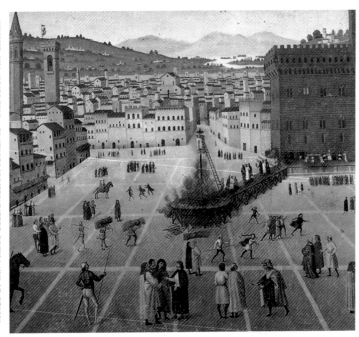

'SAVONAROLA BEING BURNT AT THE STAKE, PIAZZA DELLA SIGNORIA,
FLORENCE (1498)' — ITALIAN SCHOOL,
LATE 15TH CENTURY (DETAIL)

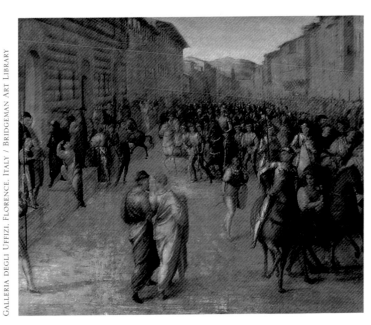

'CHARLES VIII ENTERING FLORENCE' BY FRANCESCO GRANACCI

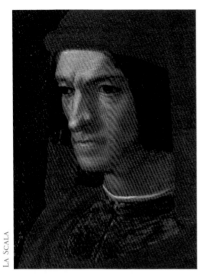

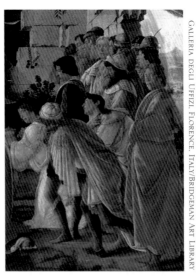

A POSTHUMOUS
PORTRAIT OF LORENZO DE' MEDICI
BY BRONZINO

SANDRO BOTTICELLI'S 'ADORATION
OF THE MAGI' (DETAIL), WITH
THE ARTIST FACING US IN
THE FOREGROUND

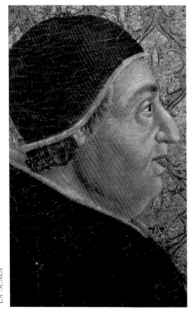

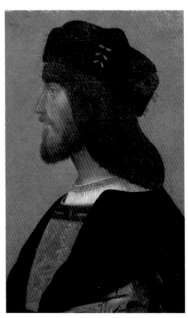

RODRIGO DE BORGIA,
POPE ALEXANDER VI
(SPANISH SCHOOL)

CESARE BORGIA

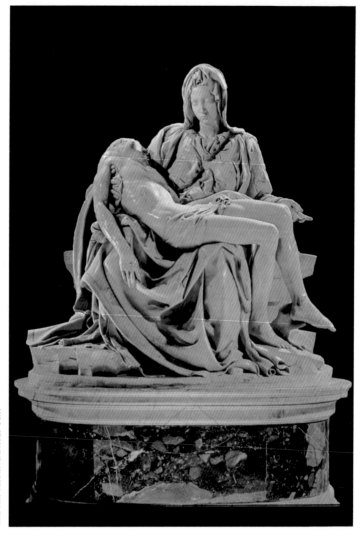

'PIETÀ' BY MICHELANGELO

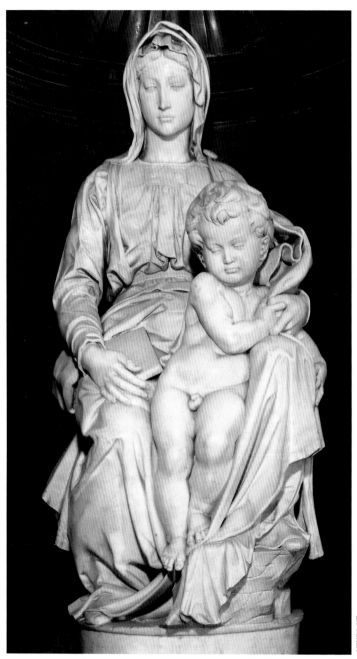

'BRUGES MADONNA' BY MICHELANGELO

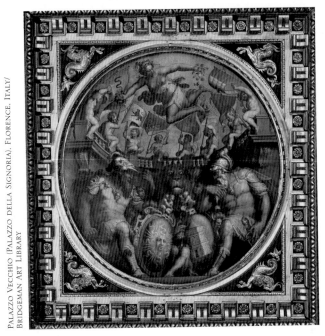

Giorgio Vasari, Michelangelo's principal early biographer,
decorated much of the Great Hall of the Signoria. This is
a ceiling piece: 'Allegory of the Districts of San Giovanni
and Santa Maria Novella' (1565)

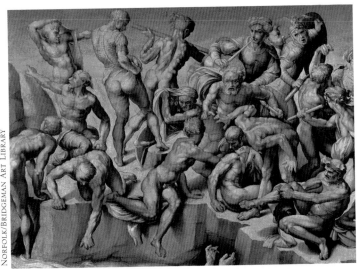

A copy by Antonio da Sangallo the Elder of
Michelangelo's cartoon for 'The Battle of Cascina'

so it seemed. Piero de' Medici, now in exile in Rome, where his brother Giovanni was safely ensconced as a cardinal, was interested in commissioning a statue; but after Michelangelo had bought the marble for it with his own money, Piero reneged on the deal. It's highly unlikely that Piero behaved like this because he wished in any way to punish the sculptor for disloyalty at the time when Piero was chased out of Florence. Like so many highly placed people then, Piero simply rode roughshod over those he would have regarded as tradesmen. In the letter quoted immediately above, Michelangelo continues:

> I had an order to do a work for Piero de' Medici and bought the marble; but I never began it as he did not do as he had promised. So I stay at home and carve a figure for my pleasure. I bought a block of marble for five ducats – but it was no good, so that the money was thrown away. Afterwards I bought another block for another five ducats, and worked at it for my pleasure, so you must believe that I too have setbacks and troubles, and you must make allowances. I will send you money, though I should have to sell myself into slavery.

It was a far from easy time for Michelangelo. He was aware of his talent; but apart from practical considerations, within him contrary forces still fought. It was hard for him to come to terms with his attraction for men, yet it was the young nude male form which increasingly attracted him aesthetically and sexually. It was equally hard for him to square what he found attractive in Rome, in terms of its appreciation of the classical antique, and its encouragement of modern art, with what he saw as its political and moral degeneracy. In Michelangelo there was always a tension between the sensuous, the stern, and the sympathetic sides of his personality.

The year 1497 slipped away. Michelangelo had acquired his own first apprentice, the first of many cherished *garzoni*, Piero d'Argenta, who'd become friendly with Michelangelo's younger brother Buonarroto during the latter's stay in Rome. In January 1498, d'Argenta wrote to Buonarroto from Rome, 'where the snow had risen up to the height of one's arse', to tell him that his brother had left Rome:

> There has been no letter from him and we have heard nothing about what may have happened. So Messer Jacopo and all of us are amazed that he has not written one line to us; and therefore I beg you if you have heard anything since his departure you should advise us of his whereabouts and what he is up to, for truly we are hungry for news of him.

In fact, after so many difficulties in finding work, Michelangelo had at last gained a valuable, major commission. The French legate in Rome, Cardinal Bilhères de

Lagraulas (known in Italian accounts of his career as Cardinal de la Groslaie), had engaged him to carve a large *Pietà* to adorn his tomb. In November 1497 Michelangelo had taken himself off to the famous marble quarries at Carrara, near Lucca, to select a piece of marble for it. He was there again the following spring; but why he left without telling even his apprentice is a mystery.

Lagraulas required the finest marble for his sculpture, and this, pure white, though brittle and hard to carve, was to be found at Carrara. Carrara was a busy place, near the malaria-infested coast, but a centre for everyone who worked in stone. It was under the dominion of the small city-state of Lucca, to whose republican government the Cardinal sent Michelangelo with, as was usual, a letter of recommendation:

We have recently agreed with Master Michele Angelo di Lodovico, Florentine sculptor and bearer of this, that he make for us a marble tombstone, namely a clothed Virgin Mary with a dead Christ naked in her arms . . . and on his presently repairing to those parts to excavate and transport here the marbles necessary for such a work, we confidently beg your lordships out of consideration for us to extend to him every help and favour in this matter . . .

The French cardinal, who'd been with Charles VIII on his campaign, had been given the see of Santa Sabina. He had selected a site for his tomb in the chapel of St Petronilla in St Peter's, since she was the legendary daughter of St Peter and, significantly, the patron of the *dauphins* of France. A contract was signed between the Cardinal and the artist on 27 August 1498, brokered by Jacopo Galli, who undertook that the piece would be completed within a year, and that it would be the finest marble statue in Rome:

Be it known and manifest to whom shall read the ensuing document, how the Most Reverend Cardinal . . . has agreed with the master Michelangelo, sculptor of Florence, that the said master shall make a Pietà of marble at his own cost, that is, a Virgin Mary clothed, with the dead Christ in her arms . . . And I, Jacopo Galli, promise to His Most Reverend Monsignore that the said Michelangelo will finish the said work within one year, and that it shall be the most beautiful work in marble which Rome today can show, and that no master of our days shall be able to produce a better. And similarly I promise the said Michelangelo that the Most Reverend Cardinal will disburse the payments as written above; and in good faith I, Jacopo Galli, have made the present writing with my own hand, according to date of year, month and day, as above.

Galli was also willing to cover the cost of the statue if the Cardinal should renege. After seeing and buying the

Bacchus and the lost *Eros*, he was perfectly confident about the bankability of Michelangelo's work.

The piece was to be life-size; and the fee was set at 450 gold Papal ducats, to be paid at the rate of 150 on commencement, then, after three months, three further quarterly payments of one hundred – the balance to be paid when the work was completed, if it took a shorter time than a year. The subject of the piece – the Virgin sitting with the dead body of her Son lying naked in her lap – was very precisely described in the contract, since it was not well known in Italy, though it had for some time been a popular religious subject in northern Europe, as one of the Seven Sorrows of the Blessed Virgin. A comparison of its contemporary treatment there, and the resolution of the problem of laying the body of a grown man in the lap of a woman, with that achieved by Michelangelo, is akin to a comparison of the medieval with the modern.

Michelangelo, who was not usually good at delivering on time and had in any case not finished the *Bacchus*, took longer to complete the *Pietà* than the contract stipulated; by the time he was polishing it, the Cardinal was dead (he died in August 1499); but Lagraulas had the distinction of having ordered what came to be regarded as the first truly great Renaissance sculptural group. The *Pietà* not only demonstrated, even more than the *Bacchus*, how great Michelangelo's understanding of the mechanics of the human body was, thanks to his study of anatomy at Santo Spirito, but also how fast he was developing. Michelangelo's biographer Ascanio Condivi writing in 1553 rebuts one criticism:

> Nevertheless, there are some who censure the figure of the Virgin as being too young in comparison with that of her Son. One day as I was discoursing of this with Michelangelo, he replied to me, 'Do you know that chaste women maintain their freshness much longer than those who are not chaste? How much more so would this be in a virgin . . .'

It has also been suggested, as in a later *Madonna and Child* now in Bruges, that the face of the Virgin recalls the sculptor's own tender memories of his mother.

The subject is a difficult one technically, as the adult figure of the dead Christ must lie convincingly across the lap of his seated mother, with all His body's weight distributed over it. In consequence her lap has to be tensed, under the folds of her dress, to take the load. Through his knowledge of anatomy, through studying Leonardo's ability to show a proper psychological relationship between figures, and through a *tour-de-force* of drapery carving which owes much to della Quercia – whose work Michelangelo had admired in Bologna – and anticipates the great seventeenth-century sculptor Bernini, Michelangelo created a believable support for Christ's body. Leonardo wrote:

How the eye cannot discern the shapes of bodies within their boundaries except by means of shadows and lights; and there are many sciences which would be nothing without the science of these shadows and lights; as painting, sculpture, astronomy, a great part of perspective and the like.

As may be shown, the sculptor cannot work without the help of shadows and lights, since without these the material carved would remain all of one colour; and . . . a level surface illumined by uniform light does not vary in any part the clearness or obscurity of its natural colour, and this uniformity of colour goes to prove the uniformity of the smoothness of its surface. It would follow therefore that if the material carved were not clothed by shadows and lights, which are necessitated by the prominences of certain muscles and the hollows interposed between them, the sculptor would not be able uninterruptedly to see the progress of his own work, and this work that he is carving requires . . .

By understanding the effect of light and shade on the surfaces he was carving, and by creating a genuine dramatic tension between grieving mother and dead son, heightening their relationship which is focused in their physical attitudes, and in turn demonstrating the psychological truth of the moment, Michelangelo in his *Pietà* created one of the most tenderly tragic sculptures ever made. Once seen, the face of

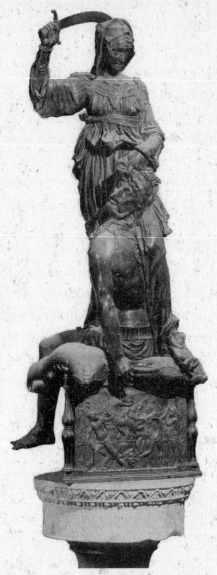

Donatello – *Judith and Holofernes*

this Virgin haunts one for life, and in it and the drapery of the head there is an echo of Donatello's Judith in that sculptor's much earlier bronze *Judith and Holofernes* in Florence. Personal influences that may be read into it are the dreadful death of Michelangelo's admired Savonarola; and a young man's ironic reflection, in this pure and chaste conception of the ultimate sacrifice, on the corruption and cynicism of Alexander's Rome.

The statue was installed in St Peter's in time for the great celebrations of the Holy Year of 1500. Marking Michelangelo, at the age of twenty-five, as one of the greatest sculptors in Italy, it was the only work he signed. The story is that he was standing near the statue when he overheard the remarks of a group of visitors from Lombardy as they were discussing who the sculptor was. One of the Lombards told another that it was by 'our Gobbo from Milan' – the nickname of the artist Cristofero Solari (*gobbo* means hunchbacked). Soon afterwards Michelangelo returned to the statue at night and by candlelight carved uncompromisingly on to the sash which runs across the Virgin's breast:

MICHAEL – ANGELUS – BONAROTUS – FLORENTIN
– FACIEBAT
(Michelangelo Buonarroti of Florence made this)

He had every right to put his stamp on his work; but no more need to advertise his talent: his reputation would do that for him from now on. The best critical summing-up on the piece is Vasari's:

> . . . the *Pietà* was a revelation of all the potentialities and force of the art of sculpture. Among the many beautiful features (including the inspired draperies) this is notably demonstrated by the body of Christ itself. It would be impossible to find a body showing greater mastery of art and possessing more beautiful members, or a nude with more detail in the muscles, veins, and nerves stretched over their framework of bones, or a more death-like corpse. The lovely expression of the head, the harmony in the joints and attachments of the arms, legs, and trunk, and the fine tracery of pulses and veins are all so wonderful that it staggers belief that the hand of an artist could have executed this inspired and admirable work in so short a time. It is certainly a miracle that a formless block of stone could ever have been reduced to a perfection that nature is scarcely able to create in the flesh.

About the same time, Michelangelo was engaged on another commission, in a medium, oil paint, which he did not particularly like. He is reputed to have dismissed it as 'fit only for women' (of whom he seems never to have had a high opinion). But painting was never a medium he took to happily, despite the decoration of the ceiling and altar wall of the Sistine Chapel, for which he is best remembered.

The painting, now in the National Gallery in London, was intended as an altarpiece for a new memorial chapel, and Michelangelo's clients were the Augustinian monks of Sant' Agostino. It was designed to be an *Entombment of Christ*. Michelangelo was paid in advance and the transaction was recorded in the ledgers of the bankers Giovanni and Baldassare Balducci, friends of Lorenzo di Pierfrancesco. Although a powerful piece that shows the sculptural weight Michelangelo was always to give to his painted figures, he left it uncompleted.

The closing years of the fifteenth century and those that opened the sixteenth, while Michelangelo was working on the *Bacchus* and the *Pietà*, continued to be volatile ones for Italy. Louis XII played diplomatic games with Venice, Florence and the Vatican and they, no longer united, played them with him as they sought individual economic, political and territorial gains. Cesare Borgia gave up his cardinal's hat in order to run an army to pursue his father's ambitions in the Romagna, where the Papal Sates showed an aversion to making themselves answerable to the Vatican. Louis made Cesare Duke of Valence and married him to the sister of the King of Navarre, while Alexander nodded through Louis' own divorce so that he could marry the widow of Charles VIII. This marriage secured Brittany for France; in return

Louis helped the Borgia pursue their subjugation of the Romagna. Meanwhile, Florence wanted French help in order to regain Pisa, and Venice formed an alliance with Louis to enable him to take Milan. It was then that Leonardo da Vinci returned to Florence, and the architect Bramante made his way to Rome.

Louis' hold on Milan was shortlived; in 1500 the Milanese welcomed back Lodovico Sforza, who took his city back with the aid of mercenaries from Switzerland, and Germany, where he had fled following his ejection; though the French soon retook the city and made Lodovico their prisoner. His power now definitively broken, he died in Touraine in 1508.

Alexander wanted to organise a crusade against the Turks, who were harassing Venice in the eastern Mediterranean, but he needed the support of France and Spain, who not only refused to help him, but forced him to connive at a secret deal they made between them to take and divide Naples.

Florence celebrated the fall of Lodovico Sforza, but the French paid little more than lip-service to aiding the Florentines in their venture against Pisa, and Machiavelli spent several exasperating months as Florentine ambassador to the French court trying to pin King Louis down to some kind of agreement. He finally returned to Florence in 1501, his mission essentially a failure.

In the meantime, on the Buonarroti domestic front, Michelangelo and his father had another exchange of letters.

In February, Lodovico Buonarroti wrote to his son defending himself against a charge of being too negative. Lodovico pointed out that he was fifty-six years old, had five grown sons, yet had to fend for himself, to the extent of baking bread and doing the washing-up. He added that if Michelangelo was doing so well, why wasn't any money forthcoming? It's difficult not to sympathise with Lodovico. He was twice a widower, he'd lost the modest Customs House job he'd had when Piero de' Medici was banished, and he was beginning to feel old.

Towards the end of that year, Buonarroto paid Michelangelo another visit in Rome. When he returned to Florence, he reported to his father that his brother was still living poorly, though Michelangelo had managed to pay 230 ducats into his bank account in September. Michelangelo had also evidently paid off his father's debt, and invested more cash in the family, as the following letter shows. Encouraged by the good financial news, but fretful that failure to take care of himself would jeopardise his son's earning potential, Lodovico wrote an awkwardly tender letter to Rome on 19 December 1500:

> . . . I know that you have advanced money, and [this representing] the love you have for your brothers is a great consolation to me. About this matter of the money with which you wish to set up Buonarroto and Giansimone in a shop, I have hunted and am still

hunting, but as yet I have found nothing to please me
. . . Buonarroto tells me how you live in Rome, very
economically, or rather, penuriously. Economy is good,
but self-denial is evil, for it is a vice displeasing to God
and Humanity, bad for body and soul. While you are
young you will be able to endure these hardships for
a time, but when the vigour of youth fails, diseases and
infirmities will develop, for these come from personal
discomforts, mean living and penurious habits . . . Live
moderately but do not stint yourself. Whatever
happens, do not expose yourself to hardships, for in
your profession, if you fall ill (which God forbid), you
are a lost man. Above all take care of your head, keep
it moderately warm, and never bathe: have yourself
rubbed down, but never bathe.

Buonarroto tells me that one of your sides is swollen,
which comes from being out of sorts or from fatigue
or eating bad, windy food, or from putting up with
cold or wet feet. I have had this myself and I am still
often troubled when I eat windy food or suffer from
the cold . . . You must guard against all these things,
because it is bad for the eardrum, which might burst,
so take care. I will now tell you about the remedies I
have found: I went for a few days eating only sops of
bread, chicken and egg, and I took by the mouth a
little cassia, and I made a poultice of thyme, which I
put in a pan with rose oil and camomile oil, and when

the poultice was ready I applied it to the front of my body, and in a few days was well again . . .

But in the end it all sounds as if Lodovico just wanted to take care of the goose that laid the golden eggs. There's no real warmth or pride in the letter. The relationship between father and son, who shared more characteristics than either would like to admit, was never close.

Irritated as he was by his father's importunity, and doubtless unwilling to return to Florence to face his feckless family again, Michelangelo was also depressed by the atmosphere in Rome. Although to a certain extent he could bury himself in his work, and carving the *Pietà* committed him to remain for the time being, he could not ignore the corruption, the violence and the jockeying for position which typified life in the Holy City.

Now a dangerous new presence entered the town. After his campaigns of 1499, Cesare Borgia, about the same age as Michelangelo, was back in Rome by early 1500 surrounded by a vast retinue clad in expensive black livery, and making quite sure that everyone knew who was boss. To underline this, Alexander made him Captain-General and *Gonfaloniere* of the Church. On Wednesday, 15 July, Alfonso Duke of Bisceglia, the second husband of Cesare's sister Lucrezia, was brutally, though not fatally, stabbed on the steps of St Peter's. He was taken home to recover, but soon afterwards was smothered in his bed by Cesare's right-hand man, Michelotto. Cesare claimed that Michelotto had acted on his own initiative, but that Alfonso had himself threatened Cesare's life. After the funeral, Alfonso's doctors and a hunchbacked valet were arrested and interrogated, but later released. 'The man who had ordered the deed was well known,' noted Alexander's Master of Ceremonies, Johann Burchard. It was clear to everyone that Cesare would brook no rivals, real or imagined. Apart from that, Alexander had a more advantageous third marriage for his nineteen-year-old daughter already in mind, who through her first two marriages had gained control of more land than any other woman in Europe except Isabella of Castile.

Cesare had also almost certainly murdered his younger brother (by one year) Giovanni, Duke of Gandia, two years earlier, when Cesare was still a cardinal. Giovanni had been Alexander's favourite, and therefore attracted the envy not only of Cesare, but of other nobles ambitious to break the dynastic hold the Borgia had over Rome. Giovanni was also a rival of Cesare in love: they both vied for the affection of their sister-in-law, Sancia. It has been suggested that Alexander favoured Giovanni because Cesare was not his son at all, but the son of Alexander's bitter rival, Giuliano della Rovere, now in exile in France, who earlier had shared a mistress, Giovanna de' Catanei, Cesare's mother, with Alexander in the mid-1470s.

The circumstances of the murder, as related by Johann Burchard, were that the Duke, having dined with Cesare and their mother, wanted to go in pursuit of private pleasure unattended, except for one servant whom he dismissed at the Piazza degli Ebrei. Soon afterwards the Duke was stabbed nine times and thrown into the Tiber near a sewage duct; the servant who had been ordered to wait at the Piazza was also stabbed, and died of his wounds soon afterwards. When the Duke's body was recovered it was still dressed in its magnificent robes and the purse on his belt still held thirty ducats (about £800 in today's money). A wood-dealer who'd seen the body thrown into the river was later questioned and asked why he hadn't reported it. His reply was that 'during his time he had seen one hundred bodies thrown into the river at that point on different nights and he had never thought anything of it'. Following the murder, though the investigation never came to any conclusion about who was responsible, the Borgia attracted intense criticism, and Alexander, to cover himself and his family, set up a reform commission to investigate means of ameliorating Papal rule. The Commission had in fact nothing but power on paper.

In the face of this cynical and decadent atmosphere, but perhaps also on account of a possible commission from the cathedral of Siena, Michelangelo finally left Rome for Florence in 1501, soon after his twenty-sixth birthday. Later in life he wrote a poem which graphically expressed his feelings about a city which for many years remained a moral cesspool for him:

Here they make helms and swords from chalices:
The blood of Christ is sold now by the quart.
Lances and swords are shaped from
thorns and crosses,
Yet still Christ pours out pity from His heart.
But let Him come no more into these streets
Since it would make His blood spurt to the stars:
In Rome they sell His flesh, and Virtue waits
Helpless, while Evil every entrance bars.
If ever I desired reward, oh now
All chance is gone. My work has come to naught.
Medusa hides beneath that mantle there.
Heaven rewards poverty, but here below
What chance have we to find the good we sought
When men are false to the great signs they bear?

CHAPTER SEVEN

The Sling and the Bow

The machinations of Cesare Borgia were not the only worry for those living in Italy in 1500. Following the deaths of Savonarola and Charles VIII of France in 1498, Charles' successor, his cousin, the thick-lipped, fleshy-nosed dandy Louis XII, had assumed among his other titles that of 'King of the Two Sicilies', which included Naples, and 'Duke of Milan', claiming the latter title through his grandmother, a Visconti princess, despite Salic Law which barred succession in the female line. At the time both Florence and Venice were on nervously good terms with France, but to cover themselves the Venetians suggested to Louis that a formal alliance with them would aid him in his pretensions to Milan and Naples. Florence, too, courted the French king in the hope that he would provide aid in their struggle against Pisa. Italian states had already forgotten that the true means of defence against a foreign intruder lay in unity, and were once more seeking to protect their own backs, but there was after all no sense yet of national Italian unity.

In July 1499 a French army crossed the Alps, capturing towns and fortresses as it made its way south. Milan fell in the autumn and its ruler, the Duke of Milan Lodovico Sforza, fled. Louis XII arrived there in October, in triumph, attended by Italian allies, diplomats and French princes of the Church.

The French army then proceeded to help Cesare Borgia in his campaign in the Romagna, but in January 1500 they had to be recalled to fight Lodovico Sforza, who, while in exile, had collected a force of German and Swiss mercenaries, and now invaded Lombardy with them. The people of Milan, who'd greeted Louis as a liberator, had quickly tired of French exploitation, and rebelled. The French lost Lombardy as fast as they had won it, but Louis was not to be beaten. He mustered and dispatched a fresh expeditionary force, which contained many Swiss mercenaries. This crushed Lodovico's mercenary army at the decisive battle of Novara, for his own, still unpaid, Swiss would not fight against their compatriots. Lodovico was captured and ended his days in French imprisonment, dying in Touraine in 1508.

Leonardo da Vinci, who had lost a patron, wrote: 'The Duke has lost his State, his possessions, and his liberty; and he has seen none of his works finished.' The metal for his never-to-be completed bronze equestrian statue of the First Duke of Milan had been lost long before when it was sent to Ferrara in 1494 to be turned into cannon for use against the previous French invasion. Now French troops were using the massive matrix for target practice.

Leonardo, who had played to the Duke on a silver lyre finished with a soundbox in the shape of a horse's head, an instrument which he had made himself, became a homeless wanderer for a short time. During his years in Milan, Leonardo had painted the portrait of Duke Lodovico's mistress, Cecilia Gallerani, as *The Lady with the Ermine*, now in Cracow, the *Virgin of the Rocks*, and the famous *Last Supper* for the Order of St Dominic at Santa Maria delle Grazie.

After brief interludes in Mantua and Venice, where he'd worked as a military engineer, Leonardo returned to Florence in April 1500 after an absence of almost two decades. He was nearly fifty, and a universally acknowledged polymath of genius throughout Italy. He would spend the next six years of his life in Florence, leaving it occasionally to take consultancy and contractual work. In summer 1502, he accepted a commission as military engineer from Cesare Borgia, who was then in the middle of his third major military aggrandisement campaign, and even threatened Florence. It is a mark of the respect accorded to Leonardo that he could get away with such conduct, though his attitude to war was that it was a grim necessity, as well as being a 'most bestial madness'.

Leonardo's thoughts on the methodology and technology of warfare were many and profound: pontoon bridges, cannon, tanks and flame-throwers were among the weapons he either invented or developed. In the service of Florence in its war with Pisa, he put forward a plan to divert the Arno from the latter town, robbing it of its water supply. He boasted that 'I can noiselessly construct to any prescribed point subterranean passages either straight or winding, passing if necessary underneath trenches or a river.' In justification of his fascination for such techniques, he wrote: 'When besieged by ambitious tyrants I find a means of offence and defence in order to preserve the chief gift of nature, which is liberty.' One can easily imagine such words in the mouth of any modern head of state.

Leonardo also used his first-hand knowledge of warfare to inform his art. Michelangelo designed defences for his home town against the forces of the Prince of Orange in 1529, following the Sack of Rome by the Emperor Charles V two years earlier. The difference between the two artists is that Michelangelo did not make a habit of designing weapons of war.

After leaving Florence in 1506, Leonardo returned to Milan, where he remained until 1513 before accepting an invitation from the King of France. He died at Amboise, on the Loire, in 1519.

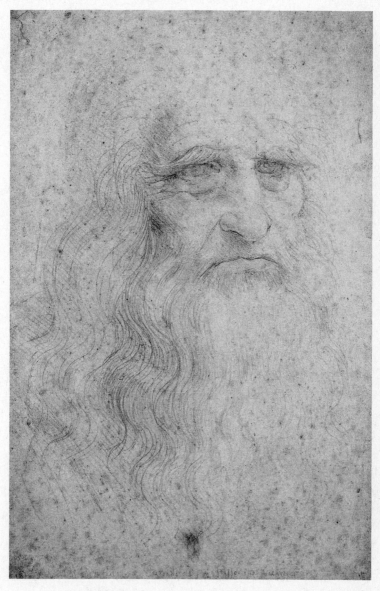

Leonardo da Vinci – a self portrait (about 1512)

His was a detached view of life. He would engage himself as a military adviser (a very useful occupation to have) to whomever would pay for his services, regardless of any other consideration of allegiance, whether it were political, moral, ethical or personal; and yet, as Vasari records, he would, when he passed places where birds were sold caged, 'often take them from their cages, pay the price demanded, and restore their liberty by letting them fly into the air. "The goldfinch," wrote Leonardo, "will carry spurge to its little ones imprisoned in a cage – death rather than loss of liberty." The significance of the note becomes clear from the fact that certain varieties of spurge form a violent poison.' Vasari adds that Leonardo had a great love and respect for all animals.

Leonardo was the illegitimate son (though acknowledged) of a lawyer from Vinci, a little town about thirty kilometres due west of Florence, under Florentine rule when Leonardo was born there in about 1451. He spent his youth and early manhood in Florence and, though receiving little formal instruction in the arts, he quickly developed an interest in the natural sciences and applied what he discovered to art, specialising early in the expression of thought and emotion in facial expressions and body language. Verrocchio was his master for a while. His obsession with creating incredibly intricate mazes, and the fact that he made all his notes in mirror-writing (he was left-handed, which facilitated this), are well-known indications of his complex character.

He was warmly welcomed back to Florence, which could just about lay claim to being his native city, though he spent only a few years of his life there. Since the death of Savonarola, there had been a resurgence in the commissioning of works from artists and craftsmen, for the patronage of artists as well as artistic creativity ran in Tuscan blood, and could not be expunged by so brief and artificial an influence as the Prior's. People had gone back to dressing fashionably, listened to music, liked painting, wore jewels, danced, ate well, used make-up and their imaginations. But in one way Savonarola had encouraged the native *forte*, in the commissioning of the new great hall of assembly, which was now complete and waiting for its final decorations to be added. Leonardo himself may have acted in an advisory capacity on its construction when plans were first drawn up in 1494.

At the time of his return in 1500, Leonardo was working on the theme of the Blessed Virgin and Child with St Anne, and may have brought a large cartoon he had made of the group with him, which interested artists, including Michelangelo – who had dealt with a similar problem in his *Pietà* – because of the difficulties it presented in terms of spatial relationships. Vasari tells us that it drew crowds, but adds, in an anecdote not corroborated, that Leonardo swiped a contract for a mural for the Servite friars from Filippino Lippi, and then failed to deliver, offering them a Virgin with St Anne cartoon in recompense. Perhaps it was this group that drew the crowds, but as Vasari is often inaccurate, it seems more likely that Leonardo would have made an immediate splash with a cartoon brought from Milan. He would have been looking for work, and would have needed to advertise, despite his reputation. Florence wasn't short of good artists.

But Leonardo was certainly a celebrity, and Vasari writes of him in terms just as glowing as those he uses for Michelangelo. One should bear in mind, however, that Vasari, born in 1511, was eight when Leonardo died. In later life Vasari became a friend of the much older Michelangelo:

In the normal course of events many men and women are born with various remarkable qualities and talents; but occasionally, in a way that transcends nature, a single person is marvellously endowed by heaven with beauty, grace and talent in such abundance that he leaves other men far behind, all his actions seem inspired, and indeed everything he does clearly comes from God rather than from human art.

Everyone acknowledged that this was true of Leonardo da Vinci, an artist of outstanding physical beauty who displayed infinite grace in everything he did and who cultivated his genius so brilliantly that all problems he studied he solved with ease. He possessed great strength and dexterity; he was a man of regal spirit and tremendous strength of mind; and his name became so famous that not only was he esteemed during his lifetime but his reputation endured and became even greater after his death.

The cartoon Leonardo brought with him is now lost; but two other examples survive: a painting in Paris and a large cartoon now in the National Gallery in London, the latter probably made in Florence around 1505. At the same time Leonardo was completing his most famous work, the *Mona Lisa*, done over two years, whose subject, the Florentine society beauty Lisa di Anton Maria di Noldo Gherardini, had married Francesco di Bartolomeo del Giocondo ten years earlier. Here the recrudescence of Leonardo's *sfumato* technique is found; and here he expresses his feeling for the mystery of life at almost his best – though some would argue that the *John the Baptist* or the *Virgin of the Rocks* transcended this portrait. The painting may have found its way to the Louvre, where it now resides, via the collection of François I, who is supposed to have paid 4,000 florins for it. (Some sources suggest that the *Mona Lisa* was made later, between 1505 and 1510.)

By the beginning of the sixteenth century, Leonardo was acknowledged as Italy's greatest painter, and the precocious Michelangelo as Italy's greatest sculptor. Despite the difference in their ages there was great rivalry and antipathy between them, though Leonardo was able to rise above any jibes the younger man, with his sense of insecurity, fired at him. And although Michelangelo may have seen Leonardo as a rival, he also acknowledged him as a master.

At the turn of the century, Michelangelo would have been as interested as any of his colleagues in what he could learn from Leonardo; when Leonardo started to draw in red chalk, Michelangelo was among the first to emulate him, and bring the new technique to early perfection. But the two men had very different characters, and for that reason alone, despite the Tuscan characteristics of independent thought and creativity they shared, it is difficult to imagine them ever really getting on. It is, however, significant that both of them often failed to finish any project completely; as if the conception were enough, and completion a bar to progression to the next idea.

Leonardo was urbane, worldly, and a convinced humanist – he had freed himself of any necessity to believe in any god, Christian or otherwise. The *Lebensanschauung* he arrived at was attained through rationalism, not a deity. He held to a natural philosophy, whereas Michelangelo remained influenced by Neoplatonism and Catholicism. Leonardo was handsome, happy in company and a good conversationalist. He was also prodigiously strong – it is said that he could straighten a horse-shoe with his bare hands.

He also loved clothes and had a magnificent wardrobe. It's interesting that although Michelangelo, like Donatello, didn't care at all about how he dressed, and generally preferred the garb of an ordinary peasant, he did leave a large number of splendid suits of clothing behind when he died. Why he had them is a mystery. It may be that the clothes were gifts, which he stored on account of their value, but never felt inclined to use.

Leonardo had little time for sculpture. Though his *Notebooks* contain serious meditations on the genre, he could also be disdainfully witty at its expense. In a manuscript *Treatise on Painting* he writes that 'the sculptor in creating his work does so by the strength of his arm by which he consumes the marble, or other obdurate material in which his subject is enclosed: and this is done by the most mechanical exercise, often accompanied by a great sweat which mixes with the marble dust and forms a kind of mud daubed all over his face. The marble dust flours him all over so that he looks like a baker; his back is covered with a snowstorm of chips, and his house is made filthy by the flecks and dust of stone. The exact reverse is true of the painter . . . [who] sits before his work, perfectly at ease and well dressed, and moves a very light brush dipped in a delicate colour; and he adorns himself with whatever clothes he pleases. His house is clean and filled with charming pictures; and often he is accompanied by music or by the reading of various and beautiful works which, since they are not mixed with the sound of the hammer or other noises, are heard with the greatest pleasure.'

Of all Leonardo's many talents, stonecarving was not one.

He concedes that 'The one advantage which sculpture has is that of offering greater resistance to time'; though he immediately goes on to argue that enamel work can last as long as a statue. For his part, Michelangelo would observe that 'the more a painting resembles relief sculpture, the better it is'. No wonder he adored Masaccio.

It's understandable that Leonardo's attitude would not have been appreciated by the earnest young Michelangelo, who had neither a strong sense of humour, nor a keen sense of irony. He was not sophisticated, except in his art, and he was, despite the talent he had and which he himself recognised, still far from having enough self-confidence to brush off undeserved criticism or other slights with disregard. Paradoxically, he was also well aware that the scared boy who'd left Florence in 1494 was returning as a lauded artist at the top of his profession at a very young age. A famous anecdote marks a pivotal point in the mutual antipathy that existed between the two artists. Leonardo was walking in Florence with his friend the painter Giovanni da Gavina, when he passed a group of men sitting at a table discussing a passage in *The Divine Comedy*. Recognising the Master, one of the men asked Leonardo to explain the passage to them.

Unluckily at that moment Michelangelo happened to pass. Leonardo, who may well have been aware of Michelangelo's profound study of Dante, replied to the man, 'Ask Michelangelo; he will explain it to you.' Michelangelo, however, thought the remark was meant sarcastically. He was aware of Leonardo's views on sculpture and didn't like the look of this aging dandy with his rose-coloured short cloak (the norm in Florence then was to wear cloaks long and black), and broad, curled beard. Angrily the young sculptor retorted, 'Don't get at me. You designed a horse to be cast in bronze, and as you couldn't manage it, you abandoned it from shame. And what's more, those stupid Milanese believed in you.' How Leonardo reacted to this sally is not recorded, but the encounter was scarcely the best footing for a relationship from which both parties could have learned much.

Painting, for Leonardo, though he could joke about its comparative qualities with carving, was the principal art, transcending music and literature; Leonardo hadn't much time for either of those disciplines. Although at the time he was writing, few ordinary people could read or sign their own names, that would be to ignore the power exerted and the influence on the intelligentsia of contemporary Italy of Dante, Boccaccio and Petrarch. On the other hand, there is no denying that the pictorial image remains the most powerful even today. One only has to look at most newspapers across the world to see how much space is occupied by image in relation to the written word; and one only has to remember, after watching a film or a play, that far more of the visual image than the spoken word remains in the memory. In his *Notebooks*, Leonardo writes:

How painting surpasses all human works by reason of the subtle possibilities which it contains:

The eye, which is called the window of the soul, is the chief means whereby the understanding may most fully and abundantly appreciate the infinite works of nature; and the ear is the second, inasmuch as it acquires its importance from the fact that it hears the things which the eye has seen. If you historians, or poets, or mathematicians had never seen things with your eyes you would be ill able to describe them in your writings. And if you, O poet, represent a story by depicting it with your pen, the painter with his brush will so render it as to be more easily satisfying and less tedious to understand. If you call painting 'dumb poetry', then the painter may say of the poet that his art is 'blind painting'. Consider then which is the more grievous affliction, to be blind or to be dumb! . . . which is the more fundamental to man, the name of man or his image? The name changes with change of country [as often happened at the time among itinerant and emigré artists]; the form is unchanged except by death.

Leonardo goes on to say that the eye is a nobler sense than the ear. He adds, 'Take the case of a poet describing the beauties of a lady to her lover and that of a painter who makes a portrait of her; you will see whither nature will the more incline the enamoured judge. Surely the proof of the matter ought to rest upon the verdict of experience!'

Michelangelo may well have been drawn back to Florence because of Leonardo's presence there, but there were other reasons, too. His success in Rome had been hard-won, and it's worth remembering that he marked the year 1497 as that in which his 'troubles began'. His father was pressing him to return, and his sense of family duty remained very strong. His brothers Buonarroto and Giovansimone were twenty-four and twenty-two years old respectively, and Michelangelo now had the means to set them up in the textile business, a prestigious and remunerative trade. The Florentine Wool Guild was still one of the most powerful in the city.

Roman society had held little to please Michelangelo, and it was probably a relief to find some excuse to leave. More tangible ones than Leonardo's arrival in his home town had also presented themselves to him: there was a contract in the offing, and the possibility of another one – of very great promise – to follow.

The first stemmed from Siena. Cardinal Francesco Piccolomini, who had seen Michelangelo's work in Rome, wanted him to carve fifteen religious statues, each about 120 centimetres high, in fashionable Carrara marble for the family chapel in the richly endowed cathedral. (White marble was in demand because it was the colour of the statuary of antiquity, and the Carrara quarry-owners, Guido d'Antonio di Biagio and Matteo di Cucarello da Carrara were doing a brisk trade.) Cardinal Francesco was sixty years old at the time, a nephew of Pope Pius II, who had made him a cardinal thirty-eight years earlier. He was a cultivated, moderate man, who had been in the running for the Papacy when Alexander VI was elected. He'd been part of Alexander's ineffectual reform commission, and also papal legate to the French king, Charles VIII.

The cardinal and the sculptor drew up a contract in June 1501, by which time Michelangelo was back in Florence. (He first mentions the possibility of the commission in a letter in May.) Michelangelo's agent and guarantor once again was the banker Jacopo Gallo. The terms of the contract were dry, detailed and strict. The figure of Christ was to be one *palm* taller than two *braccia*, as it was to go at the highest point in the chapel. Another figure of Christ for the great central recess was to be four *fingers* taller than two *braccia*. Two angels at the cornices were to be four *fingers* less than two *braccia*, and so on.

The sequence of statues was to be completed within three years; any sculpture deemed unsatisfactory was to be redone, and in addition Michelangelo was to finish a *St Francis* started (and apparently botched) by the man who'd broken his nose, Pietro Torrigiano. The fee was set at about 500 ducats, to be paid in instalments, out of which Michelangelo was to pay for the marble and all other costs, such as the provision of chisels (which Michelangelo made himself), studio outlay, and the hire of assistants.

He and his assistants did manage to finish four of the statues, of Saints Peter, Paul, Pius and Gregory, as well as completing the *St Francis* begun by Torrigiano; though only two of them can definitely be attributed to Michelangelo's own hand. He would draw up a new contract in September 1504 with Francesco's heirs for the remaining eleven statues – Francesco having succeeded Alexander VI as Pope in 1503, and reigning as Pius III, but dying a month after his enthronement. The new contract was still exacting, stipulating as before fifteen statues 'of Carrara marble, new, clean and white', but Michelangelo did little more work on it. One clause of the new contract may be quoted here as a reflection on the prevailing conditions of the times. Plague and war were factors to be taken into account:

Item, whereas the said Michelangelo, by virtue of the said agreement has bound himself to cause marble to be brought to Florence from the mountains of Carrara for the making of the said statues; and whereas, by reason of the besieging of the Pisans within the territory of Pisa, war has once more broken out; and whereas the Florentine Republic may endeavour to divert the course of the River Arno in such wise that the transport of the said marble from the mountains of Carrara to the city of Florence may therefore be hindered; and whereas also the said Michelangelo may fall ill, which God avert . . . then . . . the said [new contractual] period of two years shall be suspended during the time of the said hindrance.

Michelangelo's conscience may have been unsettled by his failure to fulfil his obligations on that occasion, but by then he was being called to greater things by the Papacy, which outranked the Piccolomini family, who had wanted a fitting monument for Francesco. It is likely, however, that Michelangelo was never truly inspired by the rather academic exercise of producing decorous draped religious figures even whose size relative to one another was delineated in the contract. His imagination's wings were already too large for such a cage.

Vasari says that 'some of his friends wrote to him [Michelangelo] from Florence urging him to return there as it seemed very probable that he would be able to obtain the block of marble that was standing in the Office of Works . . .' Certainly on 2 July 1501 the Operai had noted 'that there is a certain figure of marble named David, badly blocked out and carved, at present in the courtyard of the said *Opera*. Since . . . the Operai want such a giant to be made and put up on high by the masters of the said *Opera*, and to be put upright, in its proper place, they decided that masters competent in these affairs should investigate and determine if this matter could be completed and brought to an end.'

So the second contract awaited Michelangelo in Florence itself, and was not only of greater importance, but had far more appeal for him. A century-old sculptural programme had envisaged a series of twelve statues of Old Testament prophets to be placed high on the buttress ends of the tribunes outside the cathedral below the dome at the east end. The programme had progressed in fits and starts, often interrupted by war or funds running dry, but never wholly abandoned. It had appeared, though, to come to an end with the death of Donatello in 1466. As the passage just quoted suggests, a large block of marble, on which work had been started by Agostino di Duccio, an assistant of Donatello, about forty years earlier, still lay in the yard of the Operai dell' Opera del Duomo (Commissioners of the Cathedral Works). It hadn't been touched since, although the sculptor Antonio Rossellino had been approached on it about ten years after Agostino abandoned his effort. Contracts for both men had been drawn up, Agostino's on 18 August 1464:

The trusted and honourable Andrea di Giovanni della Stufa and Jacopo di Ugolino dei Mazzinghi, Operai of the Opera of Santa Maria del Fiore [the cathedral] of Florence, commission from the sculptor Agostino d'Antonio di Duccio, citizen of Florence, a figure of marble to be quarried at Carrara, nine *braccia* in height, at the scale of a giant, and in the appearance and name of . . . a prophet, to be placed up on one of the buttresses of Santa Maria del Fiore next to the Tribuna of the said church . . . The said figure is to be made and completed and brought to the foot of the said buttress within a period and time limit of eighteen months, beginning on 1 September 1464 . . .

This contract was retracted at the end of December 1466, but even by then it is clear that Agostino had done little work on it, though he had gone some way towards carving a space in the lower part of the block, to delineate the division between the figure's legs.

The question is, why had Agostino, a jobbing stonecarver whose principal ability was as a sculptor of architectural relief, been chosen? He had returned to his native city of Florence in 1463 from Bologna, where he had been working on the façade of the basilica of San Petronio, which had been begun some years earlier by Jacopo della Quercia. This was only a year before he was given the contract just referred to, and his talent remained modest. However, Donatello, who'd been away from Florence between 1443 and 1453, and again off and on between 1453 and 1461, returned home in 1461 and remained there until his death in 1466. It is possible that the reason for his return was to take part in the sculpture programme for the cathedral; but by then he was an old man, about seventy-five, though immensely famous and still active. A recently discovered memoir dated 1466 by Donatello's friend and physician supports the theory of Donatello's involvement in the programme.

The late Charles Seymour Jr. suggested famously in a book published in 1967 that it is probable that the true recipient of the contract was Donatello himself, and that Agostino was to work as his assistant and amanuensis, since Donatello was too old to be able to do the physical work himself. Agostino had worked with Donatello before and had trained in the cathedral 'school'. Furthermore, Agostino had completed a colossal terracotta *Hercules* in 1464, which may even have been erected on the Tribuna of the cathedral. When his contract for the marble colossus was broken off on 30 December 1466, there was no sense of rancour, or any suggestion then that he had botched the job. It seems too much of a coincidence that Donatello had died a few days earlier.

There the matter rested for a decade. The next contract, drawn up with Antonio Rossellino, is dated 6 May 1476:

The Operai, considering that several years ago the sculptor Agostino was commissioned to make a marble giant which is at present in the cellars, do commission [Antonio Rossellino], stonemason and sculptor, to finish the giant and to have it placed on one of the buttresses of the church.

Once again the project came to nothing. Rossellino, a less gifted sculptor than his much older brother Bernardo, is mainly remembered for his funerary work. He himself died in 1479, aged fifty-two; and it may be that he simply didn't have time to work on the project before he met his end. That he was approached at all may be taken as an indication of how relatively little truly great talent existed at that time.

Michelangelo would have known about the great marble block, and had probably already cast his eye over it before his departure for Rome; but whether he had early ambitions for it is a matter for conjecture.

With the Roman *Hercules*, Michelangelo had tested himself in confronting the technical demands of carving on a large scale. This commission, if he could get it, would represent a real challenge. Though contemporary ambitions were great, little had yet been achieved in replicating colossal statuary on the antique Roman scale. If Michelangelo could succeed, he might consolidate his reputation; but the challenge was also a personal one. The block of marble was not only already worked and weathered, imposing restrictions on what he did with it; it was also relatively shallow. And it was massive – nine *braccia* high – about 540 centimetres. The subject was made for him – a nude study of David. A colossal male nude in white marble, the preferred medium of classical antiquity: there could be no better way in which to make his mark definitively. It would be his first, and only,

truly colossal statue, and the first to be achieved successfully since antiquity.

Although there may have been rivals for the contract –
Leonardo has been suggested as one, and Andrea Contucci
(Il Sansovino) may also have been (a far more likely)
contender – it seems that Michelangelo, his Roman reputation having gone before him, had little difficulty in securing
the contract, which was made on 16 August 1501 with the
Arte della Lana (the Wool Guild, which traditionally under-
wrote all decorative additions to the cathedral) and the
Operai. The brief was broad: there were no artistic restrictions:

Their excellencies the consuls of the Arte della Lana
meeting together with the Operai in the audience hall
of the Opera, and being mindful of the usefulness and
honour of the said Opera, do appoint as sculptor of
the said Opera the worthy master Michelangelo di
Lodovico Buonarroti, a citizen of Florence, to the end
of making and completing, and, in good faith, finishing
a certain marble figure called the Giant, blocked out
in marble nine braccia high, now in the cathedral
workshop, and formerly blocked out by Master
Agostino . . . and badly blocked out. The work is to
be completed within . . . two years . . . beginning with
the kalends of September next, with hire and salary at
a rate of six broad gold florins per month; whatever

work is done to be carried out on the premises of the said building, and the Opera is to assist him with shelter and accommodation, with workmen of the said Opera, and wood, and all that he should need. When the said work and the said marble figure are completed, then . . . the Operai then in office will judge whether the work deserves a better price . . .

The Operai in office in 1500 had more complex reasons for restarting the David project than just the continuation of the century-old sculptural programme. Florence stood on the brink of a metamorphosis: the Academy of Plato had wanted to clear the decks through a combination of classical learning and Christian faith. Savonarola had seen salvation as being attained through a radically Christian ethic alone. Botticelli may have responded to Savonarola with at least two great religious paintings executed shortly after the Prior's death, the *Mystic Nativity* now in the National Gallery in London, and a strange *Crucifixion*, now in the USA, but it will be remembered that he was also working on a long series of illustrations for *The Divine Comedy* at approximately the same time, the last decade of the fifteenth century. Meanwhile, the grand autocracies of all the city-states of Italy were facing a gradual decline.

But there were also more immediate concerns than the social changes and political and religious polarisation in the city. For the moment rigorous military and political demands were placed on the state of Florence, which needed a response. The war with Pisa dragged on; Louis XII of France was an unsettling presence in Milan; Piero de' Medici was still a threatening force from the south; and across him was cast the sinister shadow of the Lord of the Romagna, as he had become: Cesare Borgia, who had his own ambitions to fulfil.

Florence stood alone once more: reduced from its former glory but still defiantly independent, her small forces marshalled themselves against coming threats.

The predominant feeling in 1500 was one of tension, exacerbated by the fact that this was possibly the year which would herald the Second Coming, the Year of the Half-Millennium. Once more, the Florentines looked for symbolic and morale-raising protection from its enemies to the popular Old Testament figure of David. David who in the face of all odds had killed Goliath, the apparently invincible giant, the champion of the barbarian Philistines. A visible, uniting symbol of the city was needed – who better than David? But this time a different David, one with a different attitude; a stronger David, a fighter ready for battle. No longer a willowy youth decoratively victorious, but a young man of the people, with real muscle, who, however unsure he may have been of the outcome, was ready to give his all. David the shepherd boy who would become a mighty king.

Michelangelo set to work immediately, preparing small

models and drawings. He had a specially constructed, relatively narrow wooden shed built around the marble block, so that no one should see him at work. This begs a question: was the shed too narrow to permit him to stand back sufficiently from his statue to get a good idea of its effect? But Michelangelo would not have been other than completely professional in the preparation of his ground, and he was confronting something as important to him personally as it was to the city. He wrote on a sheet of paper (which contained, among other sketches and notes, a preparatory drawing of David's right arm), in his impeccable handwriting:

> *Davicte cholla fromba*
> *e io choll' archo*
> *Michelagniolo*
> [David with his sling
> And I with my bow
> Michelangelo]

There is little doubt that not only was the *David* to be a symbol to unite the city, but that it represented something far more significant for Michelangelo himself. The bow he refers to is the small bow used to operate a sculptor's drill, a tool used since ancient times, though one which Michelangelo ceased to use as his style and personal technique matured. Just as David had confronted the giant Goliath with his

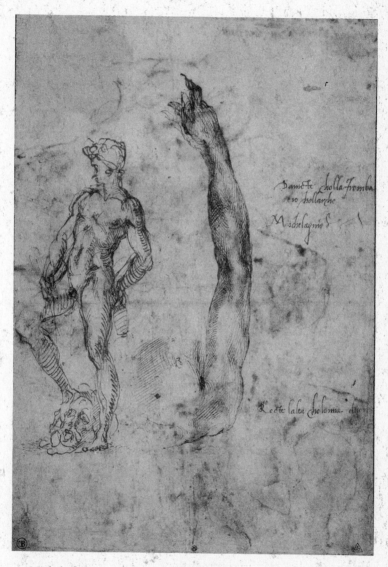

Michelangelo – sketch studies for the bronze *David* and the right
arm of the marble *David*

sling, so did Michelangelo confront the giant block of marble with his 'weapons' – the sculptor's tools. His *David* would not just be the biblical hero: he would be the embodiment of an ideal of fortitude for which Hercules had already served, and it is significant that this David is shown in readiness for the fight. Traditionally, David had been shown after the combat, in repose, his conqueror's foot on Goliath's severed head. This *David*, made at a time of general illiteracy when much political symbolism was supposed to be read into a public work of art, showed a young warrior who, although apprehensive, was ready, just as Florence was, to take on his enemies. The look of apprehension demonstrates a profound psychological and personal contribution from the young sculptor, and lifts the statue from its classical antecedents into the truly modern world. It also shows that the *David* can be interpreted as a spiritual self-portrait. And through his achievement, the sculptor himself would become a giant.

Michelangelo prepared mallets and chisels with his usual care, and he moved fast. A note in the margin of his contract states that: 'The said Michelangelo began to work and carve the said giant on 13 September 1501, a Monday; although previously, on 9th, he had given it one or two blows with his hammer, to strike off a certain *nodum* that it had on its breast. But on the said day, that is 13th, he began to work with determination and strength.'

The 'nodum' referred to may have been the beginning of

a knot or clasp for a cloak which was to have robed the original *David*. As early as 1408, Donatello had carved a marble *David* whose mantle is knotted at his breast. Alternatively, it may have simply been a mark placed by Agostino to guide him in his future work on the block. Either way, in cutting it off, Michelangelo also cut free of one of the impositions placed on him by the earlier sculptor's carving. Whatever restrictions remained could be regarded as challenges. The block was now his alone.

He would work privately and in solitude. Always addicted to, or driven by, his work, he would pause only when necessary to sleep and eat. Slowly the figure took shape.

CHAPTER EIGHT

The Triumph of David

If Michelangelo identified with David, he was well within a tradition of Renaissance thought which, following the example of the Classical World, was working its way towards an idea of Man as the sculptor of himself. But it would be a mistake to divorce the private from the public function of the statue he was commissioned to create. It is Michelangelo's triumph that both private and public functions co-exist and work equally satisfactorily, though it is the former that appeals more obviously to the modern mind. For the Florentines, and therefore to a large extent also for Michelangelo – at least in his public consciousness – the statue was a political statement, an advertisement and a symbol. Just as Donatello's bronze group of *Judith and Holofernes*, which stood outside the door of the Palazzo della Signoria, represented the triumph of the just against tyranny, and just as two previous bronze *Davids*, by Donatello and Verrocchio, had served a similar function.

Florence was well aware of its own traditions, its own traditional symbols, and its history – the story of the competition between Leonardo, Sansovino and Michelangelo for Agostino's block of marble may well have been a concoction to reflect the real competition, a century earlier, between Ghiberti and Brunelleschi, for the Baptistery doors. At that time the city had faced crisis. Now it faced crisis again. The Florentines had habitually advertised their self-confidence through beautiful artefacts which reflected their sense of liberty. There were many fine buildings as a result, but, whatever Leonardo may have felt, a great stress was laid on sculpture from the beginning of the fourteenth century. A statue could speak to the individual, and it could be erected outdoors, where everyone could see it, and if necessary it could carry an appropriate inscription. The inscription at the base of Donatello's *Judith and Holofernes*, for example, was changed three times, as the political mood dictated. This bronze group, probably commissioned by the Medici in the mid-1450s, when Donatello was already an old man, as a freestanding sculpture, was meant to be viewed from all sides, for the middle of a fountain. Its symbolism was important. Judith was a pious and chaste Hebrew widow who saved her city by ingratiating herself with the Assyrian general, Holofernes, who was attracted to her. Alone together, he got drunk and went to sleep, whereupon she cut his head off and returned with it in a sack to her people. Deprived of a leader, the Assyrians raised the siege and departed. Judith and David were both symbols of courageous and fiercely independent Florence, but Judith would become less well regarded as time passed, and the facts that she was a woman and that she achieved victory by devious means came to militate against her as a useful symbol. Passing from Medici to civic possession, the *Judith and Holofernes* group was set up outside the Signoria. It would later be replaced by Michelangelo's *David*.

Much had changed since 1400. There had been a transition from medievalism to an idealistic early modernity. At the beginning of the fifteenth century, even the word 'giant' was shunned, as associated with monstrosity and evil. But by 1500 the Florentine world had become a much more sophisticated place, due, in no small part, to the influence of the Platonic Academy and the liberal-humanist rule of Lorenzo the Magnificent. Influences on Michelangelo as he planned his massive statue were not confined to the work of Donatello and the other great masters who preceded him. He would also have been familiar with Marsilio Ficino's 1492 translation, from Greek into Latin, of Plato's follower Plotinus, the initiator of Neoplatonism, who, in his *Enneads* (1.vi), wrote:

Withdraw into yourself and look. If you do not see beauty within you, do as does the sculptor of a statue that is to be beautiful; he cuts away here, he smooths it there, he makes this line lighter, this one purer, until he disengages beautiful lineaments in the marble. Do you this too . . .

As we have seen much earlier, close association as a youth with the Medicean Neoplatonists meant that something rubbed off on Michelangelo. The Neoplatonic dictum that art must serve a moral purpose would also have appealed to the serious-minded young man who was a committed Christian; and who as an artist believed that the image of a statue was to be found within the block, just as the beauty of the soul is to be found within the physical being, if only it can be revealed, he may also have remembered, as he worked, Pico della Mirandola's *Oration on the Dignity of Man*, written in 1486, in which Pico has God address Man thus:

We have set thee at the centre of the universe that thou mayest from thence more easily observe whatever is in the world. We have made thee neither of heaven nor of earth, neither mortal nor immortal, so that with freedom of choice and with honour, as though the sculptor and moulder of thyself, thou mayest fashion thyself in whatever shape thou shalt prefer. Thou shalt have the power to degenerate into the lower forms of life, which are brutish. Thou shalt have the power, out of thy soul's judgment, to be reborn into the higher forms, which are divine.

The earliest direct influence – and inspiration – for Michelangelo was the antiquities he had been able to see in various collections during his stay in Rome, especially the newly discovered remains of colossal statues. These remains were newly discovered then, and very exciting. Most significantly, not least because the massive head has features in common with the *David*'s, were two fragments from a late imperial colossus discovered in the ruinous Basilica of Maxentius. Only the head and a huge hand remained, but they were inspiring proof of the greatness and achievement of Rome's classical past. Discovered in 1486, in 1492 the fragments were placed in the Palazzo dei Conservatori on the Captoline Hill, and it would have been there that Michelangelo saw them. The head's large eyes, thick hair, full mouth and rounded chin are all reminiscent of the *David*; only the latter statue's expression points to Michelangelo's greater genius, and modern preoccupation with inner conflict.

More recent influences can be found in the figure of *Fortitude* by Nicola Pisano, dating from 1260, which supports one of the angles of the pulpit of the Baptistery in Pisa, which Michelangelo would certainly have seen.

Fortitude, one of the cornerstones of Faith, is presented as Hercules who, in this guise, often appears among the 'prophets'. Michelangelo's *David* himself is more pagan than Old Testament, having complex affinities with Hercules; though Adam also manifests himself in the figure. Pisano's sculpture stands in a very similar pose to that of the *David,* only in mirror-image. Equally important is Niccolò di Pietro's little marble *Hercules* relief of 1393, which is found on one of the jambs of the Porta della Mandorla of Florence Cathedral, though Michelangelo's attention may have been drawn to it because one of the proposed original sites for his *David* was on the Tribuna adjacent to the Porta. Again, di Pietro's *Hercules* has a very similar stance.

It was important to Michelangelo, in his quest fully to establish himself, to be associated with the 'prophets' programme', which was the oldest sculptural programme in Florence at the time. He may have earned something of a reputation in Rome, but it was at home that he felt the need to vindicate his talent: he regarded himself as a Florentine not just by city, but by nation.

The tenacity of the Florentines in pursuing this programme for so long is astonishing. It had not got very far. The marble *David* by Donatello already mentioned is slightly over life-size, and an *Isaiah* by Nanni Antonio di Banco, of about the same size and commissioned in the same year, 1408, were both intended for the tops of the buttresses which support the three Tribune-apses of the cathedral.

Nanni's statue was placed on one of the north buttresses, as clamp marks on its base show; but it was too small for the height it was set at, and was relocated. Nanni's piece is now high up on the south aisle of the nave. Donatello's *David* was never placed on a buttress, but located in the Palazzo della Signoria in 1416. This was a significant move: in moving from the centre of ecclesiastical power to the centre of secular power, David's symbolic function changed, and to emphasise this an inscription, now lost, was added to the base: 'To those who fight bravely for the fatherland the gods will lend aid even against the most terrible of foes.' The secularising, pagan expression, 'the gods' further distances David from his religious antecedence.

At about 190 centimetres the two statues were certainly too small for the exterior prophet placements; and everyone would have been aware of the enormous technical difficulties of hoisting something the weight of a marble figure three times life-size to such a great height, let alone the correction of proportion (given that such a thing was feasible) so that the figure would look natural when viewed from far below.

The impulse to set godlike figures high up, leading the eye and through it the mind towards the sky and heaven, is one shared by many religions – one has only to look at the order of the statuary that adorns the temples of Khajuraho as it ascends – and it is a compelling one. Some success had been achieved by using terracotta – a much lighter material – and Donatello did achieve a colossal

Joshua in 1410 in that material, which was placed on the Tribuna and remained there until well into the seventeenth century. This was the first genuine colossus made in Florence. The terracotta was painted with white gesso, in deference to the custom and theory of Roman antiquity in which white marble featured prominently. Polychrome statuary was associated now with the centuries gone by – those we refer to as the Middle Ages – from which the enlightened men and women of the early Renaissance wished to dissociate themselves. Gesso needed frequent repair and repainting, and terracotta itself was not a satisfactory solution, though ways in which it could be permanently glazed white led Luca della Robbia, who died aged 82 in 1482, to evolve a technique for applying pottery glazes in various colours to terracotta figures, which could be produced relatively cheaply and in relatively large numbers. He established a successful factory which was later taken over by his nephew Andrea, and his sons. A *Hercules* was proposed to follow Joshua, and work was begun in 1415 in a collaboration between Donatello and Brunelleschi; but the project never got beyond the model stage. In any case, terracotta figures were always regarded as a stop-gap, until a technique for hoisting massive marble figures up so high was found.

Marble was always the preferred medium. It looked better, was a subtler material to work with, and stood in no need of short-term repair. The only thing against it for the prophets programme was its weight. When Michelangelo was commissioned to sculpt the *David*, the position it was nevertheless designated to take was on the Tribuna, though how the Operai thought they were going to get it up there is uncertain. Perhaps they hoped that when the time came the ingenious architect-engineer brothers, the Sangalli, would come up with something. But the idea of pursuing the prophets programme was clearly something of an obsession. The block of stone was always intended to be for a *David*; and the *David* was always intended for the cathedral.

If there was no one to compete seriously with Michelangelo among his contemporaries, he still pitted himself against the giants of the past, especially Donatello, whose influence on Michelangelo's early work is great. Donatello was working in a more confident, less volatile era, but Michelangelo's *David* marks the point of breaking away from that time. Altogether, Michelangelo's *David* is a work of art conceived at a moment of watershed: it looks forward to and belongs in the period of the High Renaissance; but nevertheless a shadow of the earlier masters passes close to it. If it is true that Donatello was involved, through Agostino, in the earlier David project, then another layer of significance is added: Michelangelo was actually working on and changing a block whose original owner and conceiver was the greatest sculptor of the fifteenth century. The thought, if it occurred to him, as well as the responsibility, would have made most twenty-six-year-olds' heads spin; but Michelangelo was invested with great confidence, together with a steadying respect for the work of past masters.

The thought of Donatello must nevertheless have been an inspiration to Michelangelo. Though Donatello was a far gentler character, the two men had many things in common, and stories about Donatello were common currency among the artists who regarded themselves as his heirs. Vasari tells us of an occasion when Donatello asked his friend Filippo Brunelleschi for his opinion of a wooden crucifix he had just completed for Santa Croce. When Brunelleschi's reaction was less than ecstatic, Donatello asked him what reservations he had:

So Filippo, being always ready to oblige, answered that it seemed to him that Donatello had put on the cross the body of a peasant, not the body of Jesus Christ which was most delicate and in every part the most perfect human form ever created. Finding that instead of being praised, as he had hoped, he was being criticised, and more sharply than he could ever have imagined, Donatello retorted: 'If it was as easy to make something as it is to criticise, my Christ would really look to you like Christ. So you get some wood and try to make one yourself.'

Without another word, Filippo returned home and secretly started work on a crucifix, determined to vindicate his own judgment by surpassing Donatello; and after several months he brought it to perfection. Then one morning he asked Donatello to have dinner with him, and Donatello accepted. On their way to Filippo's house they came to the Old Market where Filippo bought a few things and gave them to Donatello, saying: 'Take these home and wait for me. I shall be along in a moment.'

So Donatello went on ahead into the house, and going into the hall he saw, placed in a good light, Filippo's crucifix. He paused to study it and found it so perfect that he was completely overwhelmed and dropped his hands in astonishment; whereupon his apron fell and the eggs, the cheeses and the rest of the shopping tumbled to the floor and everything was broken into pieces. He was still standing there in amazement, looking as if he had lost his wits, when Filippo came up and said laughingly:

'What are you up to, Donatello? What are we going to eat now?'

'Nothing for me, thanks,' replied Donatello. 'You take what you want. But no more of this, please: I see that your job is making Christs and mine is making peasants!'

It's unlikely that Michelangelo would have reacted so good-naturedly to that kind of treatment at the hands of a fellow-artist, nor are we likely to look with much profit for the 'graciousness and courtesy', which Vasari attributes to Donatello, in Michelangelo. But both were generous to their friends, and both shared a certain unworldliness. Donatello is said to have set so little store by money that he kept what he had 'in a basket suspended by a cord from the ceiling, and all his workmen and friends could take what they wanted without asking'. In his old age, the Medicis gave him a farm as a kind of pension, but the management of it bothered him so much that he asked them to take it back. They did so, but substituted a straightforward cash allowance (Donatello was no good with banks) equivalent to the income from the farm. But Donatello still possessed a small farm of his own, which for years he had leased to a peasant. Vasari tells us that:

When Donatello was ill, shortly before he died, some relations of his came to see him. After the usual greet-ings and condolences they told him that it was his duty to bequeath them [the] farm that he owned at Prato; and although it was small and yielded very little they begged him for it very insistently. When he heard this Donatello, who had a great sense of fair-ness, said:

'I am afraid I cannot satisfy you, because it only seems right to me to leave it to the peasant who has always worked it, and who has toiled there, rather than to you, who have not given anything to it but always thought that it would be yours, and hope to do so just by this visit. Now go away, and God bless you.'

Tellingly, the contemporary bibliophile and art connoisseur Vincenzo Borghini had in his collection a large book of plates and drawings. Two facing pages showed a drawing by Michelangelo and one by Donatello. In the margin Borghini wrote (in Greek): 'Either the spirit of Donatello moves Buonarroti, or that of Buonarroti first moved Donatello.'

Donatello broke ground with his marble *David*. Before his figure, there was only one other of a victorious David standing alone, in a fresco in Santa Croce by Taddeo Gaddi, where David is shown as an older man standing on the body of Goliath. The icon Donatello invented was of a young man, relaxed in victory, the head of his giant enemy at his feet. The figure is clothed, but the tight-fitting top shows the contour of the body beneath. The face is effeminate and blank in expression – the eyes have no sculpted pupils. The contrast between the expressive body and the face which does not seem to belong to it is odd. The general effect superficially is innocuous, until one notices that the boy-hero's brow is crowned with amaranth, not laurel – amaranth being a plant known for its quality of self-renewal.

If the marble *David* of Donatello was adapted for the purposes of secular propaganda, Donatello himself cannot have minded, for he did further work for the Signoria, including, in about 1420, a *Marzocco*, the Republic's guardian lion, destined for the newel-post of the Papal apartment in Santa Maria Novella. It wasn't installed in time for the visit of Pope Martin V in 1418, but the message it was intended to send – of Florence's autonomy and power – was clear.

However, as influences on Michelangelo and his thinking about how he would approach the subject of David, two important bronzes (of about life-size for their boyish subjects) must take centre stage: the *David*s of Donatello and Verrocchio.

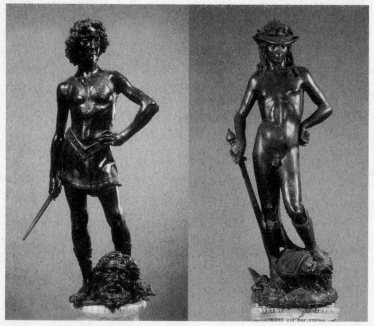

Verrocchio – *David*   Donatello – bronze *David*

Donatello's bronze *David* is as famous as it is exquisite and powerfully erotic. Little is known of its origins, or who commissioned it. For many years it stood at the centre of the courtyard of the Palazzo Medici in the Via Larga, and it has been assumed that the piece was commissioned by the Medici for the palace. But Donatello was away from Florence when the palace was being built and did not return until 1453. Stylistically the statue suggests a much earlier date, around 1430, and its quality is such that a private client is unlikely. A little over twenty years ago, the scholar H. W. Janson suggested that this *David* was a public commission with an overtly political purpose, and dates it to the mid-1420s. The reason for this is that the head of Goliath which lies at David's feet carries a winged helmet. Such a thing is very rare, but the then Duke of Milan, Gian Galeazzo Visconti, had taken the winged helmet as his symbol after his conquest of Verona, whose dukes had had it as *their* emblem. Gian Galeazzo's son Filippo Maria also took it as his insigne. Milan and Florence were rival city states and often enemies; in the mid-1420s Filippo Maria posed a threat to the Republic. Responding in the same way as they would nearly eighty years later with Michelangelo's *David*, the Signoria (arguably) commissioned a statue for propaganda purposes: a David/Florence triumphant over the defeated and destroyed Goliath/Milan.

But the threat passed, and by 1450 Florence had formed an alliance with the new Duke of Milan, Francesco Sforza.

The political *David* was as redundant as an out-of-date election poster, and even embarrassing. It was, however, a work of art. Was it now that the civic authorities decided to sell it to a private collector – someone like Cosimo de' Medici? It seems likely. We do after all know that the statue came into the possession of the Medici, and that Charles VIII's military administrator, the Maréchal de Gié, so admired it when billeted in the Medici Palace in the late 1490s that he asked for a copy to be made for him.

But just as Michelangelo took his commission and transformed the work into something original and personal, so had Donatello with his bronze *David*. He made one reintroduction and one innovation, and they intertwine. His was the first freestanding nude sculpture to be created since antiquity. But it was also the first 'nude' *David* (he is naked except for his helmet and boots). The only precedent is in the nude *Hercules* sculptures of such artists as Pisano and di Pietro, whose standing figures share the same *contrapposto* stance that most of the *Davids* adopt – the torso slightly twisted on the same axis as the legs, and the weight clearly balanced on one leg, the other being usually slightly bent.

Most importantly, there is a deeply personal involvement in Donatello's bronze *David* of the sculptor in, if not his overt theme, his inner preoccupation. This *David* is sexually provocative, effeminate, and desirable. It is one of the most powerfully erotic images ever created, and yet there is still something effete about it which Michelangelo's *David* manages to transcend. But is the effete effect deliberate? Is Donatello himself being provocative, displaying his talent with the same flamboyance that Michelangelo did when he carved the *Pietà*? And it must be deliberate that, apart from the faintly pouting mouth, the face of this boy-hero is as cool (but not quite as detached) as the face of Donatello's marble *David*, though there is a closer relationship between the expression (the pupils of the eyes are barely suggested, but their expression conveys a mixture of condescension and gentle mockery), and the languid pose. The eroticism extends to the way David's left foot, in its toeless boot, casually caresses the beard of the dead giant, just as the left wing of the helmet reaches up and caresses the inner thigh of David's right leg, its feathers extending almost to his testicles. Over a century later, Benvenuto Cellini would go some way towards creating an erotic relationship between victor and vanquished with his glorious *Perseo*, but he didn't surpass this. It isn't surprising that Donatello was himself homosexual, attracted to beautiful apprentices. Homosexuality in the Florence of the time was not unusual and was tolerated, at least by the sophisticated elite, even attracting an intellectual curiosity. The most important thing about this *David* is that Donatello, asked to create a statue for the purposes of civic and military propaganda, managed not only to achieve that (and have his offering accepted, presumably), but also to imbue his creation, for the first time in post-medieval western art, with a deeply personal preoccupation. It is in this respect most of all that he influenced Michelangelo, who not only shared his sexual proclivity, but also much of his aesthetic. The personalities, however, were different. Donatello was unworldly, gentle, fair-minded and kind. Michelangelo was always in a sort of spiritual and artistic torment, something which lent both him and his creations, starting with and succeeding the *David*, what contemporaries termed his *terribilità*.

When Donatello died in 1466, the Medici and Florence lost their principal sculptor. His mantle fell on to the shoulders of Andrea del Verrocchio, then aged about thirty, who was a goldsmith and painter as well as a sculptor. Among other things, he worked on the great tomb of Piero di Cosimo de' Medici and his brother Giovanni, commissioned for the church of San Lorenzo by Piero's son Lorenzo the Magnificent and his brother Giovanni in the early 1470s, but his principal fame today rests on two bronzes, the well-known and immensely popular *Putto with a Dolphin*, and his *David*. Both originally belonged to the Medici – the *Putto* was made for the family villa at Careggi. The *David* was sold to the Republic in 1476. The precise date of its casting is not known. There was a kind of rivalry between Donatello's *David* and Verrocchio's. Donatello's, in the very centre of the Medici Palace, became increasingly associated with the family, whereas Verrocchio's, installed in the Signoria, symbolised the power of the independent Republic.

It may even be that Lorenzo commissioned a *David* for the Republic to counterbalance his own – a kind of sop to Cerberus.

Whatever the truth of the matter, and the political tensions of the late 1470s do not play a role in the artistic consideration of Verrocchio's contribution to the *David* corpus, his *David* differs greatly from either of Donatello's versions. It is smaller – only 125 centimetres in height – and though realistically that could be the height of a boy (people were smaller in those days), the proportions are reduced, so that this *David* has the appearance more of a statuette than of a life-size figure. If it is hard to give a precise age either to Donatello's or Michelangelo's versions of David, it is virtually impossible in the case of the Verrocchio. Like the others, he stands in a *contrapposto* pose, but he is clothed in a decorative, tight-fitting tunic and kilt, which nevertheless reveal all the contours of his body, even to his ribcage, beneath. His pose lacks the tension of the Michelangelo and the suggestiveness of the bronze Donatello, and like the Donatello he is portrayed after the fight, the head of Goliath at his feet. But there is no relationship between victor and vanquished, no erotic flirtation between victory and defeat. Verrocchio's David holds a neat short sword at a negligent angle, unlike the massive weapon Donatello's *David* holds, and his expression is, if anything, rather smug.

This hero is far less complicated than Donatello's, and although it is a beautiful piece of work technically, it is

essentially decorative, and seems to lack the personal investment which informs the work of the other two sculptors. It
may be that this piece taught Michelangelo, if anything,
what to avoid. But his genius, like that of Donatello,
outstripped Verrocchio's. Oddly, Verrocchio's *David* seems
to belong to a later time, when ornament became more
important than sense. It is proto-Baroque.

While Michelangelo worked, the threats to Florence that
had helped shape the commission were gathering pace. More
than ever, Florence had need of a symbol which would stress
the Republic's independence, as well as its pride in liberty.
Events on the political and military scene beyond the
Republic were unfolding fast; the Signoria knew that
Florence would not remain unaffected by them.

Hitherto, it had always been the policy of the Papacy that
Naples should remain unmolested, but in June 1501
Alexander signed a secret treaty with France and King
Ferdinand of Spain, agreeing to the division of Naples
between those two countries. This he did to counter the
machinations of some of the major Roman families, principally the Orsini, and the Colonna, whose intrigues were
always supported by Naples.

A French army marched to Rome and pitched camp
outside the city, where it was joined by Cesare Borgia and
his forces. The combined operation wasted no time in
attacking Naples. There was no opposition, and King

Federigo fled. He subsequently surrendered to the French, who gave him a dukedom to fob him off and then proceeded to split his kingdom, as arranged, with Spain. Meanwhile in Rome, the Colonna were summarily excommunicated and their possessions confiscated by the Pope, who gave some of them to the Orsini family, who were their bitter rivals, but retained most for the Borgia.

Cesare continued his campaigns with utter ruthlessness, marching into Florentine lands at Val di Chiano and taking Urbino in mid-1502. At the very end of the year he took Senigaglia, but afterwards had his generals, who were plotting against him because they thought him too powerful, arrested and executed. One of them had belonged to the Orsini family, which gave Alexander in Rome the excuse to arrest all the members of the Orsini clan he could lay hands on. Cesare turned his army on to the Orsini lands and devastated them, attacking their stronghold, Bracciano. The defenders appealed to the French for aid, but by now the French had their own problems, having fallen out with the Spanish who, with an army under Gonsalvo de Cordoba, seized control of Naples in May.

Piling success upon dubious success, and operating – to Alexander's fury – more and more independently of his father, Cesare began treating with the Holy Roman Emperor to take over Pisa, Lucca and Siena – all very close to Florence – as fiefdoms. Perugia had just fallen to his marauding soldiers when, after a banquet in Rome in mid-August 1503, both Cesare and Alexander contracted – apparently – a virulent form of malaria. Alexander died on 18 August. Because of the reputation of the Borgia, a story circulated that the father and son had inadvertently drunk wine from a flagon specifically prepared for Cardinal di San Crisogno, one of their guests at dinner. But Frederick Corvo, in his study of the Borgias, says that Alexander and Cesare themselves rode out to dine *al fresco* at the Cardinal's villa outside Rome on 5 August: 'It is said that the Holiness of the Pope was much heated by the exertion of riding there; and that, while he was in this condition, he drank a cup of wine for the sake of coolness. No more hazardous action can be imagined; except on the part of one desiring to court a malarial fever.' Whatever the cause, and it may be that the accidental taking of poison intended for another was a story deliberately circulated by enemies of the Borgia after their fall, Alexander appears to have been seriously ill from that point.

The bloated and unpleasant corpse of Alexander – his body the wrecked result of a lifetime of excess – lay in state in St Peter's for three days. That summer was particularly hot – many died of plague, and the streets were fetid. Three days was long enough to make Alexander's dead body swell so much that when the time came to put it into its coffin, it would not fit. One contemporary witness, the Orator of Venice, Antonio Giustiniani, who had chronicled the progress of the Pope's illness in a series of missives to the Doge, noted that 'his corpse was more hideous and monstrous than words can tell, and without human form'.

Rome did not mourn this foreign intriguer and tyrant unduly. The late Pope's own Master of Ceremonies, Johann Burchard, describes a mêlée that took place when the corpse was borne into St Peter's – an indication of the near-anarchy that followed Alexander's death; and tells graphically of the deterioration of the corpse as it awaited burial:

> . . . the body of the Pope had remained for a long time, as I have described, between the railings of the high altar. During that period, the four wax candles next to it had burned right down, and the complexion of the dead man became increasingly foul and black. Already by four o'clock on that afternoon when I saw the corpse again, its face had changed to the colour of mulberry or the blackest cloth, and it was covered with blue-black spots. The nose was swollen, the mouth distended where the tongue was doubled over, and the lips seemed to fill everything. The appearance of the face was far more horrifying than anything that had been seen or reported before. Later, after five o'clock, the body was carried to the Chapel of Santa Maria della Febbre and placed in its coffin next to the wall in a corner by the altar. Six labourers or porters, making blasphemous jokes about the pope in contempt of his corpse, together with two master carpenters, performed this task. The carpenters had made the coffin too narrow and short,

and so they placed the pope's mitre at his side, rolled his body up in an old carpet, and pummelled and pushed it into the coffin with their fists. No wax tapers or lights were used, and no priests or any other persons attended to his body.

Alexander's funeral and burial were shunned by almost all the cardinals in Rome.

The much younger and more robust Cesare survived, but he was too weakened by illness to influence the election of his father's successor. He had made too many enemies for them not to take advantage of his illness, and Alexander's old enemy, Giuliano della Rovere, was waiting in the wings. The College of Cardinals ordered the still desperately ill Cesare's departure from Rome prior to the election of the new Pope in September, and the aged and ailing Cardinal Piccolomini was chosen by the Conclave as a safe stop-gap, becoming Pius III (he represented no faction and so satisfied everybody while the real jockeying for power could take place), until the Borgia problem could be fully resolved. They did not have long to wait. Cesare's star was on the wane. Leaderless, his largely mercenary army melted away, quickly reducing in size from 12,000 to 650 men. He was allowed back into Rome but in order to escape arrest and the fury of the now-resurgent Orsini, he had to take refuge in the Castel Sant' Angelo.

Pius III died on 18 October 1503 and the new Pope was

swiftly elected: Giuliano della Rovere, aged sixty, took his place on the Papal throne as Julius II at the end of the same month. He was a tough man who had climbed a long ladder. His father had been a fisherman, which, he occasionally joked, more than qualified him for St Peter's throne. He was unschooled but energetic, fighting his enemies and the syphilis that ate him from within with equal rigour. When, much later, Michelangelo came to make a statue of him, he said, 'Put a sword in my hand, not a book.' Most at home as a soldier and administrator, Julius seems an unlikely patron of the arts, but in the Renaissance, the arts were far more integrated into politics and propaganda than they are today, and it should be reiterated that most people looking at a work of art then would be seeing its public message, rather than any personal and intimate interpretation with which the artist had invested it. Julius would later become Michelangelo's most demanding and exacting patron.

His first undertaking as Pope was to break the remaining power of the Borgia once and for all, and that meant getting rid of Cesare. (Cesare himself had cheated his sister and former ally Lucrezia out of most of her possessions and lands, and she had been married off to Alfonso d'Este of Ferrara. Lucrezia, despite her infamous reputation, died peacefully, aged thirty-nine, in 1519, a well-respected and loved patroness of learning and the arts, and celebrated by Lodovico Ariosto, among other poets.)

Julius also needed to win back the Papal States alienated

by Alexander VI, bring the rebel cities of Perugia and Bologna to heel, and block any attempt by Venice to seize control of the Romagna under the pretext of liberating it from Cesare's rule. He also proposed to clean up Rome, which remained a sink of iniquity and vice. It was said that in a population of 50,000, there were 7,000 prostitutes. Cesare at least posed no threat. Robbed of his power, the man who had lived by the principle that, if one had to choose, it was better to be feared than loved, found himself without a friend and surrounded by vengeful enemies. Julius had him imprisoned as a rebel in the Borgia Tower at the Vatican, and issued a Bull of Deprivation, stripping him of all his lands, titles and personal property.

Just after Christmas, 1503, the last French forces were routed on the banks of the River Garigliano, about fifty kilometres north-west of Naples, by the army of Gonsalvo de Cordoba. The French claims on Naples were finished. Cesare had no cards left to play except his Spanish family connection. He gave up any thought of winning back the Romagna and managed to escape, disguised, to Naples via Ostia. Once there, however, he was sent to Spain where he was held prisoner in the Castle of Medina del Campo, thereby ending the short, meteoric rise of the Borgia in Rome. Cesare had not quite played his last card though. He escaped from his prison and joined his brother-in-law, King Jean of Navarre, in October 1506, taking service in his army. If he dreamed of any kind of comeback, and it's reasonable to suppose that he did, given his energy and the fact that he was still only thirty-one, the dream wasn't to come true: Cesare died in a minor skirmish near the Castle of Viana in May 1507.

During Cesare's depredations in northern Italy, Florence had been wary and alert, but its uneasy alliance with France had saved it. When Cesare invaded the Florentine lands in 1502, the Republic had recourse to Louis XII. Louis was quite happy for Cesare to make himself master of territory which he did not himself want or need as trustworthy bases for his own military enterprises; but Florence was one such place. Louis deployed troops under the Maréchal de Gié in Tuscany, and the *Signoria* were able to buy Cesare off at the gates of the city. He then withdrew.

Since Savonarola's death, the reinstated Republic had reverted to the system of a great council whose members held office for two months at a time. The dangerous times that dominated the years at the turn of the century persuaded them, however, that a more stable government was needed for the security of the state, and on 1 November 1502 a prominent member of the *Signoria*, Piero Soderini, was elected *Gonfaloniere* for life. He was a moderate man and a good administrator, who had the sense to depend heavily on one of his administrative assistants, Niccolò Machiavelli, under whom Florence would finally abandon its habit of hiring troops as and when needed, and build up its own, reliable national militia.

Soderini was also greatly helped by the withdrawal of the

threat posed by Cesare Borgia, and by the removal of another thorn in the Republic's side.

Ever since his exile from the city, Piero de' Medici had planned his return. He had met with varied fortune, but had never succeeded in attracting enough support for a real assault on the Republic, though he'd accompanied Cesare to the city's gates in 1502, in the hope that the Borgia would be able to reinstate him, in return for money. He never gave up, however, and remained a real danger. It was a relief for Florence therefore to hear the news of his death. He had drowned during the Battle of Garigliano, where he had allied himself to the French in the hope of doing a deal with them. In the retreat across the Garigliano to Gaeta, the boat on which Piero had embarked capsized. He was thirty-two years old.

There was now little left to fear from the Medici, it seemed; but the fortunes of the family now lay in the hands of Lorenzo the Magnificent's younger son, Cardinal Giovanni, who would later become Pope Leo X, and reign from 1513 to 1521; and his cousin Giulio, who reigned as Pope Clement VII from 1523 to 1534. Both were able men and did not lose sight of their family's lost patrimony.

Thus, during the period when Michelangelo was working so furiously on his *David* – it was nearing completion within eighteen months of his having started – two of the Goliaths that threatened Florence, the Borgia and the Medici, fell.

Though he was aware of the political events unfolding around him, Michelangelo had little time to reflect on them, even if he had been so inclined. As well as the *David*, he still had the Piccolomini contract to think about, and now he took on two more pieces of work.

The *Signoria* had long neglected the request from Maréchal de Gié for a copy of Donatello's bronze *David*, which the Maréchal had so admired during his billeting at the Medici Palace. As the man whom many spoke of as Italy's greatest sculptor was a Florentine, and presently at work in Florence, now seemed a reasonable time to secure his services for a bronze *David* for the Maréchal. The contract was drawn up with Michelangelo on 12 August 1502. It stipulated that the figure should be 2.5 *braccia* in height, and finished within six months. The *Signoria* undertook to supply all needful materials, and to pay the artist fifty florins.

A preparatory drawing for the bronze *David* still exists, on the same sheet of paper (now in the collection of the Louvre in Paris) on which Michelangelo drew the pendant right arm of the marble *David*. It shows a helmeted figure with his foot planted on Goliath's head, but it scarcely suggests a copy of Donatello: this David is far more robust and far less sexy. The reverse of the same sheet of paper has a sketch by Michelangelo of the *Adam* sculpted by the fifteenth-century master Jacopo della Quercia for the façade of San Petronio in Bologna – another possible influence on the marble *David*. Another clue to Michelangelo's thinking at the time is suggested by a fragment of verse he wrote next to the sketch of the bronze *David*: it is the beginning of a line from a well-known sonnet by Petrarch: *'Rotta l'alta colonna . . .'*. It means, 'Broken is the tall column . . .', and it refers to the death of a member of the Colonna family who was a patron of Petrarch. However, the line concludes: *'. . . e il verde lauro'*. This means: '. . . and the green laurel'. Petrarch may have been referring to Laura, whom he loved passionately but chastely, and who is the inspiration for almost all his poetry. Michelangelo, as Charles Seymour Jr. has pointed out, would have been thinking of Lorenzo the Magnificent and the golden days of Florence that had ended a decade earlier, but, writing as he was in 1502, would scarcely have completed Petrarch's line for fear of the anti-Medici feeling which ran high in Florence then. That this hypothesis is probably correct is borne out by the Latin elegy Angelo Poliziano wrote to Lorenzo, which has the lines:

> *Laurus impetu fulminis*
> *Illa illa iacet subito*
> *Laurus omnium celebris*
> *Musarum choris*
> *Nympharum choris*

> [Lightning has struck
> Our laurel tree

Our laurel so dear
To all the Muses
To the dances of the nymphs]

(from the translation by John Addington Symonds)

Michelangelo did complete the bronze *David* (it was cast by the master bronze caster, Benedetto da Rovezzano), but too late for it to be presented to de Gié, who by then had fallen from favour. Instead it was presented to the French king's principal adviser on foreign affairs, Florimond (or Florimard) Robertet, and was kept at the Château de Bury until many years later when, according to some sources, it was transferred to Villeroy, and subsequently melted down to make cannon some time after 1650. Whatever the cause, it is now lost. Contemporary descriptions of works of art, even great ones, are rare, but Benedetto Varchi, writing in 1564, confirms the supposition which the drawing suggests, that it was made in competition with Donatello's version.

A second contract, dated about eight months later, 24 April 1503, stemmed once more from the cathedral. By then the marble *David* was nearing completion and the Operai were evidently pleased with the result, for the new job involved the carving of all twelve Apostles, each to be 4.5 *braccia* tall. It may be that the Operai hoped by this to bind Michelangelo to them permanently, since the duration of the contract was for twelve years. The Operai would meet all Michelangelo's expenses, including journeys to and from Carrara, and they would build a workshop for him on the Via da' Pinti, near the Servite Monastery, up to the value of 600 florins. Any excess, the contract warned, would have to be met by Michelangelo himself, whose fee was to be paid at the rate of 2 florins a month over the 144 months. A minatory final clause read: 'If he fails to carry out the contract he is liable to a fine of 1000 florins.'

These were not the only works which Michelangelo undertook, and, as will appear, he was working on other projects at around the same time that he was working on the *David*. His desire to prove himself, and his creative energy, were both insatiable; but he could not possibly complete all that he had promised. In the case of the Apostles, the first block of marble arrived in 1503, and some time thereafter he started work on a *St Matthew*, which survives in Florence as a magnificent work-in-progress, demonstrating vividly Michelangelo's method. Michelangelo would draw the figure he intended to carve in charcoal on one face of the block, and then work inwards from that face, always working from that one side, drawing the figure out of the stone. Not only did he work on the *St Matthew* in that manner, but he must have used the same method with the *David*, owing to the shallowness of the block.

Benvenuto Cellini, who knew Michelangelo in later life, describing the technique of marble sculpture in his *Autobiography*, notes that:

The best method ever was used by the great Michelangelo; after having drawn the principal view on the block, one begins to remove the marble from this side as if one were working on a relief and in this way, step by step, one brings to light the whole figure.

The method also allows greater freedom of expression than working from a marked-up block, though it requires vast talent and assurance of the sculptor, and tends to produce statues that suggest one main viewpoint, though in the case of Michelangelo's work that is debatable. However, the production of figures designed to be viewed from all sides was only beginning to be rediscovered.

Michelangelo made more elaborate use of the claw chisel than any other artist before or since. He worked with it as if he were working with pen and ink on paper, and just as in his drawings he quickly and confidently revealed the vitality of the human body and muscles that seem to ripple before the eye, so in stone he unhesitatingly draws out life through the depiction of sinews and muscle and skin through which one fancies one can see even to the bone. He cross-hatches with the claw chisel just as he would have cross-hatched on paper with a pencil; and this method of interpreting form by modelling and remodelling through clarifying lines – a method which appeals to rational understanding – is typically Tuscan.

It may seem that Michelangelo's procedure had much in

common with that of the ancients, since with them he 'released' his work from its marble block, patiently, layer after layer. But while, as the art historian Rudolf Wittkower has pointed out, 'in both cases the work reaches finality by means of an intense process of uninterrupted creation, the differences are of vital importance'. Ancient sculptors used the punch, or pointed 'chisel'. Michelangelo could never have achieved his fluidity with such a tool. The claw chisel allowed him to define and redefine natural form. By running over contours of muscle and sinew, the chisel in its course freed the form from the stone by a quasi-organic process. The unfinished St Matthew looks as if it might have been designed as a relief, and it could stand as one; but we know that it indicates Michelangelo's technique of approaching the stone from one side only. Vasari also describes this technique, comparing the gradual emergence of the figure from the marble block to a model sunk under water that is slowly pulled up, revealing the topmost parts first and then, part by part, the rest.

Michelangelo's *David* had begun to emerge by the beginning of 1503. In February of that year, the figure was so advanced that the Operai met to determine how much should be paid to the artist on its completion, and talks began about where it should be placed.

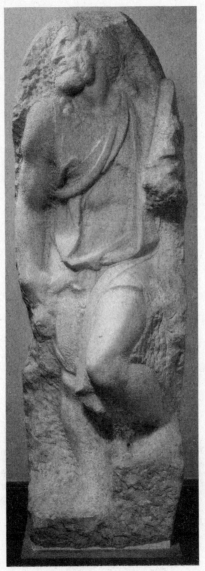

Michelangelo – *St Matthew*

CHAPTER NINE

Il Gigante

Little remains of the preparatory work for the marble *David*. But at nine o'clock on the morning of his seventy-second birthday, 22 May 1986, the American Michelangelo scholar Frederick Hartt received a telephone call at his home in Charlottesville from a professional acquaintance based in Paris, but at the time in New York, to inform him that a private foundation had in its possession a 'document' relating to the artist, which it had acquired the previous year from the heirs of the composer Artur Honegger (who had written a *King David* oratorio). Intrigued, Professor Hartt invited the caller to visit him with photographs of the 'document'.

In French, the word 'document' can cover any work of

art. The photographs disclosed, to Hartt's great excitement, an exquisite fragment, the torso and upper thighs of what Hartt took to be a damaged statue from Greek antiquity. 'The subject was a bony, rangy young man, tense and proud,' Hartt recalled in his monograph on the subject. He asked how large the figure was, and was told, 'the same size that you see in the photographs'. In other words, this was a model for a statue. Slowly, and with increasing excitement, it dawned on him what this might be. He had seen a drawing by Michelangelo of the same figure – 'the same young man, perhaps a marble-cutter at Carrara. The bony structure, the vibrant muscles, the wonderful, ungainly grace . . . all were the same'. He realised that he could well be looking at the only genuine, small-scale finished model by Michelangelo in existence, as opposed to the half-dozen or so *bozzetti* – rough sketches in clay or wax – he had left behind. What was more, this piece, made of an alabaster stucco, seemed clearly to be a late study for the *David*.

Hartt managed to contain his excitement with a certain professional scepticism, but the likeness of the model to the *David* was too evident, and from its form he could see what final adjustments Michelangelo had made to the finished sculpture: the slightly different pose, the slingshot strap not quite in the same place. These adjustments demonstrated that this was no later copy, but the real thing. Furthermore, he consulted Ugo Procacci's painstaking catalogue of the holdings of the Casa Buonarroti Museum in Florence, which contains a wax *bozzetto* which purports to be for the *David*. Procacci records that an original model in stucco had been recorded in an inventory of the later Medici collections on 3 November 1553: *un modello di stucco del gigante di michelagnolo*.

Despite infirm health and a heavy work schedule, Hartt preferred to fly to Geneva, where the Foundation that owned the piece was located, rather than entrust it to be flown over with a representative of the Foundation to the USA. He arrived in Geneva on 9 June, and that evening held the model in his own hands: 'Within its tiny compass I could feel in germ not only the marble *David* but the whole race of heroic beings with whom Michelangelo populated his famous, classic compositions.' Though the model had, at some point in its history, been buried, been in a fire, and lost its head and limbs, the twenty-centimetre torso that remained shone with the genius that had created it. After subjecting it to the most careful scrutiny, Hartt was convinced. It was a model moulded from a stucco created from an alabaster gesso. Joint marks from where the mould was removed are still visible on the model, and this too is indicative of Michelangelo's method. Even in apparently finished works, he would leave a small area rough here and there, just as he painted the shadow his scaffolding cast on to the Sistine ceiling, and just as, in the marble *David*, he left the very top of the head uncarved, to show that he had used the whole block. This roughness was removed when the statue was cleaned during the eighteenth century, and though Vasari reports that Michelangelo also left some of Agostino's original work untouched 'on the edges of the marble', there seems little trace of it now.

Writing fifty years after the event, Vasari says of the work confronting Michelangelo when faced with Agostino's 'botched' marble: 'all things considered, Michelangelo worked a miracle in restoring to life something that had been left for dead'. It's possible that Vasari was simply prolonging a myth, for some early accounts say that Agostino had 'bosked out' the work – 'bosk out' simply meaning to 'rough out'.

The fine detail of the little model – down to the rings around the nipples and the ornamental curls of the pubic hair which crown the penis – suggests that 'after moulding' it was finished with delicate tools made of wood or bone. When new and complete, the effect of the model must have been stunning. Hartt surmises that either the wax figure on which the mould would have been based, or the cast model itself might have been used by Michelangelo to convince the Operai and the Arte della Lana to give him the contract: 'The gesso model could stand in the workshop, impervious to summer heat, which would have softened a figure in wax to the point where it would no longer be usable. By means of squaring with horizontal and vertical rules crossed at right angle, which Vasari also describes, Michelangelo proceeded to enlarge the small model and project it systematically on to the block of marble.'

But did Michelangelo base his sculpture on a living male nude whom he used as a model? For the body, if not the face, he probably did, and from the development of the muscles, Hartt has suggested 'one of the mountaineer quarrymen from Carrara. Such a lean build, especially the contrast between the broad, muscular shoulders and the taut, tiny waist, would be the normal result of habitually rotating the torso while swinging a heavy hammer against the iron point used to split the marble.' Nevertheless, the *David* is not as monumental in build as some of Michelangelo's later male nudes, for example the *Adam* and the *Christ* in the Sistine Chapel. But it was not until 1506 that Michelangelo first saw the *Laocoön*, and from then on adopted a more monumental approach, although this would have been inappropriate for a *David*.

The depiction of pubic hair, however stylised, in a massive statue, raised questions of contemporary taste. Its portrayal in smaller pieces, especially of narrative art, was not unusual, but earlier large nudes, such as figures of Adam and Eve, hid their genitalia under decorous fig-leaves. The influence of the Church on the matter of sex and the concealment of sex organs was strong. The only other large nude figure commonly visible was that of Christ Crucified, and of the few that existed in Florence, only one, by Michelozzo, has pubic hair. Michelangelo's own version for Santo Spirito only suggests the pubic hair by a few brushstrokes. But it was probably always the intention to drape these crucifixes with real loin cloths. How the *Signoria* dealt with the problem as presented by the *David* will appear later. But if they saw the model before Michelangelo started work, then they must have approved it. Perhaps they only got cold feet when they saw it enlarged to 540 centimetres.

In preparation for his work, which started in mid-September, just as the hot Florentine summer was beginning, though only gradually, to give way to softer weather, Michelangelo would have had the marble block tilted back so that he could work at it without having chips fly into his face. He had to adapt what he had visualised in the model to the shallowness of the block. The left arm, whose hand holds the end of the sling, was originally extended, but to retain that pose would have meant making the arm separately, so Michelangelo conceived the idea of bringing the hand back to the shoulder, which not only makes the figure more compact and dramatic, but means that the whole can be carved as one piece. The sculptor's generally held belief that only one block should be used for a statue was adhered to by Michelangelo all his life, and this respect for the integrity of the block made him adopt a method of composition which always managed to contain vivid movement within a closed form. What was a professional dictum for most sculptors became an aesthetic *sine qua non* for him. In this he followed Donatello once more, who is supposed to have said that a perfect sculpture should be able to stand the test of being rolled down a hill without damage; and even Donatello's bronzes seem to obey this rule. What is at stake is the fundamental integrity of the form. The block contains the statue, and the statue echoes the memory of the block.

The marble *David* seems too exquisite for its sculptor ever to have meant that it should go up high on the cathedral Tribuna, on the north side, where the light would not set it to its best advantage, and where no one would be able to see it properly. Though the disproportionately large head and hands had led people to believe that these were deliberate exaggerations which would balance out when viewed from below at a distance, the widely spaced, slim legs and narrow torso would have been lost if viewed from far below. The extremely large right hand may in fact be a reference to the *manu fortis* description applied routinely to David during the Middle Ages, but it may also have derived its inspiration from the description of the lost Colossus of Rhodes by Pliny the Elder, 'few men can embrace the thumb in the span of both arms'. Also the intense expression of the face would have been lost if the statue had been sited high up on the cathedral, though only recently, through the means of photography, can we see David as Michelangelo saw him, face to face.

There is no mention in the contract of where the statue was to be placed, but that does not mean that there was

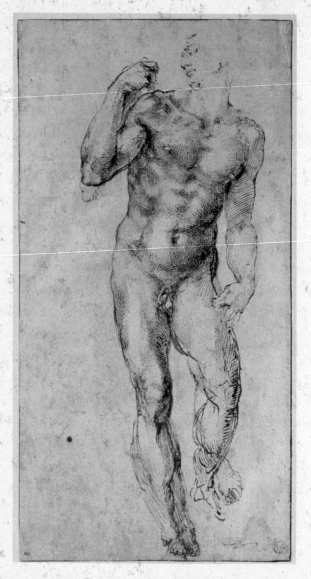

Michelangelo – a sketch of David with his sling
(about 1503)

not an unspoken and understood agreement about the siting when the contract was signed. In the couple of years it took Michelangelo to complete his statue, working through the heat of summer and the cold of winter in his private shed, alone and sharing his work with nobody, much changed in the world around him, and those changes influenced shifts of emphasis within Florence. Among others, one was a moving away from ecclesiastical to temporal authority.

The *David* is as much a secular figure as a religious one – more so. When you look at it, you think of a Greek god more than of an Old Testament prophet; but the more you look, the more you realise that this is the embodiment of an ideal as well as being a realistic portrait of a beautiful naked man. This *David* has elements of Hercules and Adam within him, and it is worth remembering that, although he probably did use a live model for the body, the overall conception here is Michelangelo's own, deriving from an idealised image in his mind's eye. As Charles Seymour Jr. has written, 'Studies from the life were only a first step towards a long-pondered conclusion.'

Michelangelo's inspiration may have been drawn from the Roman statuary he had seen, but spiritually no one had paid such original tribute to the sense of man-created-in-God's-image since the Greek sculptors of 1900 years earlier. And the interpretation of the god made flesh was focused in the male nude. Michelangelo's few female nudes are executed with less passion than his men, though they share the same monumentality. The Virgin Mary represented virtuous women, Eve represented fallen women. Goddesses like Venus would be represented as acceptable models for the female nude, viewed without moral judgment, and other classical deities and nymphs – Europa, Daphne, Diana – would become acceptable subjects for the depiction of the female nude, as would the very popular Judgment of Paris. Michelangelo's preoccupation was centred on the form of the male nude, not always in perfect physical condition, but always, to borrow Vasari's phrase, 'something divine'. It was the idea of a godhead represented in Man, as much as an

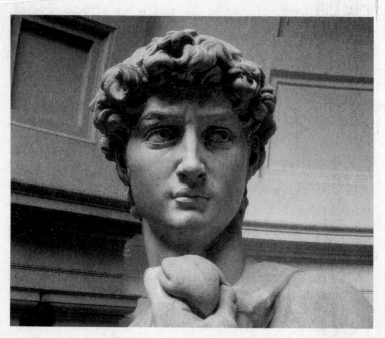

Michelangelo's *David* – detail of face

externalisation of sexual desire, that drove Michelangelo's genius.

Although he drew inspiration from classical models, his psychological approach was modern. Even though in the early *Bacchus* he was interested in reproducing what Kenneth Clark has called 'the lifeless surface of a marble copy', the sheer energy he invested in his sculpture transcends the more formal and detached work of antiquity. This David is still young enough to be ungainly; his hands and head are too big for his body. One eye is slightly larger than the other. He has a slight strabismus. Close up the knitted brow seems exaggerated, but as Howard Hibbard points out in his book on Michelangelo: 'The head breaks the antique spell of the abstract torso by investing the figure with the human thought and consciousness so prized in humanist Florence.' All Michelangelo's drawings, from early on, are full of this energy, and it finds mature and individual expression, for all the technical accomplishment of the *Pietà*, for the first time in the *David*, which is why, though an early work, it still remains one of his greatest, and enchants our imaginations and inspires us.

If Michelangelo had really thought his statue would end up thirty metres above ground, why did he give the face such an intense expression? The exaggeration of the knitted brows and the set of the mouth suggest anxiety and aggression, and the weak Roman chin carries a further complication: a sense of apology. Such complexity would scarcely have been visible if the statue had been set on high. This is difficult territory, for we are in the realm of surmise: was Michelangelo content to show what he could do, not minding if no one else would see it once the statue was up on the Tribuna? Were the complications of hoisting so massive a piece already felt to be so great that everyone knew full well that it would never be placed on the Tribuna? Isn't the whole sculpture too top-heavy to work as one designed to be viewed from below? Although these questions suggest themselves, no one can answer them fully. And is the famous squint so many have noticed in the eyes meant to add to the narrative content? Is David perceived by Michelangelo as squinting at his enemy into the sun?

David is also Apollo. His torso is in direct line of descent from the *Apollo Belvedere*, though it transcends it, being filled with a pulsating tension, from the tendons of the neck to the bulging veins in the forearms and hands, which the *Apollo*, with its formal musculature, lacks. Apollo, however, is a god, above emotions such as fear and nervous anticipation. Perhaps closer to the midriff of the *David* comes the fragment, nearly sixty centimetres tall, called the *Belvedere Torso*, attributed to Apollonius, son of Nestor, from about 150 BC and in the collection of the Vatican. Frederick Hartt has commented that this 'was Michelangelo's favourite work of ancient art. In the tonus of the muscles and particularly in the tension of the diaphragm, he could find, translated into physical terms, that inner warfare, that battle in the soul which was his deepest concern. For, according to his writings, the "beautiful and mortal veil" of human flesh clothed the movement of the spirit but reflected the divine will'. This would have satisfied Michelangelo's own philosophy in every point.

Michelangelo's *David* is a real person, tense as hell, the body reflecting the mind in every fibre: a man, not a god, but at the same time a man who could become a god, and who certainly reflects the godhead in Man. He also retains, just, the convention of the exaggerated muscles which lie above the pelvis and separate the thighs from the torso, allowing torso and legs to operate independently. It was Donatello who broke away from this convention in his bronze *David*, by concentrating the junction of the body at the waist; but his boy David was still a boy, with underdeveloped muscles, despite the formality of the torso.

This is a legacy of the development of sculpture in about 500–450 BC, when a break was made from the stiff pose of the earlier standing male nudes, the *kouroi*. *David*'s torso, though without doubt naturalistic, still echoes the old *cuirasse ésthéthique*, a formal depiction of the muscles used in antiquity that was later used as a basis for the design of body armour, and has remained an ideal male model, from the days of the masque, when the hero might be clad in a suit of such impossibly perfect musculature, down to the recent 'pecs chest and six-pack stomach' of the modern 'super-hero', such as can be seen in Batman's costume in the films of the 1990s, though there the *cuirasse* is deliberately taken to a degree which courts caricature.

The Tuscans loved movement, energy, drama. In a sense, Michelangelo's marble *David* isn't just a great piece of state propaganda imbued with an individual significance. It is, for all that it has only one character, a narrative, dramatic work: through the figure you can see the battlefield, see Goliath, approaching from afar, and be uncertain, with David, of the outcome of the fight, despite the fact that you know it: for David doesn't. His eyes, one slightly larger than the other and seeming to squint into the sun, are anxious. His fate is as uncertain as Florence's was when Michelangelo first put mallet to chisel.

As has been noted, the tool Michelangelo preferred above all was the serrated claw chisel, the *gradina,* but in his early works he still used the drill, which is evident in the *David's* hair and in the pupils of his eyes. The drill had been used by the ancients and had never been forgotten, but Michelangelo was one of the first to abandon it in favour of a more roughly sculpted surface – though the *Pietà* and a related piece, the Bruges *Madonna,* are both highly polished.

Michelangelo must also have been aware of another aspect of sculpture which Leonardo, for all his contempt for it, had astutely pointed out: that a statue to look to its best advantage needed to be placed in the correct light. In his paintings he is almost obsessive in his control of light. This would have been impossible to arrange for a statue due to be placed in the open air, where light changes capriciously. Is it possible that when the final position for the *David* was decided on, facing south, it enjoyed the best lighting the open air of Italy could provide? In a later age Bernini, most of whose works were made for indoor display, was very aware of the importance of correct lighting and always tried to ensure that his work was properly lit.

Michelangelo would not be bound by the theories of perfect proportion originally promulgated by the fourteenth-century architect and art theorist Leoni Baptista Alberti, whose *Della Pictura* contained the first description of perspective in depiction. Alberti was a follower of the architect Vitruvius, whose *De Architectura*, written some time before AD 27, is the only Roman treatise on architecture extant.

Alberti's precise laws of artistic proportion, his *exempedum canon*, a modular system of dividing the human figure into defined proportions, were developed by Leonardo, whose famous drawing of a man in perfect relation of torso to limbs, and so on, is well known (and the face is a self-portrait). Leonardo backed up the drawing with a lengthy and detailed theoretical essay which leaves no stone unturned, for example: 'The arm when bent will measure twice the head from the top of the shoulder to the elbow, and two from this elbow to where the four fingers begin on the palm of the hand. The distance from where the four fingers begin to the elbow never changes through any change of the arm.'

Michelangelo's philosophy was less cool and less detached than Leonardo's, who had little time for Neoplatonism and saw the universe (and man with it) engaged in a cosmic cycle of destruction and renewal, which no one could do anything to influence. There is however a formality about the composition of the *David* which is subject to aesthetic grammar: the right arm hangs straight down, the left is bent and raised: thus a closed right-side contrasts with an open left-side, balanced by the attitude of the legs, for the weight is cast back and on to the right leg. The right calf is supported by the tree-stump; the left foot is elegantly raised, and is on the point of slipping off the pedestal of rock, so that the figure appears almost to float. As with the *Bacchus*, but even more convincingly, it would not surprise us if this *David* began to move.

Just as Shakespeare, born in the year that Michelangelo died, took a well-known theme, the revenge tragedy, and of it made something as original as *Hamlet*, simply by twisting its basic premise round, so Michelangelo took the well-known theme of *David* and, as we have seen, made his boy-hero human, vulnerable and afraid, but determined to go through with his task. ('The Lord is my light and my salvation; whom then shall I fear?') He achieved this by the simple expedient of portraying his figure alone and before the battle, not after it. *David*'s physical imperfections, the slight but significant disproportions, humanise him. There are no props: no sword, no head of Goliath, not even the stone, which Donatello's *David* holds casually in his hand, and Verrocchio's *Goliath* has embedded in his forehead. The sling is indicated. David stands alone on a roughed-out bit of rocky ground, a dead tree stump behind him. And yet the figure contains a world.

If the *David* represents a great leap forward, not only for Michelangelo, but for the representation of the personal in art, it is nonetheless hard to chart the artist's progress steadily. What the *David*'s immediate forerunners have in common with it – the *Bacchus*, and to a greater extent the *Pietà* – is an innate sense of drama. This would not ever leave Michelangelo's work, though, as Martin Weinberger profoundly points out: 'The young artist is at first unable to bring into display in any one work all the possibilities that lie within him. The *St Proculus* and the Bologna *Angel*, produced within a few months of each other, represent very different artistic tendencies and yet are equally Michelangelesque. Awareness of the work of other artists deflects the path of straight evolution, and new and unexpected forces disturb the course of early development at almost every point.'

But the *David* represented a turning-point. Just as, when in Rome, Michelangelo absorbed the lessons of the late fourteenth-century Florentine sculptors, so, back in Florence, he felt the influence of the statues of ancient Rome which he had recently seen. But the *David* is not just a turning point for Michelangelo; it is a turning point for all of us: eschewing any medieval influence, it is at once a farewell to the cool detachment of classical art, and a salutation to the personal involvement of the artist with his creation which we have experienced (except perhaps in the narrow field of Socialist Realism) ever since. And it is very important for us to bear in mind that this was all new. The Medici and the *Signoria* were patrons and collectors of modern art. One only has to compare Michelangelo's *Pietà*, for example, with contemporary German polychrome woodcarvings on the same theme, to see what progress Italy had made.

As with his earlier pieces of freestanding sculpture, the *David* presents one dominant view, from threequarter left, although it is possible to appreciate the figure from all sides. The outwardly bent left elbow relieves the piece of any columnar effect, but at the same time there are no clumsy, disrupting angles. Everything is in perfect balance. Though he contains memories of all those artists who had influenced Michelangelo, from the ancients to Pisano and Masaccio and Donatello, the *David* is not a copy of another style nor a synthesis of several; but a fusion of elements into a new, original whole.

The *David* defines Michelangelo's working ideal, which he described many years later, in spring 1547, in a famous letter to the humanist Benedetto Varchi, who delivered two lectures on the artist's poetry to the Florentine Academy. In his letter Michelangelo confirms the definitions of the best manner of sculpting offered by Cellini and Vasari. He also had the benefit of hindsight, for in the intervening years he had painted two huge commissions: the Sistine Chapel ceiling and, twenty-nine years later, the vast fresco that adorns the altar wall. By 1547, aged seventy-two and still working hard, he could speak of painting with more authority and more sympathy than he had hitherto, though his first love remained sculpture. His reply to Varchi is not without irony, however. It is a model of how a creative artist should reply to a theorist, and it demonstrates that he still felt that the art of reduction was greater than the art of addition:

So that it may appear that I have received, as I have, your little book, I will answer something to it as you ask me, although ignorantly. I say that painting seems to me the more to be held good the more it approaches relief, and relief to be held bad the more it approaches painting; and therefore I used to think that sculpture was the lantern of painting, and that between the one and the other was that difference which there is between the sun and the moon. Now, since I have read in your little book, where you say that, speaking philosophically, those things which have the same end, are the same thing; I have changed my opinion: and I say that if greater judgment and difficulty, impediment and labour do not make greater nobility, that painting and sculpture are the same thing; and that it should be so held, that every painter should not do less sculpture than painting; and likewise, that every sculptor should do no less painting than sculpture.

I understand sculpture, that which is made by force of taking away. That which is made by force of adding on, is similar to painting: enough, that one and the other [come] from the same intelligence . . . He [Leonardo] who wrote that painting was more noble than sculpture, if he had understood so well the other things he has written, my maidservant would have written better. Infinite things, still not said, there would be to say of similar sciences, but as I have said, they need too much time, and I have little, not only because I am old, but almost in the number of the dead: therefore I pray you to hold me excused. And I recommend myself to you and thank you as much as I can and know how for the honour is too great you do me, not appropriate to me.

In his 1568 version of Michelangelo's biography, published four years after Michelangelo's death, Vasari tells a story which might have drawn a rebuke from Michelangelo had he included it in his 1550 edition, since it casts Piero Soderini, the *Gonfaloniere* of Florence, in a foolish light. Soderini has been characterised variously as weak and lacking conviction, but he did manage to guide the fragile Republic through choppy water until it collapsed again in 1512 and he was banished, as the city passed into Medici hands once more. During his ten years in office, he seems to have been a moderate and firm controller of the city's destiny. He was rich, influential, and had good contacts. What was more, he was over fifty and had no sons, so the danger of his ambition getting the better of him and encouraging him to found a Medici-like dynasty was negligible. He was a noted patron of the arts, and the lavish banquet he gave to usher in his rule was a statement of hope that Florence, relieved of its enemies, might now enter a new, republican and democratic golden age. It is sad to reflect that such a hope was so soon to be dashed, and that the Medici would gain autocratic command of the city within three decades, though never again to acquit themselves as gloriously as Lorenzo the Magnificent. Michelangelo would have frowned on Vasari making a cheap joke at Soderini's expense many years later, and the story does not have the ring of truth. However, well known as it is, it is worth repeating here for the sake of historical completeness:

When he saw the David . . . Piero Soderini was delighted; but while Michelangelo was retouching it he remarked that he thought the nose was too thick. Michelangelo, noticing that the Gonfalonier was standing beneath the Giant and that from where he

was he could not see the figure properly, to satisfy him
climbed on the scaffolding by the shoulders, seized hold
of a chisel in his left hand, together with some of the
marble dust lying on the planks, and as he tapped
lightly with the chisel let the dust fall little by little,
without altering anything. Then he looked down at the
Gonfalonier, who had stopped to watch, and said:

'Now look at it.'

'Ah, that's much better,' replied Soderini. 'Now
you've really brought it to life.'

And then Michelangelo climbed down, feeling sorry
for those critics who talk nonsense in the hope of
appearing well-informed. When the work was finally
finished he uncovered it for everyone to see. And
without any doubt this figure has put in the shade every
other statue, ancient or modern, Greek or Roman.
Neither the Marforio in Rome, nor the Tiber and the
Nile of the Belvedere, nor the colossal statues of Monte
Cavello can be compared with Michelangelo's *David*,
such were the satisfying proportions and beauty of the
finished work. The legs are skilfully outlined, and the
slender flanks are beautifully shaped and the limbs are
joined faultlessly to the trunk. The grace of this figure
and the serenity of its pose have never been surpassed,
nor have the feet, the hands and the head, whose
harmonious proportions and loveliness are in keeping
with the rest. To be sure, anyone who has seen

Michelangelo's David has no need to see anything else by any other sculptor, living or dead.

Discussions by the public authorities, which must have included representatives of the Operai and the Arte della Lana, were already taking place about where to place the *David* as early as February 1503, when, as we have seen, the statue was well advanced. Although notionally the idea of placing it on the Tribuna was still alive, it does not appear to have entered into any serious argument. Perhaps the technical difficulties of raising it *were* insurmountable, though that may also have been a welcome excuse, for there seems little doubt that most of the city fathers, having seen the piece, also realised that it would have far greater value as a political and propaganda tool if it were well in view. For these reasons, as much as aesthetic ones, sites closer to the ground were considered.

However, by the beginning of 1504, when the statue was all but finished, no decision about where to place it had yet been reached. During the preceding years, and perhaps particularly since Soderini's appointment as permanent *Gonfaloniere* from towards the end of 1502, power in the city had shifted from the Church to the State. Not only was this a natural reaction to the extremism of Savonarola, but with the expulsion of the Medici the Republic sought to reassert itself as a secular and democratic power. So the question of where to place the *David*, whose subject was religious, but whose political message was secular, narrowed to two locations: near the cathedral, or near the Palazzo della Signoria. Specifically, the cathedral location would have placed the statue between the Baptistery and the West front of the cathedral; the Palazzo location provided a further choice: the *David* could either go under the central arch of the Loggia dei Lanzi (which some have argued was Michelangelo's own choice, though he took no part in the discussion), or into the courtyard of the Palazzo, or on the *Ringhiera*, the raised stone platform outside the main door to the Palazzo, where Donatello's *Judith and Holofernes* stood. The significance of the last site was that it was not only the actual entrance to the building, but symbolised a gateway for suppliants for the state's justice. Speeches and public announcements were also delivered from the *Ringhiera*.

The Loggia location, on the other hand, would have given the statue greater protection from the elements, and under the central arch it would have commanded a dramatic and dominating position. The courtyard position would also have provided protection, but would have condemned the *David* to relative obscurity, which was not what anyone wanted.

A large and democratically selected committee of artists and artisans was convened to determine the best location. They ranged from such luminaries as Leonardo da Vinci through to minor craftsmen who were scarcely articulate; but it is worth listing the names of the principal people who

sat down to discuss the matter on 13 January 1504, to give
some indication of the kind of artistic concentration that
existed in Florence at that time:

Andrea della Robbia (the nephew of Luca)

Francesco Filarete (First Herald of the *Signoria*)

Giovanni Cellini (a piper in the city orchestra, and the
father of Benvenuto)

Francesco d'Andrea Granacci (the painter, and
Michelangelo's old friend)

Biagio d'Antonio Tucci (painter)

Piero di Cosimo (painter)

Gallieno (master-embroiderer)

Davide Ghirlandaio (the painter, and younger brother
of Domenico)

Simone del Pollaiuolo (architect)

Filippino Lippi (painter)

Cosimo Rosselli (the painter, and master of Piero di
Cosimo)

Sandro Botticelli (painter)

Giuliano da Sangallo (architect, engineer and sculptor)

Antonio da Sangallo (the architect, Giuliano's
brother)

Andrea 'il Sansovino' (painter)

Leonardo da Vinci (painter, sculptor, architect, engineer, musician, theoretician)

Pietro Perugino (painter)

The Herald, Francesco Filarete, made an opening statement in which he outlined the government's view. He argued for the *Ringhiera* site, saying that the statue would be seen there to its best advantage, and suggested that they should replace *Judith and Holofernes* with it. The latter, he said, no longer seemed fitting, since the subject of a woman killing a man, for all its symbolic importance in the context of the Bible story, was nevertheless hardly a suitable emblem for the city. The new *David* was far more appropriate. Besides, he added, ever since the *Judith* had been set up, it had brought Florence bad luck. This last argument was designed to strike home, for, as already suggested, superstition, especially a belief in the beneficent or malign influence of the stars, was still taken very seriously in those otherwise enlightened days; and it was true that the closing years of the fifteenth century and the opening ones of the sixteenth had been difficult for Florence.

Francesco was supported by the embroiderer Gallieno. Only Botticelli and Cosimo Rosselli spoke in favour of a location outside the cathedral. Giovanni Cellini was for placing it in the courtyard of the Palazzo, where it would have replaced Donatello's bronze *David*. The majority, including Filarete's nephew Angelo, were in favour of the Loggia. Leonardo's testimony was brief and cool, but he countered the Herald's argument against placing the statue in the Loggia 'because it would get in the way of official ceremonies held there' by stating somewhat back-handedly that the statue could be placed somewhere at the back against a wall. 'I confirm that it should be in the Loggia, where Giuliano [da Sangallo] has said, on the parapet, where they hang the tapestries on the side of the wall, with decent adornment and in a manner that does not spoil the ceremonies of the officials.'

Leonardo was probably too grand to be envious of Michelangelo, but in truth may not have cared much about the fate of the statue. A sketch he did at the time looks very like a drawing of the *David*, though far more thickly muscled.

Piero di Cosimo, that strange and reclusive creature, whose few surviving paintings testify to a very particular genius, and who, as Vasari recalls, designed a huge and popular 'Triumph of Death' for one of the city's carnivals, voted for the Loggia, but concluded that Michelangelo himself should be consulted about the best place for his statue. In this opinion Piero was joined by his great friends Giuliano and Antonio da Sangallo.

The Loggia appealed to all those who put aesthetics before politics because, they argued, the dark background of the place would set the white marble of the statue off to its best advantage. Although there is a strong argument to suggest that Michelangelo favoured the Loggia position, equally convincing ones have been advanced to indicate that he wanted the statue to go on to the *Ringhiera*.

Despite the fact that the vast majority of members of the

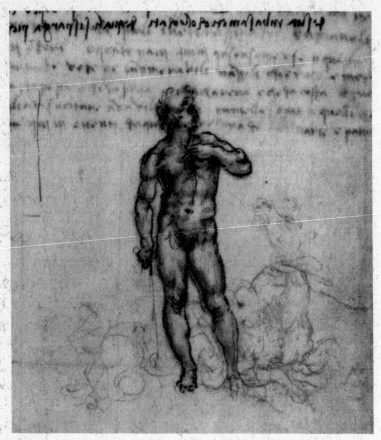

Leonardo – possibly of Michelangelo's *David*

committee plumped for the Loggia, in the end, in the way of these things, their deliberations were shelved, and the city fathers went for the location they had no doubt determined on all along: the position which gave the statue the greatest visibility and the greatest political significance: on the *Ringhiera,* facing south, across the Arno, in the direction from which Florence's enemies traditionally came, and until recently, in the form of Cesare Borgia and Piero de' Medici, had come. The *Judith and Holofernes* was transferred to the Loggia.

Towards the middle of May 1504, the Giant, as everyone still nicknamed the *David*, was ready to be transported to its appointed place on the *Ringhiera*. Everyone in the town was agog to see it, and the streets bristled with excitement. Michelangelo was always very jealous of his work, perhaps fearful that it would be copied, that his ideas would be stolen; and his future reputation hung on the reception by the public of his latest creation. He knew, of course, that he had the approval of the *Signoria* and of most of his peers. The general populace was proud of the reputation of their gifted young countryman, and willing to be well-disposed to whatever he had made, but there were some dissident voices.

The first problem to be overcome was the technical one of moving the statue at all. No one had been faced with such a task before. Antonio and Giuliano da Sangallo were equal to the challenge. As Vasari describes it, they 'constructed a very strong wooden framework and suspended the statue from it with ropes so that when moved it would sway gently without being broken; then they drew it along by means of winches over planks laid on the ground, and put it in place. In the rope which held the figure suspended [they] tied a slip-knot which tightened as the weight increased: a beautiful and ingenious arrangement. (I have a drawing by [Giuliano's] own hand showing this admirable, strong and secure device for suspending weights.)'

The work of moving the statue was begun at midnight on 14 May 1504. First of all, they had to break the top of the gateway to the Cathedral Works in order to let the colossus pass through, and that very same night some young men threw stones at it, though no damage was done. What their motivation was is unknown. Perhaps they represented the rump of a pro-Medici faction who objected to such a massive symbol of republican independence; or they may have acted from mere superstition, for some still believed that magical qualities, and not necessarily benign ones, could attach themselves to a carved figure; alternatively again it may have been a simple act of vandalism. The *David* was guarded for some time after it had been placed on the *Ringhiera*, but no further harm befell it then.

Its progress, bound upright with ropes and encased almost to the head in a wooden framework, was painfully slow. It took four days to cover the few hundred metres that separated the workshop from the Palazzo, arriving at its site at midday on 18 May. More than forty men were employed to move it, deploying fourteen rollers beneath it, which were replaced from behind to the front. Once it had arrived, it took another three weeks or so to place it on the plinth from which the *Judith* had been removed, using another hoist designed by the Sangallo brothers. When the last sections of wooden superstructure were finally removed on 8 June, and the statue was at last open to the view of everyone, most Florentines welcomed it with great enthusiasm.

The *Signoria* could be forgiven a moment of triumph. In the space of time between the commissioning and the completion of the statue, the Republic's dangers had diminished considerably; there was, however, still a need to remain on guard. It was felt that the statue had already brought the city luck, and this was reflected in the fact that as it was originally displayed, both the sling and the tree-stump behind the right leg were gilded, and the head was crowned with a garland of gold leaves. Also, because of the *David*'s very masculine nudity – the penis was not reduced in scale in relation to the body – it may be that the authorities feared that the statue might be attacked and disfigured. Another reason for their action may have resulted from their own prurience, but whatever the cause, the loins were covered and the genitalia totally concealed by another garland, of brass, hung with twenty-eight copper leaves, which was attached to the statue before it was unveiled to the public. This covering remained in place at least until the middle of the sixteenth century. Were these additions the 'decent adornments' to which Leonardo had referred?

By 1508 Michelangelo, by then deeply preoccupied with other projects, seems to have registered satisfaction with the siting of his statue. The *David* remained unmolested until 1527, the year in which the Holy Roman Emperor, Charles V, sent an army to sack Rome. The reasons for this action are complex. Both François I of France and Pope Leo X (Giovanni de' Medici) had tried to block the election of Charles following the death of the Emperor Maximilian in 1519. However, once the nineteen-year-old Charles was elected, Leo X dropped his alliance with the French and entered into secret negotiations with Charles, whose help he enlisted in an attempt to have Luther, who had already been excommunicated, executed. Charles agreed, but his German vassals objected. Charles told Leo he would override his vassals if the Vatican lent its support to his intended attack on French possessions in Italy, including Milan. But Leo died in 1521, and after a brief reign, Adrian VI was succeeded by Clement VII (Giulio de' Medici). Clement reverted to an alliance with France, but regretted it when Charles defeated the French, took François prisoner, and stood in a position to threaten Rome. When François was released, Clement attempted to enter into secret negotiations with him against Charles, but once Charles' spies informed him of this he sent an army, under his envoy Cardinal Colonna, in September 1526, which occupied the Roman suburbs.

Clement fled, signed a treaty abandoning support for François, but reneged on it almost immediately and sent Papal troops to seize and destroy Colonna's estates. This triggered an inevitable reaction from Colonna who aligned himself with Charles de Lannoy, the Emperor's envoy at Naples. Meanwhile, the German general, Georg von Frundsberg, had assembled an army of *Landsknechte*, mainly Lutheran mercenaries from Bavaria and Franconia, whose aim was to destroy the Pope, whom they regarded as the Antichrist, and relieve him of his valuable possessions. Clement managed to stave off Colonna and de Lannoy, but the German army was unstoppable and would not be bought off. Worse, the Roman citizenry failed to support the Pope. Rome was duly taken in 1527.

The Medici had slowly but surely consolidated their grip on Florence ever since the expulsion of Soderini in 1512, but the German incursion and the evident recalcitrance of Pope Clement – a Medici – triggered a moment of revolution against the family in the same year. On 16 May 1527 – nine days after the Sack of Rome began – the Medici were once again overthrown in Florence, and they would be out of power for a decade. Shortly before that, however, towards the end of April, anti-Medicean rebels had occupied the Palazzo della Signoria and, during a siege of the building, hurled a bench down from one of the windows which hit the *David*'s raised left arm and broke it in three. A few days after this accident, Vasari, then aged about sixteen, and his friend Francesco de' Rossi (some scholars say it was Francesco Salviati) managed to retrieve the broken pieces and carry them to a nearby church (possibly San Piero

Scheraggio) for safekeeping. The arm was later carefully restored.

From the early 1530s the *David* was crowded by Baccio Bandinelli's *Hercules and Cacus*, placed on the other side of the Signoria door to balance Michelangelo's masterpiece – an ironic stroke. Bandinelli, a man who later gave rise to the French word *bandinellisme*, which refers to work of especial vacuity and pomposity, regarded himself as Michelangelo's equal in talent, but is chiefly remembered as the bitter enemy of Benvenuto Cellini. The *Hercules and Cacus* is a very unhappy piece of sculpture.

The *David* remained in situ until 1873, when, in order to protect it, it was transferred to a specially prepared space in the Accademia, where despite an environment which tries to be sympathetic it still seems a little like a caged bird. It was replaced on the *Ringhiera* by a copy, set up in the original position, in 1882, which, however accurate, does not breathe in the same way as the original.

In the nearly four hundred years that the *David* stood protectively outside the Signoria, whoever its occupants were, the people of Florence regarded the statue as a tutelary deity of the city. Although the Republic would never be revived, and Florence waned in importance, ultimately to lose an absolute sense of national identity as Tuscany was subsumed within a new country, the unified nation of Italy, the *David* remained, as a reminder of the city-state's last glorious days of independence, when it was still the cradle and the home of the greatest creative talents of the country. It is ironic that such a powerful symbol of the city appeared just as the most splendid period of its history was coming to an end.

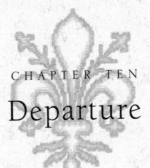

CHAPTER TEN

Departure

Apart from the four commissions he had taken on – the marble and the bronze *David*s, the Piccolomini series for Siena and the Apostle series – the second of which he failed to complete by far and the third of which he barely started – Michelangelo took on other work during the period, 1501 to 1505, that he remained in his home town, staying in the family house, and, as always, supporting his plaintive father and improvident brothers with the bulk of his earnings.

In those active four years – but what years of his long life were not? – Michelangelo also painted the so-called *Doni Tondo*, a circular painting of the Holy Family with the young St John the Baptist, probably made in 1503 for the marriage of Angelo Doni with Maddalena Strozzi, which took place late in 1503 or early in 1504. He also carved two further *tondi*: the *Taddei Tondo*, showing the Virgin with the Christ Child and the infant St John the Baptist, now in the Royal Academy of Arts in London, and the *Pitti Tondo*, a Virgin and Child now in the Bargello in Florence. Neither of these is fully finished, but another Mother-and-Child, the so-called *Bruges Madonna*, acquired in Florence between 1504 and 1505 by a visiting Flemish cloth-merchant called Mouscron for the church of Notre-Dame in his home town of Bruges, where it still stands, is as highly polished, and shows the same degree of finish, as the *Pietà*, as well as having certain stylistic affinities with it. It should be added that Mouscron, who would have seen the *David*, probably bought the *Madonna* on the back of the other statue's fame. It was by no means unusual for a wealthy merchant when travelling to buy a statue by a famous local artist because of that fame, rather than on account of any aesthetic appeal of the work per se. In Bruges, as John Hale has pointed out, it would be a generation before anyone appreciated the *Madonna* as a work of art in her own right, rather than simply as an object of devotion. However, Bruges was a very sophisticated city with a highly developed artistic community of its own.

This *Madonna* has been the subject of some speculation, since it had not been sent to Bruges before Michelangelo was obliged to return to Rome at the behest of Julius II.

From there he sent an anxious letter to his father, who was left in charge of its dispatch, to say that no one should be allowed to see the work. In the letter, dated 31 January 1506, he wrote: '[Have] the marble Madonna taken to the house and let no one see it'.

His behaviour has been seen as an indication that this Madonna had originally been intended to form part of the Piccolomini series, and that he was afraid that he might be accused of bad faith if it were discovered that he had sold the statue opportunistically following the death of Pope Pius III – who, as Cardinal Piccolomini, had been the original commissioner of the series – in 1503. This doesn't chime well with the general tenor of Michelangelo's character, however, and in any case the statue clearly had already been seen by outsiders. It had impressed the young Raphael, for example, only eight years' Michelangelo's junior, who'd arrived in Florence at about that time. It may be that the desire for secrecy stemmed from Michelangelo's jealousy of his own work, and his secretive and private nature, but wasn't he therefore shutting the stable door after the horse had bolted? Another reason may be found in the fact that the marble is faulty: there are visible bluish 'veins' across the Madonna's forehead and cheeks, which may have caused Michelangelo anxiety lest his purchaser or his agents should become aware of them before delivery, and back out of the contract: but this can only be conjecture. For some reason, both Michelangelo's contemporary biographers, Condivi and Vasari, refer to this *Madonna* as a bronze relief, something which the artist never had them correct. Is this a further indication of a desire for secrecy?

It's likely that he began work on the statue as early as 1501, because of its closeness in feeling to the *Pietà*; though the *Madonna* is much smaller, less ethereally flamboyant and less theatrical. She is grave, and seems older and less obviously attractive than the Virgin of the *Pietà*, and there is a more monumental quality about her pose, as she holds the enormous, robust Christ-Child, who, equally grave, stands between her knees. Rolf Schott, in his work on Michelangelo, comments that 'upon the Madonna's head, Michelangelo has focused every tender memory of his mother', who bore him when she was nineteen, and died aged twenty-five. The thought is charming even though there is no way of proving the intention. For stylistic reasons, experts believe that Michelangelo worked on the statue between 1501 and 1504. He could seldom bring himself quite to finish a piece, as if he could always leave room for improvement; but these two early Virgins are the exquisite exception to that tendency.

The two other marble works which feature the Virgin are both *tondi* – circular marble reliefs that had been used as tomb furniture for many decades, but which also reflected the circular form of mirrors, and of the painted salvers traditionally given to new mothers. The origin of these two works is that both were done on commission for private patrons who admired Michelangelo's work, and were not intended for use as tomb ornaments. The most likely reason that they are unfinished is that Michelangelo ran out of time; but it is possible that they were left deliberately so: a new aesthetic suggested that something which was *non-finito* carried with it an artlessness and informality which enhanced the overall impression.

The *Pitti Tondo* is considerably the smaller of the two – about two-thirds of the diameter of the *Taddei*. It was made for Bartolomeo Pitti, a member of another dominant Florentine family, whose ancestors would soon build the grandiose Pitti Palace in the city district of Oltrarno (on the south bank of the Arno). It is more fully finished, and the crown of the head of the Madonna breaks the circle. Behind her is the sketched-in head of the young St John the Baptist, and below him (barely more than the head is delineated) are dramatic low diagonals of rough claw-chisel marks. The lap of the Madonna is voluptuous and the Christ-Child on her left, bending over the book she holds, is again robust but is also, perhaps deliberately, unfinished. There seem to be three main foci: the near-finished faces of the Virgin and the Christ-Child, and the Virgin's left hand which tenderly supports the Christ-Child beneath his left arm – the attitude of her fingers, and the tension in them, though barely sketched in, is remarkable.

The face of the Virgin is heavy, formal, and unlike Michelangelo's other characterisations – the expression is vivid, but it is less realistic. It reminds you of Leonardo, and the formalised expressions of his subjects; and from that real-isation you see that the whole group is influenced by Leonardo. Was Michelangelo trying out a technical exercise, not only in the close-grouping which Leonardo had experi-

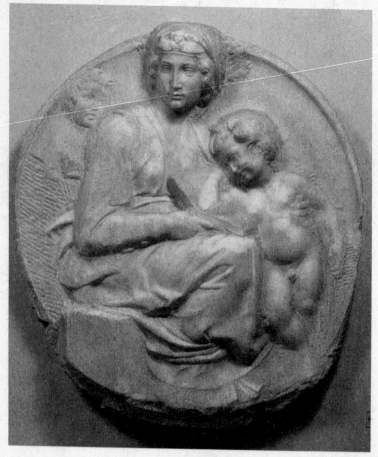

Michelangelo – *Pitti Tondo*

mented with in his Virgin-and-St-Anne relation, or was he trying to emulate the older Master?

The influence of Leonardo is also felt in the other two *tondi*. The *Taddei*, made for another discriminating collector, Taddeo Taddei, aged about thirty in 1500 and the son of Soderini's predecessor as *Gonfaloniere*, is much truer to Michelangelo's own genius. It is informal and active. A tender Virgin again nestles Christ on her lap, as he shrinks

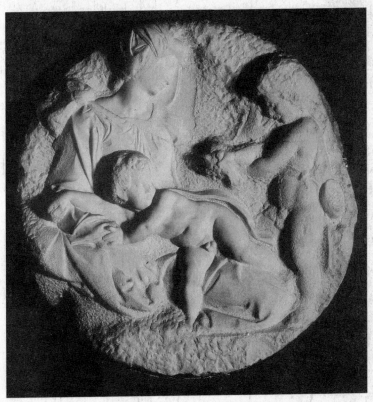

Michelangelo – *Taddei Tondo*

from a goldfinch – symbol of Christ's Passion – which the stocky little St John the Baptist offers him. The vigour and sense of movement in the Christ-Child here, and even the early realistic appreciation of the texture and muscle tone of an infant, are original and impressive. Nevertheless his pose recalls the Christ-Child of Leonardo's cartoon of the Virgin with St Anne and their two children, now in London. One vivid departure is the barely sketched-in right hand of the Virgin as she reaches out to John, perhaps, despite his evident diffidence, gesturing that it is too soon to tell her Son of his destiny. Here too the psychological homogeneity is purely felt, not rationalised. It is a pity that the Royal Academy did not choose to display this valuable piece to better advantage.

The third *tondo* is the painting for Angelo Doni, one of the few freestanding works by Michelangelo, and the only one that can be dated definitely before the Sistine Ceiling. Doni was very rich, and a keen and perceptive collector of both antiques and modern art.

The painting is formal, and again influenced by Leonardo's theory and practice: of a closely knit central group involved in one idea. This time there is no question of any 'unfinished' impressionism. The painting is lit gently but precisely from the left, and the main figures are highly defined: their expressions seem orchestrated, not spontaneous. The central group, of Joseph, Mary and Christ-Child, still have something of the statuesque: this is sculpture conceived as painting. But painting can include significant background, and here there is the infant St John the Baptist passing by, his eyes seemingly raised beyond the central group to heaven; and in the distance behind him, five statuesque young male nudes, perhaps representing the unregenerate pre-Christian age, the age unmistakably identified here with classical antiquity, which Michelangelo cannot represent as unenlightened, for, strong as his Catholic conviction was, he was still influenced by liberal humanism. His love of the male nude here represents fully his love of and belief in human integrity, *an und für sich*. But interestingly, in this tempera work, for Michelangelo tended to avoid oil, St John is partially 'out of focus' and the young men in the far background even more so. It is impossible to prove that this was intentional, though, and even if it were possible, Michelangelo would have proved the most difficult of interviewees; but the young Baptist seems to be a link between two worlds.

The *Doni Tondo* story carries a materialistic coda. Doni, who had apparently contracted a price of seventy ducats for it, decided, when he saw the piece, that it was worth only forty ducats, which he therefore offered, and gave to the man who delivered the picture on Michelangelo's behalf. Outraged at this, Michelangelo sent the delivery-man back, with a message that either the picture should be returned, or that Doni, in breach of contract, should pay 100 for it. Doni, who wanted the picture but was careful with his money, offered the original seventy. Michelangelo, furious by now, riposted by demanding 140 ducats, which is what the wretched Doni had to pay. However, the difficulty over price may have arisen not only from Doni's meanness but from Michelangelo's own pride. He found it difficult to set proper prices, and had at the time no agent. It is quite likely that he had originally given in to a low offer, but later felt that his work was worth more. At any rate Doni finally had the grace, or the cupidity, to pay double what had originally been agreed.

Towards the end of Michelangelo's time in Florence, Piero Soderini turned his attention to the new Great Hall of the Palazzo della Signoria (now politically rechristened the Palazzo del Popolo), whose decoration was still unfinished, though it rejoiced in the addition of wonderfully carved woodwork by Baccio d'Agnolo and Filippino Lippi. Given that both Leonardo and Michelangelo were resident in the city, it was logical to commission both of them to paint great triumphal battle scenes on walls there. Once more the motivation for the commissions was propaganda, emphasising the Republic's readiness to see off enemies, and designed to aid Machiavelli's plans to create a permanent militia, by raising both morale and a military consciousness.

Leonardo's theme was the *Battle of Anghiari*. Despite his grandeur it was the first public commission the city had offered him, and, much as he might have longed to return to Milan, it was not in his nature (or that of any other freelance at the time) to refuse a commission. The battle had been fought near Arezzo in 1440, where an allied Florentine and Papal army had defeated an army of mercenaries employed by the Milanese, with the miraculous assistance of St Peter. It had been a cavalry battle, or at least that was how Leonardo chose to portray it. Ever the theorist, Leonardo provides several pages of advice in *Precepts of the Painter* on how to represent a battle, yet his advice is clearly based on observation, and he was able to execute it himself in a masterly way:

> You should give a ruddy glow to the faces and the figures and the air around them, and to the gunners and those near to them, and this glow should grow fainter the farther away it is from its cause. The figures which are between you and the light, if far away, will appear dark against a light background, and the nearer their limbs are to the ground, the less they will be visible, for there the dust is greater and thicker. And if you make horses galloping away from the throng, make little clouds of dust as far distant from one another as is the space between the strides made by the horse, and that cloud which is farthest away from the horse should be the least visible, for it should be high and spread out and thin, while that which is nearest should be most conspicuous and smallest and most compact.

Leonardo also left copious historical notes, showing that he had researched the battle before depicting it. Surviving sketches show vividly shouting men and rearing horses meshed in close combat, and merging into a monumental whole. Vasari describes the work, which must have survived into his time:

> He showed a group of horsemen fighting for a standard, in a drawing which was regarded as very fine and successful because of the wonderful ideas he expressed in his interpretation of the battle. In the drawing, rage, fury, and vindictiveness are displayed both by the men and the horses, two of which with their forelegs interlocked are battling with their teeth no less fiercely than their riders are struggling for the standard, the staff of which has been grasped by a soldier who, as he turns and spurs his horse to flight, is trying by the strength of his shoulders to wrest it from the hands of four others. Two of them are struggling for it with one hand and attempting with the other to cut the staff with their raised swords; and an old soldier with a raised cap roars out as he grips the staff with one hand and with the other raises a scimitar and aims a furious blow to cut off both the hands of those who are gnashing their teeth and ferociously defending their standard. Besides this, on the ground between the legs of the two horses, there are two

figures, foreshortened, shown fighting together; the one on the ground has over him a soldier who has raised his arm as high as possible to plunge his dagger with greater force into the throat of his enemy, who struggles frantically with his arms and legs to escape death.

The fresco was to cover a huge area: almost eight by twenty metres; Michelangelo's was to cover a corresponding area of similar size.

In October 1503 Leonardo was appointed studio space in the Sala del Papa at Santa Maria Novella – a large enough room to accommodate the full-scale drawings for the fresco. Evidently he didn't start work with gusto, because in May the following year a new contract was drawn up, among whose counter-signatories was Machiavelli – urging him on, and stipulating that the cartoon at least must be finished by the following February, that is, in 1505. Leonardo did ultimately begin work on the painting, but, experimenting with fresco technique, his attempt failed, and soon afterwards he left again for Milan, his work barely started and his contract unfulfilled. Soderini later complained that Leonardo had received a lot of money for negligible work. But he did complete his contract in part, and as recently as 2000 considerable excitement was generated by the possibility that his fragment still exists in the Palazzo della Signoria (now the Palazzo Vecchio), under a thick layer of plaster applied by Vasari to protect it when he was later commissioned to decorate the Great Hall with his own mighty, but less accomplished, battle scenes. It has been suggested that Vasari even left visual clues about where the lost Leonardo fragment can be located, but as yet (at the time of writing) no conclusions have been reached.

Michelangelo's theme was *The Battle of Cascina*, a victory over the perennial enemy, the Pisans, which had been won on 29 July 1364, ending five years of warfare between the two cities. The victory was regarded by the old Guelph Party as a triumph, and its anniversary was celebrated annually. An indication of how busy and how popular Michelangelo was is that the block of marble for the first of the Apostle series arrived in Florence from Cararra in 1503, at the same time as Michelangelo was finishing the *David* and doing his preliminary sketches for *Cascina*. These drawings are among his most beautiful and expressive works.

Michelangelo's *Cascina* contract was a challenge, because it gave him a chance to rival Leonardo in the art of painting, and he worked on the full-scale cartoon energetically in a large hall at the Ospedale Sant' Onofrio. In February 1505 he received his first advance payment – 3000 ducats – on the painting. Soderini got even less for this outlay that he'd had from Leonardo, though for a moment it looked as if both masters were about to start work at the same time on their separate sections of the walls of the Great Hall. However, although Leonardo worked on his picture until August 1505, Michelangelo did not have time even to start

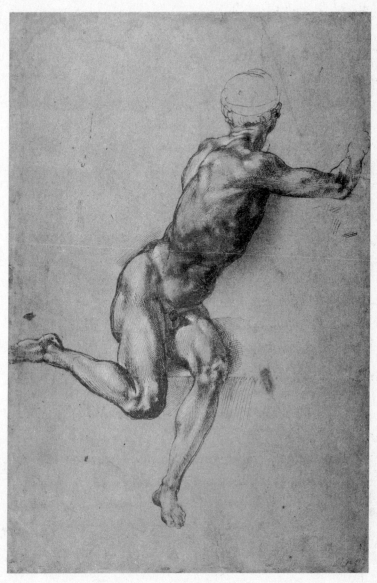

Michelangelo – a study for *The Battle of Cascina*

on his fresco before being summoned back to Rome by
Julius II.

If there was room for a moment of envy of the younger
by the older man, this was it; but Leonardo's character and
self-confidence were such that he was not the type to descend
to so vulgar an emotion. As for Soderini, he was in no position politically to stand in the way of the Pope's will.

Michelangelo had originally decided to portray a famous,
but isolated moment *before* the battle of Cascina itself, and
therein the originality of his imagination manifested itself
once again. Instead of a formal conflict, the moment he
showed was a kind of surprise manoeuvre, which enabled
him to display once again his *forte* of showing naked men
in tense action, harking back to his *Battle of the Centaurs*,
but showing how far he had developed such art since
Pollaiuolo's *Battle of Naked Men* of 1465, which had not
been so long before, though there is still something academic
about the work, as far as we can tell from the copy which
survives of the central scene, which recalls Pollaiuolo's
didactic piece.

Michelangelo chose to show the moment when the
Florentine army was camped by the banks of the Arno. As
the weather was suffocatingly hot, the men had stripped off
to bathe in the river. Their general lay ill meanwhile. The
hero of the hour was an officer called Manno Donati, who,
realising that the army was ill-prepared and undefended,
raised a false cry of alarm. Believing that the Pisans were

attacking, the Florentines struggled to get their wet limbs back into their tight clothes and panicked. Manno thus revealed the weakness of his side, and as a result the Florentines posted a guard and kept themselves in readiness thereafter. The next day they pierced the Pisan flank and swept the enemy from the field. The busy activity of a large number of naked men hurriedly trying to struggle into their armour gave Michelangelo a wonderful opportunity to show off his expertise with his favourite subject, from a variety of angles and viewpoints. It is almost a technical exercise, and was much admired and copied by his colleagues. Benvenuto Cellini much later described it in this way:

[Michelangelo] showed all their actions and gestures so wonderfully that no ancient or modern artist has ever reached so high a standard. Leonardo's as well . . . was wonderfully beautiful . . . and while they [the cartoons] remained intact, they served as a school for all the world.

Vasari fills out the historical background, as well as describing sections of the cartoon forever lost to us: 'And as the soldiers rush out of the water to dress themselves Michelangelo's inspired hand depicted some hurrying to arm themselves in order to bring help to their comrades, others buckling on their cuirasses, many fastening other pieces of armour on their bodies, and countless more dashing into the fray on horseback. Among the rest was the figure of an old man wearing a garland of ivy to shade his head; he is sitting down to pull on his stockings, but he cannot do so because his legs are wet from the water, and as he hears the cries and tumult of the soldiers and the beating of the drums he is straining to pull on one stocking by force. The nerves and muscles of his face and his contorted mouth convey the frenzied effort and exertion he is making with his whole body. There were some drummers and other naked figures, with their clothes bundled up, hurrying to get to the fighting, and drawn in various unusual attitudes: some upright, some kneeling or leaning forward, or half-way between one position and another, all exhibiting the most difficult foreshortenings. There were also many groups of figures drawn in different ways: some outlined in charcoal, others sketched with a few strokes, some shaded gradually and heightened with lead-white. This Michelangelo did to show how much he knew about his craft. When they saw the cartoon, all the other artists were overcome with admiration and astonishment, for it was a revelation of the perfection that the art of painting could reach. People who had seen these inspired figures declare that they have never been surpassed either by Michelangelo himself or by anyone else, and that no one can ever again reach such sublime heights. And this may readily be believed, for after the cartoon had been finished and, to the glory of Michelangelo, carried to the Sala del Papa, with tremendous acclamations from all the artists, those who subsequently studied it and made copies of the figures (as was done for many years in Florence by local artists and others) became excellent painters themselves. As we know, the artists who studied the cartoon included Aristotile da Sangallo (Michelangelo's friend), Ridolfo Ghirlandaio, Raphael Sanzio of Urbino, Francesco Granacci, Baccio Bandinelli, and the Spaniard Alonso Beruguete. They were followed by Andrea del Sarto, Franciabigio, Jacopo Sansovino, Rosso, Maturino, Lorenzetto and Tribolo, when he was a child, and by Jacopo da Pontormo and Perin del Vaga. All these men were outstanding Florentine artists.

'The cartoon having thus become a school for craftsmen, it was taken to the great upper room of the house of the Medici. But this meant that it was unwisely left in the hands of the craftsmen: and when Duke Giuliano fell ill, without warning it was torn in pieces. And now it is dispersed in various places. For example, there are some fragments still to be seen at Mantua in the house of Uberto Strozzi, a Mantuan gentleman, who preserves them with great reverence; and certainly anyone who sees them is inclined to think them of divine rather than human origin.' Though the cartoon is lost, a copy of the central scene by Aristotile da Sangallo can be found at Holkham Hall in Norfolk, England.

Although neither Leonardo's nor Michelangelo's picture was ever completely transferred to the walls of the Great Hall, each artist, as Cellini and Vasari state, left beautifully drawn studies which have survived. Surviving sketches from both artists show astonishing bravura, though the large, fragile originals were broken up, soon after they had been abandoned, by fellow-artists eager to own models of what they themselves aspired to. As Charles Morgan relates in his *Life of Michelangelo*:

> Ultimately both cartoons were transferred to their respective positions in the Great Hall, where they caused a popular sensation, flapped and tore, were relegated to less conspicuous settings, cut up and dispersed by students and souvenir hunters . . .

Neither artist would stay much longer in Florence. In March 1505 Michelangelo received a summons from Pope Julius II to come to Rome to work on His Holiness' monument, a project referred to by Ascanio Condivi as 'the tragedy of the tomb', since off and on it preoccupied Michelangelo for four decades, and never came to an entirely satisfactory conclusion. But there was also his greatest project for Julius, and the one for which, even more than the *David*, most people know him, although the way it came about was almost accidental: the painting of the ceiling of the Sistine Chapel.

Michelangelo lived in an age when travel and exploration were becoming increasingly current. In 1492, Christopher Columbus sailed west on a voyage that would lead him to discover America, establishing one of the most famous dates in history, though he himself was convinced he'd discovered the Indies. Four years earlier, the Portuguese Bartolomeu Diaz rounded the Cape of Good Hope. Six years later than Columbus, in 1498, Vasco da Gama used the Cape route to cross the Indian Ocean and make landfall at Calicut, and almost exactly a year earlier than that, Giovanni Caboto, a Genoese pilot sailing as John Cabot under letters patent from Henry VII of England, arrived on the coast of Nova Scotia.

Within Europe and the Near East travel was commonplace. Artists and artisans moved about freely. Pico della Mirandola travelled widely to learn languages, and as early as 1436 Paolo Uccello had painted an equestrian portrait of a celebrated Florentine *condottiere*, Giovanni Acuto, born John Hawkwood, of Castle Hedingham, Essex, England, a most resourceful soldier of fortune who, after service at Crécy and Poitiers, was knighted by King Edward III and then made his way south with a band of mercenaries. He hired himself out to the Republic, where he remained, fighting its battles in return for an annual pension. The proto-travel book, *Sir John Mandeville's Travels*, had appeared in 1356 and quickly became hugely popular throughout Europe. There was a copy in Leonardo's library.

Michelangelo, however, wasn't interested in travel. His journeying took him only around Tuscany and the Papal States, though he travelled as a young man as far as Bologna and Venice. His travels were internal, of the mind and heart, but no less audacious or risky than those of the explorers. In March 1505, on the verge of his thirtieth birthday, with one of his greatest works already achieved, he stood on the brink of another great adventure.

With heart of sulphur and with flesh of tow,
With bone designed of dry and rotting wood,
With spirit lacking any guide to show
Which impulses are evil and which good,
With reason which displays itself so weak
Confronted with a world so full of snares,
It is no wonder that my flesh should break
When it first stumbles on such furious fires.
With glorious art – that gift received from heaven –
That conquers nature and in every way
Clings to all human longing and desire;
If such a gift I truly have been given
And yet, divided, torn, still burn and stray,
He is to blame who fashioned me for fire.

Michelangelo

Select Bibliography

AGNES ALLEN: *The Story of Michelangelo*, Faber, London, 1953

GLEN M ANDRES, JOHN M HUNISAK AND A RICHARD TURNER: *The Art of Florence* (2 vol), Artabras, London and New York, 1988–1994

PAUL BAROLSKY: *Michelangelo's Nose*, Pennsylvania State University, 1990

CYRIL BERTRAM: *Michelangelo*, Dutton, London, 1964

GIOVANNI BOCCACCIO (TRL G. H. McWILLIAM): *Decameron*, Penguin, Harmondsworth, 1972

GEORGE BULL: *Michelangelo*, St Martin's, New York, 1998

MICHELANGELO BUONARROTI (TRL ELIZABETH JENNINGS, JOHN FOLGER): *Sonnets*, Carcanet, Manchester, 1988; *Letters* (trl E. H. Ramsden), Owen, London, 1963

JOHANN BURCHARD (ED/TRL GEOFFREY PARKER): *At the Court of the Borgia*, Folio Society, London, 1963

JACOB BURCKHARDT: *The Civilisation of the Renaissance in Italy*, Phaidon, London, 1965

ROBERT W CARDEN (ED/TRL): *Michelangelo: a Record of His Life as Told in His Own Letters*, Constable, London, 1913

KENNETH CLARK: *The Nude*, Pelican, London, 1964

BENVENUTO CELLINI (TRL GEORGE BULL): *Autobiography*, Penguin, London, 1966

CHARLES CLÉMENT: *Michelangelo*, Sampson Low, Marston, Searle and Rivington, London, 1885

JOHN CLEMENTS: *The Poetry of Michelangelo*, Owen, London, 1966

FRANCESCO COLONNA (TRL JOSCELYN GODWIN): *Hypnerotomachia Poliphili*, Thames and Hudson, London, 1999

ASCANIO CONDIVI (TRL HERBERT P HORNE): *The Life of Michelangelo Buonarroti*, Merrymount Press, 1905

FREDERICK BARON CORVO: *A History of the Borgias*, Carlton House, New York, 1935

DANTE (TRL ALLEN MANDELBAUM): *The Divine Comedy*, Everyman, London, 1995

R DUPPA: *The Life and Literary Works of Michel Angelo Buonarroti*, John Murray et al, London, 1806

A FALENI: *Notize Storiche del David*, Firenze, 1875

DONALD LORD FINLAYSON: *Michelangelo the Man*, Putnam, London, 1935

SIGMUND FREUD (TRL ALAN TYSON): *Leonardo*, Pelican, London, 1963

JOHN HALE: *The Civilisation of Europe in the Renaissance*, Fontana, London, 1994

FREDERICK HARTT: *David by the Hand of Michelangelo: the Original Model Discovered*, Thames and Hudson, London, 1987; *The Drawings of Michelangelo*, Thames and Hudson, London, 1971; *Michelangelo: the Complete Sculpture*, Thames and Hudson, London, 1969

HOWARD HIBBARD: *Michelangelo*, Allen Lane, London, 1975

CHRISTOPHER HIBBERT: *The Rise and Fall of the House of Medici*, Penguin, London, 1979

ROSS KING: *Brunelleschi's Dome*, Pimlico, London, 2001

MICHAEL LEVEY: *Florence: a Portrait*, Pimlico, London, 1997

NICCOLÒ MACHIAVELLI (TRL GEORGE BULL): *The Prince*, Penguin, London, 1966; *Discourses* (ed Bernard Crick, trl Leslie Walter SJ, revised Brian Richardson), Pelican, London, 1974

LORENZO DE' MEDICI (ED JOHN THIEM, TRL JOHN THIEM ET AL): *Selected Poems and Prose*, Pennsylvania State University Press, 1991

CHARLES H MORGAN: *The Life of Michelangelo*, Weidenfeld and Nicolson, London, 1960

LINDA MURRAY: *Michelangelo*, Thames and Hudson, London, 1992

WALTER PATER: *The Renaissance*, Ward Lock, London and Sydney, 1969

GIOVANNI POGGI (ED): *Il Duomo di Firenze*, Bruno Cassirer, Berlin, 1909

A E POPHAM: *The Drawings of Leonardo da Vinci*, Reprint Society, London, 1957

ELIZABETH RIPLEY: *Michelangelo*, OUP, New York, 1953

ROLF SCHOTT: *Michelangelo*, Thames and Hudson, London, 1963

HEIN.-TH. SCHULZE-ALTCAPPENBERG (ED, ET AL): Catalogue for *Sandro Botticelli, the Drawings for Dante's Divine Comedy*, Royal Academy, London, 2001

CHARLES SEYMOUR JR.: *Michelangelo's David – a Search for Identity*, University of Pittsburgh Press, 1967

IRVING STONE: *The Agony and the Ecstasy*, Doubleday, New York, 1961

IRVING AND JEAN STONE (EDS) (TRL CHARLES SPERONI): *I, Michelangelo, Sculptor – an Autobiography through Letters*, Collins, London, 1963

GIORGIO VASARI (TRL GEORGE BULL): *Lives of the Artists* (2 vol), Penguin, London, 1987

LEONARDO DA VINCI (ED/TRL EDWARD MacCURDY): *Notebooks* (2 vol), Cape, London, 1938

MARTIN WEINBERGER: *Michelangelo the Sculptor* (2 vol), Routledge and Kegan Paul, London, and Columbia University Press, New York, 1967

ROLF C. WIRTZ (TRL BARTON, COX, MÜLLER): *Florence*, Könnemann, Cologne, 2000

RUDOLF WITTKOWER: *Sculpture*, Peregrine, London, 1979

Index